PROFICIENCY
EXPERT
COURSEBOOK

Megan Roderick and Carol Nuttall with Nick Kenny

Contents

Contents

Exam overview

▶ See the Exam reference on page 167 for more detailed information and task strategies.

The *Cambridge English: Proficiency*, also known as the *Certificate of Proficiency in English (CPE)*, has four papers. The Reading and use of English paper carries 40% of the marks, while Writing, Listening and Speaking each carry 20% of the marks. Candidates who receive a grade A, B or C in their exam will receive the *Certificate of Proficiency in English* at Level C2. Candidates who perform below C2 level, but at the C1 level, will receive a certificate certifying that they are at the C1 level.

Paper	Part	No. of questions/ Length	Task type	Task description
Reading and Use of English	Part 1	8	Multiple-choice cloze	Choosing the correct word or phrase to fill gaps in a text; focus on vocabulary.
Reading and Use of English	Part 2	8	Open cloze	Filling in gaps with the appropriate word; focus mainly on grammar; some focus on vocabulary.
Reading and Use of English	Part 3	8	Word formation	Changing the form of given words to make them fit the gaps in a text; focus on vocabulary.
Reading and Use of English	Part 4	6	Key word transformations	Using a given word to complete a sentence so that it means the same as a previous sentence; focus on grammar, vocabulary and collocation.
Reading and Use of English	Part 5	6	Multiple choice	Answering four-option multiple-choice questions on a text.
Reading and Use of English	Part 6	7	Gapped text	Deciding where jumbled paragraphs fit into gaps in a text.
Reading and Use of English	Part 7	10	Multiple matching	Matching a prompt to elements in a text or several short texts.
Writing	Part 1	240–280 words	Writing an essay with a discursive focus	Summarising and evaluating key ideas contained in two texts.
Writing	Part 2	280–320 words	Contextualised writing task	Writing for a specific reader, using the appropriate format and style as required in the instructions.
Listening	Part 1	6	Multiple choice	Answering two questions about each of three short extracts.
Listening	Part 2	9	Sentence completion	Identifying specific information and stated opinion from a monologue.
Listening	Part 3	5	Multiple choice	Listening for specific information, attitudes and opinions in a conversation.
Listening	Part 4	10	Multiple matching	Listening to monologues and selecting the correct options from a list of possibilities.
Speaking	Part 1	2 mins	Short interview	Showing ability to use general interactional and social language.
Speaking	Part 2	4 mins	Two-way conversation	Sustaining an interaction in a decision-making task.
Speaking	Part 3	10 mins	Individual long turn	Developing topics, expressing and justifying opinions and organising discourse.

1 Performing arts

'Music is the most universal language we humans have ... every person on the planet has the ability to understand great music.'

'There is a bit of insanity in dancing that does everybody a great deal of good.'

'I love acting. It is so much more real than real life.'

'There are no limits. There are plateaus, but you must not stay there, you must go beyond them.'

Lead-in

1 Discuss the quotations. Which do you like best? Why?

2 What different types of performing arts can you think of? Brainstorm your ideas and draw up a list. Which ones do you prefer?

3 How important are the following factors in becoming a successful performing artist?

training   a mentor   upbringing   arts   family background   innate talent   determination
a lucky break   participation in talent contests

4 Who do you think are some of the best performers around today? How do you think they achieved excellence in their particular field?

5 Which type of performing arts do you think has the most secure future? Which are the most accessible to young people?

Have you got what it takes?

Reading 1 (Paper 1 Part 5)

Before you read   **1**   Some cultural events involve participants who remain anonymous, where the individual is only important as part of a whole.

     1   Can you think of any more examples of this, other than what is shown in the photographs?

     2   Do you generally prefer to be anonymous or to stand out in a crowd?

Skimming and scanning: reading for main idea (gist) and reading for detail

2   Reading a text and answering questions on it require two basic skills working together: the understanding of gist and the ability to comprehend the detail of a text.

     1   Quickly skim the text on page 9 for gist, focusing on the beginning of the sentences, particularly in the first half of each paragraph.

     2   Match the summaries below to the paragraphs. Support your choice with details from each paragraph. There is one extra summary sentence you do not need.

A source that never runs dry	The dangers of fame
Complaints are useless	A financial dilemma
A harsh reality	It's who you know, not what you know

➤ EXPERT STRATEGIES page 168

Multiple choice   **3**   Read the strategy, then do the task.

EXPERT STRATEGY

When you answer questions on a text, keep the overall context and the writer's intention in mind.

You are going to read an article about dancers in London. For questions 1–6, choose the answer (A, B, C or D) which you think fits best according to the text.

Task analysis   **4**   Analyse any problems you had with the multiple-choice questions.

   • Was it difficult to understand the writer's intention?

   • Did any unknown words give you problems?

   • Did you find the question options confusing?

   • Once you know the correct answers, go back and study the text to make sure you understand the rationale behind the answers.

Discussion   **5**   Have you ever performed in public? How did you feel? If you haven't, would you like to? Why/Why not?

6   Check the meaning of these key words from the text.

EXPERT WORD CHECK

tatty   hustle   resilience   prerequisite   sartorial   mediocrity   lousy
ruthlessness   jaded   notorious

A dancer's lot

1 All across London, they emerge from underground stations and buses; bags slung over their shoulders and taut stomachs beneath thick winter overcoats. Nobody recognises them, as they head for freezing upstairs rooms in tatty gymnasiums or
5 slink into backstage theatre doors, even though they appear regularly in sold-out musicals and favourite television shows. They earn precious little, even those who perform live with famous singers, and have no real prospects, doing what they're doing, despite having hustled and sweated themselves to the
10 heights of one of Britain's most demanding professions. But still they go, every morning, to their grim upstairs rooms in gyms and their backstreet, backstage doors, to dance.

2 Most have left behind worried parents in faraway towns and villages; made repeated promises to look after themselves and
15 taken trains, in their late teenage years, for London. There's much to despise about the city, where talent and a reptilian grade of resilience, although prerequisites, provide no guarantee of success. Even auditions are becoming rare. Conscious of deadlines and financial constraints, choreographers call in talent
20 from the blessed pool of their own chosen. If you aren't the right height, don't have the right face, hair or sartorial style, then don't expect a look in. Although choreographers occasionally seek out the beautiful, they're mostly instructed to hunt the bland: those least likely to outshine the stars. And, as many
25 dancers will tell you, it's getting to the point where mediocrity is acceptable; there'll be someone over there out of sync, someone over there who can't hold her arm still.

3 And if they get a part, increasingly dancers are turning up for jobs where the choreographer just stands there and works
30 them endlessly, fingers clicking: 'Again, again, again'. As one dancer, Melanie Grace says, 'You dance for the love and the passion, and keep your mouth shut because you don't want to get a reputation.' It's not always easy, though. You think the television shows provide changing rooms? For dancers? Even
35 the big budget ones have them disrobing in a corner of the canteen – and the pay's lousy. But you have to ignore it, keep your head down. You're in London now. You're one of many; one of nothing. The sooner you accept that, the better you'll get on. Of the fleets of talented dancers who try, only a quarter
40 make it, the rest simply can't process the ruthlessness – to dance in London is hard on the soul.

4 Yet most of the dancers have agents, who you might think would negotiate a better fee or conditions for their dancers, but no. You'll never meet a dancer who thinks their agent deserves
45 their twenty percent cut of the fee. Mostly you'll just get a text or email notifying you of an audition and a single agent might have as many as two hundred dancers on their books. As Melanie says, 'It's catch-22, because you won't hear about the auditions without one.' Here's the job, take it or leave it, and if
50 you leave it, they'll just hire someone straight out of college and pay them even less.

5 Oh, the annual churn of the colleges. The dancers hear it constantly, the sound of the machine in the distance, its ceaselessly grinding gears that, with every coming year, push
55 out hundreds of new dancers, each one younger and hungrier and less jaded than you. And with every release of fresh limbs into the stew of the city, things get harder. The worst thing the kids can do is accept a job for no pay. They do it all the time. One website has become notorious for television and pop-
60 video production companies scrounging for trained people to work for nothing but 'exposure'. And if the youngsters are fresh out of dance school, despairing of their blank CV and craving the love of those ranks of sparkle-eyed strangers, they'll leap at the chance. It's the reason things are getting harder.
65 How to describe the London dance scene today? The word Melanie chooses is 'savage'.

1 In the first paragraph, the writer paints a picture of dancers who are

A careful not to be recognised by fans in the street.
B deserving of the fame they have achieved.
C unlikely to be making further advances in their careers.
D hoping to find work on stage alongside established stars.

2 What do we learn about auditions in the second paragraph?

A Increasingly higher standards are expected of dancers.
B The best dancers do not necessarily get the jobs on offer.
C It's difficult for dancers to find the time to attend very many.
D Dancers with family connections in the business get invited to more.

3 What is implied about choreographers in the third paragraph?

A They expect dancers to do as they are told.
B They dislike it when dancers criticise each other.
C They are intolerant of dancers who make mistakes.
D They are sensitive to the pressures that dancers are under.

4 What point is made about agents in the fourth paragraph?

A Dancers are largely satisfied with their service.
B Most dancers recognise that they are essential.
C They tend to represent only the less experienced dancers.
D They make every effort to get the best deal for dancers.

5 The writer uses the image of a machine in line 53 to underline

A the attitude of training institutions.
B the dubious activities of a website.
C the constant supply of new talent.
D the exploitation of young people.

6 In the text as a whole, the writer is suggesting that dancers in London

A should demand much better pay and working conditions.
B have to regard the experience as useful for the future.
C should be rewarded for dedication and perseverance.
D have to accept the realities of a competitive industry.

Vocabulary

Words connected with the performing arts

1a Read the dictionary definitions below from the *Longman Exam Dictionary* and use the 'How to use the dictionary' notes at the beginning of your dictionary to help you answer the following questions.

1 What tells you which part of speech the word is?
2 What helps you to pronounce the word correctly?
3 What do the symbols [C], [I] and [T] tell you about?
4 What does [+ **for**] tell you about the word?

> **audition** [/ɔːˈdɪʃən/] *n* [C] a short performance by an actor, singer, etc., that someone watches to judge if they are good enough to act in a play, sing in a concert, etc. [+ **for**] *I've got an audition for the Bournemouth Symphony Orchestra on Friday.*

> **audition** *v* **1** [I] to take part in an audition: [+ **for**] *She's auditioning for Ophelia in 'Hamlet'.* **2** [T] to watch and judge someone's performance in an audition: *We auditioned more than 200 dancers before deciding on Carole Ann.*

b Look up the following words in your dictionary, then give a full explanation of their pronunciation, symbols and use to the rest of the class. Write an example sentence for each one to show how they are used.

° choreography   auditorium   °inspire
backstage   °preview

Nouns + prepositions

2 Complete the text with the prepositions below.

on   for (x3)   to   with   in   of

Phrases with *jump/leap/bound(s)*

3a The phrase *leap at the chance* appears in the text on page 9. The words *jump*, *leap* and *bound(s)* are sometimes used in phrases to add emphasis to a reaction or situation. Discuss the meaning of the phrases in *italics* in the following sentences.

1 His determination to become a dancer *knew no bounds* and he practised for eight hours a day. *limit*
2 Kathy *jumped for joy* when she heard she'd got the part in the play. *extremely happy*
3 Paul's move from Liverpool in the hope of becoming a professional dancer was *a leap in the dark*, as he had no idea what would happen. *take a risk / completely unknown*

b Replace the underlined phrases in the sentences with the correct form of a phrase below.

jump to conclusions   jump down my throat
leap at the opportunity   by leaps and bounds
out of bounds   know no bounds

1 Sara's enthusiasm for the stage was endless, and by the age of twelve she had already performed in two musicals, both as a dancer and actor. *knew no bounds*
2 'OK, I know you've been working really hard but there's no need to yell at me just because I pointed out a mistake!' *jump down my throat*
3 If you are invited to audition for a West End production, you should accept immediately, as it may be a while before you get another chance. *leap at the opportunity*
4 Kevin's performance in his first few concerts was rather wooden and unnatural but he's improved immensely since then. *by leaps and bounds*
5 The area backstage is off limits to the public during the performance but certain members of the audience are sometimes invited to visit performers after a show. *out of bounds*
6 There have been rumours that the leading lady is romantically involved with the lighting technician but perhaps we shouldn't assume too much. *jump to conclusions*

FILM VILLAINS

Home | News | Archive | Log-in

It appears to be a prerequisite **(1)** _____ *for* screen villains to love classical music, and magnificent examples abound. Take, for instance, Malcolm McDowell's insistence **(2)** _on_ listening to Beethoven while he kills people in *A Clockwork Orange*. Glenn Close's thirst **(3)** _for_ revenge is fuelled by music from *Madame Butterfly* in *Fatal Attraction*, while the gangster Al Capone finds reason **(4)** _to_ shed a tear when listening to Leoncavallo's *I Pagliacci* in *The Untouchables*. Hollywood's interpretation **(5)** _of_ evil genius

comprises villains who are highly intelligent, often slightly aristocratic beings, and their sensitive tastes **(6)** _in_ art and music are placed in sharp contrast **(7)** _with_ the crude brutality of their acts of violence. Hans Zimmer's score for *Hannibal* enhances the dramatic effect of Dr Lecter's talent **(8)** _for_ displaying a veneer of refined elegance just before he murders his victims. Perhaps, more than any other kind of music, the range and complexity of classical music reflects the tangled psychological workings of the criminal mind.

Collocations

4 Complete the collocational phrases in the sentences with the words below.

stage   dress   emotional   standing   backing
curtain   live   cue   limelight

1 Theatre companies always claim that a disastrous ___dress___ rehearsal usually means an outstanding first night.
2 Some actors find that being in the _limelight_ ~~curtain~~ can put a strain on family relationships.
3 Bidji sang _backing_ ~~stage~~ vocals for Manu Chao on his CD *Mister Bobby*.
4 It is not unusual for accomplished movie stars attempting to perform on stage to suffer from _stage_ ~~cue~~ fright on their opening night.
5 The opera was so moving that the principal singers received a _standing_ ovation from the audience at the end of the performance.
6 Despite the struggle to get into her costume, Helena managed to enter the stage on ~~limelight~~ _cue_.
7 The pianist gave an inspiring _live_ performance in Hyde Park, in front of a large audience.
8 Actors often make excellent use of _emotional_ recall to enhance their portrayal of a character.
9 After a riveting charity performance, U2 were joined on stage by all the other artists for a moving ~~backing~~ _curtain_ call.

Compound words

5a The words *backstreet* and *backstage* in the text on page 9 are compound words. The words *over* and *under* are also used to form compounds. Discuss what *overstatement* and *understatement* mean.
exagerate   \ *not full picture / less strongly than you should*

b Match the words in column A with a word from column B to form compound nouns. Some of the words combine with more than one other word.

A
1 under f e a d
2 sound c f
3 play   b d
4 over   d ...
5 screen a
6 back   f c

B
a writer
b wright
c track
d act
e study
f stage

Word formation

1 Read the strategy, then do the task.

> **EXPERT STRATEGY**
> Remember to read each sentence in the context of the paragraph and the text as a whole.

▶ EXPERT STRATEGIES page 167

For questions 1–8, read the text below and the task strategy. Use the word given in CAPITALS at the end of some of the lines to form a word that fits in the gap in the same line.

How do you say 'Mamma Mia' in Chinese?

The **(0)** _widely_ acclaimed *Mamma Mia* is to be the first major Western musical to be translated for the Chinese stage. But is it possible to produce a successful **(1)** _Adaptation_ of a Western show in Chinese? The world is about to find out. When the **(2)** _playwright_ Catherine Johnson wrote the original plot, based on the music of the Swedish band Abba in 1999, she couldn't have imagined that it would come this far. It remains to be seen what the band's **(3)** _lyricists_ ~~lyricsed~~, Benny Andersson and Bjorn Ulvaeus, will make of the translation. Some words were initially **(4)** _misinterpreted_ ~~uninterpretable~~ and had to be corrected. Some of the Western choreography considered to be of **(5)** _questionable_ ~~questioning~~ taste in China has given way to traditional folk dances to render the show more appropriate for local audiences. 'It's certainly been an **(6)** _unprecedented_ ~~precesive~~ challenge,' laughs one member of the British production team, 'but so far the show's been received enthusiastically by everyone who has seen the **(7)** _preview_ showing. So we'll have to wait and see.'

Meanwhile, **(8)** _backstage_ in the dressing rooms the atmosphere is tense, as the curtain rises on this ambitious production.

WIDE

ADAPT

PLAY

lyrical (like a poem)
LYRIC

INTERPRET

QUESTION

PRECEDE (*happen before*)

VIEW

STAGE

the CULTURE supplement   **11**

2 Write a short review of a film, theatrical performance or concert you have seen recently. Use words from this section to help you.

Listening 1 (Paper 3 Part 2)

Before you listen   **1**   Discuss the following questions.

     1   Make a list of the kind of jobs connected with the film industry.
     2   What role does each one play in the making of a film?

Listening for information: **2**   🎧 T1.02   Read the exam question in Exercise 3. Listen and note
taking notes   down any experiences that helped the speaker become an
animator.

Sentence completion   **3**   🎧 T1.02   Look at the task below. Read the questions and the
strategy carefully, then do the task.

EXPERT STRATEGY

In Paper 3 Part 2, you are listening for concrete pieces of information. On the recording, you will hear the words or phrases you need to complete the gaps but they will not be in the same sentences. Before you listen, think about:
• the type of word or phrase which is missing in each gap
• the sort of information you are listening for.

You will hear an animator called James Quigley giving a talk about his work. For questions 1–9, complete the sentences with a word or short phrase.

James Quigley: animator

Before being introduced to animation, James had been hoping to make [people laugh] **1** his career.

           illustration   *imperfections*
James' college tutor showed him how retaining [movings] **2** in his drawings helped to achieve a sense of movement.

James uses the word [realistic] **3** to describe the type of animation he favours in films.

James' success at a [film festival] **4** led to opportunities to work as an animator.

Money made from work on [advertisements] **5** allows James to finance his own films.

                              collaboration
James says he particularly enjoys the level of [motion frowns] **6** required to create an animated film.

People are surprised to learn that much of James' drawing is done [by hand] **7** and that this suits him best.

James feels that [observation] **8** is the most important aspect of an animator's work.

James mentions that the [actors] **9** involved in a film can prove a source of inspiration for drawing the characters.

---

4   You are interested in becoming an animator. Based on what you heard, and the notes you made in Exercise 2, write down some questions you would like to ask James.

Language development 1

Present and past tense review: state verbs

➤ EXPERT GRAMMAR page 172

1 Tick the acceptable sentences and correct the sentences containing mistakes. Sometimes both might be possible. Discuss your answers.

1a Unfortunately, it <u>isn't looking</u> *[doesn't look]* as if that dance company needs me at the moment – and I really wanted to be in their show!

b They <u>look</u> for someone who can sing really well.

2a I really <u>am not seeing</u> *[don't see]* what you mean by 'professionalism'.

✓ b I'm seeing some actor friends tomorrow.

3a They <u>are having</u> *[have]* a lovely villa in France.

✓ b <u>Do</u> you <u>have</u> a lot of studying to do at the moment?

✓ 4a This matter <u>doesn't</u> really <u>concern</u> *[involve / business]* him.

✓ b What <u>is concerning</u> me is her lack of stamina.

✓ 5a I <u>don't mind</u> singing and acting as part of our amateur performance but my dance skills need a bit of work.

b I'm <u>minding</u> *[mind / take care of]* my neighbour's dog while she's away.

Time words

2 Complete the short dialogue with the correct time word and form of the verb. There are two extra time words you do not need.

before	currently	first	just	last	lately	long
since	still	yet				

Chrissy and Dana are chatting before a performance.

Chrissy: Ever **(1)** _since_ I first **(2)** _met_ (meet) Ryan, he's wanted to become a performer.

Dana: Yes, he says he's **(3)** _yet_ [has] **(4)** _to find_ (find) anyone with an extraordinary talent who has really inspired him. However, he **(5)** _still_ **(6)** _hasn't travelled_ (not travel) much abroad, I suppose.

Chrissy: He **(7)** _has been doing_ (do) a lot of hip-hop classes **(8)** _lately_ . How **(9)** _long_ do you think it will be before he **(10)** _becomes_ (become) a dance teacher?

Dana: He **(11)** _is_ **(12)** _currently_ **(13)** _doing_ (do) masterclasses with a top dancer, so I think it will be soon!

After the performance.

Chrissy: It's the **(14)** _first_ time that I **(15)** _have seen_ (see) Ryan dance that well.

Dana: He left by the backstage door **(16)** _before_ .I **(17)** _had_ (have) time to congratulate him! Let's send him a text!

Use of English 2 (Paper 1 Part 2)

Open cloze

1a Read the newspaper extract about mobile phone use during concerts. How do you feel about Sir Peter's comments?

b Read the strategy below, then do the task.

> **EXPERT STRATEGY**
>
> Read through the whole text quickly to get the general idea, before trying to find the missing words.

For questions 1–8, read the text below and think of the word which best fits each gap. Use only one word in each gap. There is an example at the beginning (0).

➤ EXPERT STRATEGIES page 167

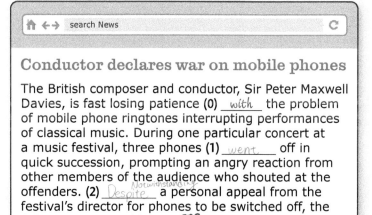

search News

Conductor declares war on mobile phones

The British composer and conductor, Sir Peter Maxwell Davies, is fast losing patience **(0)** _with_ the problem of mobile phone ringtones interrupting performances of classical music. During one particular concert at a music festival, three phones **(1)** _went_ off in quick succession, prompting an angry reaction from other members of the audience who shouted at the offenders. **(2)** _Despite_ *[Notwithstanding]* a personal appeal from the festival's director for phones to be switched off, the following evening **(3)** _one_ [they] rang in the middle of a piano sonata. **(4)** _What_ made matters worse was the fact **(5)** _that_ the owner was sitting close to Sir Peter himself.

'I've just about **(6)** _had_ enough!' Sir Peter said, branding those failing to comply with the polite request 'artistic terrorists' intent **(7)** _on_ committing an act of vandalism. All it takes is a **(8)** _few_ [phone] calls or message bleeps for everyone else's enjoyment of the music to be spoilt. 'Some people,' he continued, 'just can't bear having their mobile turned off. It's like they feel disconnected from the world, or not wanted!'

2 Discuss these comments. Do you agree or disagree? Give reasons to support your opinion.

> People should not be allowed to take mobile phones into theatres or concert halls.

> Concert etiquette should be taught by parents.

> Technology is causing young people to have shorter attention spans.

Writing 1 (Paper 2 Part 1: Essay)

Summarising and evaluating

▶ **EXPERT STRATEGIES** page 169

1 Read the strategy and the exam task below, then answer the following questions.

  1 What type of writing task is it?

  2 Which two tasks must you include in your answer?

EXPERT STRATEGY

For this type of writing task, make sure your answer contains the following:
- key points of the two texts (a summary)
- your opinion of their content (an evaluation).

Also, use your own words, not 'chunks' from the texts.

Write an essay summarising and evaluating the key points from both texts. Use your own words throughout as far as possible, and include your own ideas in your answers.

You should write **240–280** words.

1 Performing techniques: stage vs. screen

Gesture, movement and physicality are vital on stage. Whereas tiny gestures can be magnified in close-up film shots, as a stage actor you will use your body very differently. You will need to communicate a physical energy and develop a 'stage presence'. The film close-up permits subtleties of facial expression and movement that don't work on the stage.

Camera work and editing achieve effects on the screen that the stage actor must create largely by using the body. In film, props and settings are also used extensively to convey meaning and atmosphere. On the stage, it's down to you to do that work.

2 Acting: finding your voice

Consider the actor's voice for a moment. Vocal expression is as much about movement and emotion as sound, and nowhere is this more noticeable than on the stage. Achieving resonance in your voice requires physical as well as vocal effort. For the screen, the emphasis may be on perfecting a range of accents rather than pitch, yet even here embracing cultural body language makes the accent sound more authentic. Interestingly, in the recording studio many voice actors imitate the movements of their animated characters to achieve better vocal results. The right training can help you develop such skills to find work in any medium.

2 Read the model answer to the question in Exercise 1. Does it address the two tasks successfully? Why/Why not?

The two texts **(1)** _discuss_ / _assess_ techniques required for different styles of acting. Firstly, the first text **(2)** _examines_ / _evaluates_ the use of physical expression on stage as opposed to film and **(3)** _conveys_ / _compares_ the value of facial expression in close-up film shots with the need to use the whole body on stage to **(4)** _exemplify_ / _communicate_ feeling. It **(5)** _suggests_ / _asserts_ that whereas film actors are supported by the setting and camera work, the stage actor is unaided, and must therefore exude stronger physical energy to achieve the same result.

There is no doubt that the two media **(6)** _demand_ / _need_ different styles of acting but now that technology has entered the theatre, set designers and directors are able to make use of special effects and more sophisticated props to create atmosphere. So, while it may have been true 50 years ago, I feel it is a gross exaggeration to suggest that the stage actor is totally unsupported today.

The second text, on the other hand, looks at the importance of the voice in acting, and emphasises the need for aspiring actors to **(7)** _acquire_ / _achieve_ a range of vocal skills to be able to sustain a career in any medium. It **(8)** _assumes_ / _acknowledges_ the relationship between vocal expression and body movement and **(9)** _advocates_ / _concludes_ following a training course to develop such skills effectively.

To my mind, the two texts examine specific skills needed for different types of acting but we should not ignore recognising the essential connection between vocal and physical expression, and the value of gaining the proper kind of training in order to become a versatile performer, capable of working on both stage and screen.

3 Circle the most suitable verb in _italics_ in the model answer. Explain your choices and say why the other options do not work.

4a Look at how the essay is organised. Underline the paragraphs which summarise the two texts. Has the candidate used their own words effectively?

  b Highlight the paragraph(s) in which the candidate evaluates the texts.

5 Discuss. Do you agree with the candidate's evaluation of the texts?

6 Do the extra writing task on page 192. Use the writing strategy to help you.

1B It's live!

Listening 2 (Paper 3 Part 4)

Before you listen

1 🎧 T1.03 Listen carefully to what the speaker says about studio vs. live performance and answer the following questions.

1 Name three advantages of recording music in a studio that the speaker mentions.
2 Which does the speaker prefer: studio recordings or live performances? How do you know?

EXPERT STRATEGY

Before you listen, carefully read the rubric and then the options for each part.

Multiple matching

2 🎧 T1.04 Read the strategy, then do the task.

➤ EXPERT STRATEGIES page 171

You will hear five short extracts in which people are talking about different free-time activities they take part in.

Task One

For questions **1–5**, choose from the list (**A–H**) each speaker's main reason for doing the activity.

Task Two

For questions **6–10**, choose from the list (**A–H**) what each speaker plans to do in the future.

You will hear the recording twice. While you listen, you must complete both tasks.

A a wish to excel at something	G	G 1
B nostalgia for a former interest	H	H 2
C feeling in need of a challenge	C	E 3
D proving someone wrong	E	C 4
E a love of entertaining people	F	A 5
F a need to impress others		
G the chance to improve fitness		
H wanting to develop existing skills		

A learn new techniques	C	H 6
B meet like-minded people		F 7
C find work in a related field	E	E 8
D initiate a local project	G	D 9
E participate in a major event	F	B 10
F put original work on show		
G gain a qualification		
H pass on expertise		

➤ **HELP**

• Speaker 1 refers to a friend's reaction – but was this the reason why she did the activity?

• Speaker 2 mentions getting a qualification. Is he talking about the past, the present or the future?

• Speaker 4 refers to an activity she used to do – but why did she take it up again?

Discussion

3 Which of the activities you heard about do you find interesting? Why/Why not?

4 Check the meaning of these key words and phrases from the audioscript.

EXPERT WORD CHECK

hard-pressed   counteract   inevitable   sedentary   tag along   hark back   passable   thrive on   hilarious   get your teeth into (sth)

A

B

C

Speaking (Paper 4 Parts 1 & 2)

Vocabulary 1: music and entertainment

1a Think of different ways in which music is used to entertain, either on its own or in combination with other activities. Which interests you the most?

b Discuss these questions.

1 What's on your iPod or your phone?
2 Have your tastes in music changed at all over the last couple of years? If so, in what way?
3 What do people's tastes in music reveal about their culture or generation?

2 Read the question and the four possible answers.

1 How much information is given in the answers?
2 What answer would *you* give to the question?

> Do you ever go clubbing?

Answer 1

> No, it's <u>not really my scene</u>, although I enjoy dancing generally.

Answer 2

> I've been on the odd occasion with friends. It's quite fun!

Answer 3

> Yes, every summer! We sometimes go to Mykonos where the clubbing scene is really good!

Answer 4

> I can't dance to save my life so this is not something I'd choose to do in my spare time!

Part 1

3 In pairs, ask each other the following questions, taking turns to ask and answer. Use the strategy to help you.

1 In what way does music make a difference to your life?
2 What would the world be like without music?
3 Is musical talent something you are born with or can you acquire it through hard work?
4 How do you think musical training might enhance other areas of your life?

EXPERT STRATEGY

Don't forget to expand your answers by giving additional information or a reason for your answer.

Vocabulary 2: describing music

4a 🎧 T1.05 Listen to a conversation between Maggie and Tom, then choose from the adjectives below to express their ideas.

deafening	depressing	discordant	harmonious
inspiring	mind-blowing	rhythmic	soothing
uplifting/moving	upbeat		

Tom likes _deafening_ heavy metal. He hates _discordant_ 20th century classical music.

Maggie likes _uplifting/moving upbeat_ _____ rock or pop; she doesn't really like _depressing soothing_ music. She finds classical composers such as Bach _inspiring_ .

b Who do you agree with?

D

E

Useful language: agreeing, disagreeing and weighing things up

5a 🎧 T1.05 Listen to the dialogue again, then complete the table below with phrases the speakers use to agree or disagree.

Agreement	Disagreement/ Partial disagreement	Weighing things up
although I agree with you	I hear what you're saying but I've never ~	Don't forget ~
	I'm not sure about that	
You're right there	to be honest	I bear that in my mind
	I'm bear in my mind ?	
absolutely		

b Now write the following expressions in the table.

A Ð I can't disagree with that ...
w Ð I think we ought to take into consideration ...
D That may be the case but ...
W We can't rule out (the possibility that) ...
w Have you considered ...?
D You've got a point but ...
A I'd go along with that.
A Absolutely!

6 Write a chat message in response to the statements below, using phrases from Exercise 5.

1 Listening to really loud music on a hands-free or on headphones is bad for your hearing. Be careful!

_____

2 There's nothing better than a live concert!

_____

3 I don't think I'd like to give a performance online and be watched by millions of people! How about you?

_____

Part 2
Collaborative task: planning a summer arts festival

> **EXPERT STRATEGY**
> Maintain a dialogue with your partner and use appropriate phrases for agreeing and disagreeing.

7 In pairs, do the task, using the strategy to help you.

a First, look at photographs A and B and talk together about how popular these activities might be during the summer where you live. You have about one minute to talk about this. ⏱ Time yourselves!

b Now look at all the photographs (A–E). Imagine that the organisers of a performing arts festival are producing two advertising posters and these pictures have been used for one of them.

Talk together about the different types of performing arts these photographs show. Then decide what other activities should be shown on the second poster. You have about three minutes to talk about this. ⏱ Time yourselves!

Part 2 Sample task

8a 🎧 T1.06 Read the Speaking assessment criteria on page 204. Then listen carefully to two students, Luisa and Max, doing the first part of the task. Identify any areas where they, in your opinion, fall short of the required standards.

b 🎧 T1.07 Now listen to the same students doing the second part of the task and use the same criteria to judge their performance.

c How did you do compared with Luisa and Max? How was your timing?

Task analysis

9 What was the most difficult part of the task for you? Why? How could you improve on that?

Language development 2

Future tense review

▶ **EXPERT GRAMMAR** page 173

1 In pairs, decide which follow-on sentence, a or b, is the most suitable in the following contexts. Give reasons for your decision.

1 Oh no! The electricity's gone off!
   ✓a What are we doing now?
   ✔b What are we going to do now?
2 You know he can't be trusted, so don't expect any sympathy from me!
   ✓a If you will keep on seeing him, you're bound to get hurt.
   b If you see him, you'll get hurt.
3 Don't worry about being late! When you get to the station,
   ✓a Paul will be waiting for you.
   b Paul will have waited for you.
4 Oh, good! You're here!
   ✓a I was just about to call you.
   b I'm going to call you.

Other forms with future meaning

2a Complete the dialogue with the phrases below. Use each phrase only once.

wouldn't be	were supposed to	was just about to
might	were due to be	was going to

Gemma: Oh, hi, Matt! I (1) _was just about to_ ~~was going to~~ call you shortly. I thought I (2) ~~was going to~~ _might_ go and see Kevin Spacey in *Richard III*. Do you fancy it?
Matt: Well, lucky you caught me, really. We (3) _were due to be_ rehearsing today but Bob called to say that Carla's sprained her ankle and so we (4) _wouldn't be_ going after all. I (5) ~~might~~ _was just about to_ go and see her now, as a matter of fact, but wanted to let you know about the situation first.
Gemma: Thanks. Shame about Carla, but lucky for you! A day off!
Matt: I'm not so sure about that, Gemma. We (6) _were supposed to_ finish rehearsing the first act today, so this is bound to set us back quite a bit. It could be days before she's able to rehearse again now.
Gemma: Sorry to hear that, then. Anyway, what do you say to *Richard III*? Shall we go?
Matt: Yeah, why not?

b 🎧 T1.08 **Listen and check your answers. Discuss.**

Use of English 2 (Paper 1 Part 4)

Key word transformations

1 Read the strategy on page 168, then do the task.

For questions 1–6, complete the second sentence so that it has a similar meaning to the first sentence, using the word given. Do not change the word given. You must use between three and eight words, including the word given. Here is an example (0).

0 Shall we get Harry a present? He's retiring next month.
   (due)
   Harry _is due to retire next month_ , so why don't we get him a present?
1 If the star hadn't caught the flu, there would have been a cast party tomorrow.
   (was) (due)
   There _was supposed to be a_ cast party tomorrow but the star has caught the flu.
2 Competition is fierce but Tilda Swinton is a firm favourite to win the award for Best Actress.
   (set)
   Despite _fierce competition ... Tilda Swindon is set to_ win the award for Best Actress.
3 Profits from Justin Timberlake's worldwide tour will probably exceed one billion dollars.
   (stands)
   Justin Timberlake's worldwide tour _stands to make in excess_ of one billion dollars.
4 A problem has forced the director to cancel this week's meeting with the scriptwriter.
   (supposed)
   The director _was supposed to attend_ a meeting with the scriptwriter this week but a problem has forced him to cancel it.
5 Sandra was fully intending to send a photograph with her application form but she forgot.
   (had) _had fully intended to send_ _had every intention of sending_
   Sandra _had every intention of sending_ a photograph with her application form but she forgot.
6 They're auditioning for the new musical on Monday, so no doubt hundreds of dancers will turn up.
   (bound) _turn up to/for_
   Hundreds of dancers _are bound to come to_ the auditions for the new musical on Monday.

steal the limelight

Use of English 3 (Paper 1 Part 1)

Lead-in

1 Do you have a favourite comedian? What do you find funny about him/her?

Developing skills: words in context
> EXPERT STRATEGIES page 167

2a Read the task and the text below. Then look at the example answer (0). All the options fit grammatically but only A fits the context. Discuss why the other options are not possible.

Multiple-choice cloze

b Read the strategy, then complete the task. Use the Help notes for support with certain items.

For questions 1–8, read the text below and decide which answer (A, B, C or D) best fits each gap. There is an example at the beginning (0).

A 'GRAND' RETURN TO STANDUP COMEDY

Comedians Pete Barnes and Dave Reid are (0) __A__ into the spotlight once more. After a twelve-year (1) __A__ in TV sitcoms, the comic duo are (2) __A__ up to appear live at the Grand Theatre, Leeds, on 15th August. 'We're delighted to be returning to the stage after such a long time and it seems fitting to be (3) __A D__ our comeback at the venue where we gave our debut performance,'

says Dave. 'We've (4) __D B__ a long way since then, and have added some great new material to our (5) __C B__ in preparation for going on tour in the autumn.'

The duo will be performing alongside other big names in a one-off gala performance which aims to (6) __C__ money for charity. Pete and Dave have gone viral with a promotional sketch, to give people a taste of what to expect in the show. Look out for 'Pete and Dave: The Traffic Warden' on all the major networking sites. At least one member of the Royal family is (7) __D__ to be attending the show, which is bound to (8) __C__ further interest. So, to be sure of a seat, buy your tickets early!

EXPERT STRATEGY

Some options have a similar meaning but only one fits the context of the passage.

come a long way

> **HELP**

1 This is a word that means 'an amount of time spent doing something specific'.

3 You are looking for the word that collocates with *comeback*.

4 All options fit grammatically but only one forms an idiom which means 'make great progress or improvement'.

		short		
0	A stepping	B tapping	C slipping	D popping
1	(A) stint *a period of time*	B shift	C turn	D go
? 2	(A) lined	B planned	C booked	D laid
? 3	A breaking	B doing	C holding	(D) making *make a comeback*
? 4	A reached	(B) come	C gained	D got
5	A role	(B) act	C play	D turn
6	A gather	B attract	(C) raise	D achieve
7	A gossiped	B suggested	C alleged	(D) rumoured
8	A enhance	B induce	(C) generate	D initiate

Task analysis

3 Answer the questions about the task.

1 Which of the gapped words in the text form part of a collocation?

2 Which words form part of an idiom or fixed phrase?

Writing 2 (Paper 2 Part 1: Essay)

Lead-in **1 a** How do you listen to music?

- radio
- live performance
- iPod
- internet streaming
- file-sharing websites
- other

b How has access to music on the internet affected the kind of music we listen to?

Task analysis **2** Read the exam task and texts below. Which of the following statements best sums up text 1?

1 Many people believe that illegally downloading music is destroying the industry, as people no longer need to buy CDs.
2 File-sharing sites have marginalised minor artists and diminished their chances of success.
3 Music piracy has brought about a shift of focus in the industry, by allowing music lovers a greater range of music to listen to.

Write an essay summarising and evaluating the key points from both texts. Use your own words throughout as far as possible, and include your own ideas in your answer.
You should write **240–280** words.

1 'File-sharing' impact on the music industry

Many people believe that file-sharing sites allowing users to share music across the globe have had a detrimental effect on the music industry, with record companies suffering as a result of declining CD sales.

The truth is, however, that most artists are not signed to major companies, and so often don't get much radio play. Uploading their songs onto file-sharing sites ensures they get exposure they might not otherwise receive as it allows music lovers to download their songs for free. Also, it affords listeners greater freedom of choice in what they listen to, thus offering the potential for CD sales across a broader spectrum of musical tastes.

2 The allure of live performance

In this age of high-definition sound, why do people still crave the sweaty atmosphere and crush of the crowd that a live concert provides? Is it perhaps to serve some inherent need to make a connection with others?

A live performance is a communal experience, shared by people of similar tastes. Passion for the same kind of sound generates energy and excitement often described as electric. Members of the audience sing along with the artists, and strangers forge a bond based on mutual appreciation and awareness. Also, bands often vary the way they play a song at concerts, so there is that promise of a unique experience never to be relived.

Plan your essay

3a Summarise: List the key points in the two texts. Then use them to build up a summary. Look back at the summary paragraphs in the model answer in Writing 1 on page 14 to help you.

b Evaluate: Compare the content of the two texts, by considering the following:
- any similarities – in style, theme, opinion
- any differences – in perspective, opinion, style
- to what extent you agree/disagree with the points they make

4 Decide how you wish to organise your answer. Look at the model answer in Writing 1 and the writing strategy to help you.

EXPERT STRATEGY

Here are two ways you can organise your answer.

Either
- summarise text 1
- evaluate text 1
- summarise text 2
- evaluate text 2

or
- summarise text 1
- summarise text 2
- evaluate texts 1 and 2

➤ EXPERT STRATEGIES page 169

Language and content

5a Complete the summary of text 2 with the correct form of the words below.

while	attract	suggest	despite	stem	experience

The second text looks at why live concerts continue to **(1)** _attract_ large audiences **(2)** _despite_ the high quality of recorded music today. It **(3)** _suggests_ this tendency **(4)** _stem_ from a fundamental need to physically **(5)** _experience_ the atmosphere and share their love of music with others of similar tastes, **(6)** _while_ at the same time hoping to hear something slightly different.

b Refer back to your notes and write a paragraph evaluating the two texts. The following words and phrases may help you.

While the first text suggests …
The second text, on the other hand, argues …
We cannot ignore the fact that …
To my mind …
There is no doubt in my mind that … live performance brings you a unique experience you've don't usually have from listening to CDs, such as
While I agree with this point to a certain extent, there are other factors to consider. facial expression the singers make or original arranges for the songs
Undoubtedly, there is some truth in this view but … file-sharing sites are unlikely to encourage people to buy CDs

Write your essay

➤ EXPERT STRATEGIES page 169

6 Now write your essay, using the ideas and some of the language above. Write your answer in **240–280** words.

Check your essay

➤ EXPERT WRITING page 191

7 Edit your essay, using the checklist on page 191.

Review

1 Complete the sentences with the correct form of the verbs below.

acquire   convey   assert   demonstrate   assess
recognise   demand   conclude

1 During next week's seminar, students of the drama school _will acquire_ the skills necessary to promote themselves, as well as perform on stage.

2 Today, professional dancer Miguel Zotto _is demonstrating / demonstrates_ the modern style of the Argentine tango for us, with his lovely partner, Eva Viron.

3 Training to become a professional ballet dancer _demands_ dedication, hard work and natural talent.

4 After examining the damage caused by the fire, the experts _concluded_ that it had been caused by a discarded cigarette.

5 _Recognising_ the need to inject new life into the declining theatre, the manager decided to hold a hip-hop and breakdance festival.

6 At the end of the course, students will _be assessed_ on their ability to adapt to a variety of acting roles, including song and dance routines.

7 Mona _asserted_ her right to demand compensation for the accident, after some loose floorboards were discovered in the stage.

8 The haunting music of the ballet _Swan Lake_ _conveys_ the sense of _anguish_ that the protagonist feels.   └ _painful feeling of loss_

2 Replace the underlined phrases in the sentences with a suitable collocation or fixed phrase.

1 The _final practice_ of the play was disastrous but fortunately, the first evening performance went off very smoothly.   _dress rehearsal_

2 The audience cheered as all the artists returned to the stage for a _final bow_.   _curtain call_

3 The actress took one last look in the mirror before sweeping onto the stage right _on time_.   _on cue_

4 The audience gave the cast a _wonderful send-off by rising from their seats to applaud them_.   _standing ovation_

5 Just because I didn't agree with his view, there was no need for the director to _shout at me_!   _jump down my throat_

6 I would _grab the chance_ to perform alongside Johnny Depp, if I were you.   _leap at the opportunity_

7 Some performers relish being _in the public eye_, while others crave some privacy.   _in the limelight_

8 According to some critics, Spanish actor Javier Bardem's talent _is unlimited_.   _knows no bound_

3 Circle the correct form of the verb to complete the sentences.

1 Sally _is studying / studies_ graphic art and hopes to become a set designer.

2 The London Symphony Orchestra, which _was performing / has been performing_ at the Royal Albert Hall since May, is giving its final concert this evening.

3 David's debut performance as Hamlet was magnificent. Until then, he _was only ever performing / had only ever performed_ in minor roles.

4 Helena _was training / trained_ to be a ballet dancer when an accident put an end to her dreams.

5 A preview performance of Richard Beecham's new play at the Barbican theatre _is to be shown / is showing_ on Friday.

6 Alice works at Pixar, and so far _has been working / has worked_ on five major animated movies.

7 George and Dave _have been collaborating / collaborated_ for four years before setting up their own Light and Sound studio.

8 Molly _had been hoping / has hoped_ to make a career in film but her father wouldn't let her.

4 Read the text below. Use the word in CAPITALS at the end of some of the lines to form a word that fits in the gap in the same line.

ITALIA CONTI ACADEMY

The world-renowned Italia Conti Academy in London is a centre of (0) _excellence_ in the training of students whose dream is to work in the performing arts. The overall standard of (1) _tuition_ is very high and teaching staff typically use the most up-to-date methods with great (2) _enthusiasm_ and dedication.

EXCEL

TUTOR

ENTHUSE

The Academy offers a variety of courses. What these have in common is the level of both physical and mental (3) _commitment_ they demand from students. But they are all designed to be (4) _accessible_ to anyone with a high level of ambition combined with (5) _extraordinary_ talent.

COMMIT

ACCESS

ORDINARY

Students get the chance to attend both formal classes and practical workshops with the emphasis on preparing for public performance. Indeed, many successful students do go on to perform first as (6) _understudies_ and then as lead artists in (7) _prestigious_ theatrical productions in London, whilst others bring the same level of (8) _professionalism_ to more specialist fields, such as choreography. Little wonder, therefore, that the Italia Conti Academy enjoys such an enviable reputation.

UNDER

PRESTIGE

PROFESSION

2A

- **Reading and Use of English:** Gapped text (Part 6); Word formation (Part 3)
- **Listening:** Multiple-choice questions (Part 1)
- **Language development:** Passive forms
- **Writing:** Article (Part 2): Skills for article-writing; Descriptive vocabulary

2B

- **Listening:** Sentence completion (Part 2)
- **Speaking:** Individual long turn (Part 3): Food production/environmental issues
- **Reading and Use of English:** Open cloze (Part 2)
- **Language development:** General verb phrases; Phrases with *have*; Prepositional phrases
- **Writing:** Article (Part 2): Planning and organising; Analysis of introduction

Lead-in

1a Where would you normally find the animals in the photographs?

Africa   Asia   Canada   Denmark   Germany   Mexico   Norway   Russia   the Arctic
the UK   the USA

b Which three animals would you most like to see in the wild?

c Which would you say are threatened or endangered species?

d What aspects of the natural world do you appreciate the most? Which aspects of modern society do you enjoy the least?

2 One of the dangers of modern society is the threat to the world's natural resources. What do you think we should do about this?

3 Which environmental organisations do you know? What do they do?

Reading (Paper 1 Part 6)

Before you read

1 The Amondawa are an Amazonian tribe of about 150 people.
- They live by hunting, fishing and farming.
- They have no words for concepts such as 'next week' or 'last year'.
- Nobody in the tribe has an age; they just change their name when they become an adult.

2 Compare how the tribe lives with how we live in the modern world. Think of some of the advantages and disadvantages of living as they do.

Skimming

3 Read through the text quickly (ignore the missing paragraphs at this stage).
1 What is the main topic of the text?
2 How would you describe the attitude of the tribes mentioned in the text towards contact with the outside world?

Gapped text

> EXPERT STRATEGIES page 168

4 Read the strategy on page 168, then do the task.

You are going to read an extract from an article. Seven paragraphs have been removed from the extract. Choose from the paragraphs A–H the one which fits each gap (1–7). There is one extra paragraph which you do not need to use.

Task analysis

5 Compare your answers.
1 Highlight sections in the text and in the gapped paragraphs that gave you the clues or the links.
2 In what way was an understanding of the overall text structure important in finding the answers?

Discussion

6 Give your opinion on the following question.
Should we try to bring 'civilisation' to these uncontacted peoples or do they have a right to follow their traditional way of life in peace?

7 Check the meaning of these key words from the text.

EXPERT WORD CHECK

ravage clamour tributaries resurgent indigenous enmeshed
slaughter logger dredge up concessions

The last stand of the Amazon

Novelist Edward Docx has spent almost a decade travelling to the Amazon, watching as multinational companies ravage the land he loves. Here is his heartfelt dispatch on the forest's final frontier – still home to as many as 100 uncontacted tribes.

Deep in the Brazilian Amazon, there are no horizons and so the dawn does not break but is instead born in the trees – a wan and smoky blue. The crazed clamour of the night – growls, hoots, croaks – has died away and for a moment there is almost hush. This is also the only time of cool. Then, suddenly, the great awakening begins and the air is filled with a thousand different songs, chirps, squawks and screeches – back and forth, far and near, all around. Nothing anywhere can prepare you for this unique experience in a supremely challenging part of the world.

1 | G |

The area of the Amazon rainforest is larger than Western Europe and the forest stretches over nine countries. There are approximately 1,250 tributaries that service the main river, 17 of which are more than 1,000 miles long. Roughly a fifth of the earth's oxygen is produced in the Amazon rainforest and more than two-fifths of all the species in the world live there. Surprisingly enough, oil is one of the main resurgent threats to the region.

2 | F |

Major disruption and destruction to the forest usually follows, starting with seismic testing and then helicopters, roads, crews, and so on. And inevitably, there are catastrophic spills and accidents. Health studies have found that 98 percent of the children of the indigenous Achuar tribe have high levels of cadmium in their blood, and two-thirds suffer from lead poisoning. A lawsuit is currently being brought to court by some of their members due to the contamination of the region.

3 | B |

Beatriz Huertas Castillo, a writer and researcher, explains: 'They are indigenous peoples who, either by choice or by chance, live in remote isolation from their national societies. There are at least 14 such tribes in Peru. We think 69 in Brazil. Maybe 100 in the Amazon area as a whole.' They are among the handful of peoples left alive on the planet who have next to no idea of what the world has become and who live as they have done for thousands of years.

4 | C |

'I spoke to Mashco-Piro women when they were first contacted,' says Castillo. 'And they were terrified of disease, of being slaughtered, of their children being taken into slavery. In the past, every encounter has brought terror for them – they have no immunity to our diseases and they were thought of as animals, even hunted. Now they see the loggers and the oil companies coming in a little further every year. And for them it's the same thing so they flee into neighbouring territories.'

5 | H |

The problems of this new threat, as explorer, writer and Amazon expert John Hemming explained, are these: the territories of tribes such as the Kayapo will be flooded; vast amounts of the greenhouse gas methane will be released, due to rotting vegetation; further roads and colonisation will happen in their wake; they change the flow and run of all the river systems, which affects untold numbers of aquatic species, meaning that more food will have to be imported for consumption, more roads will have to be built, and so grimly on.

6 | A |

'Since the 2004 peak of 27,000 sq km of forest destroyed, matters have improved with regard to deforestation,' he says when I call him at his home in Manaus, the great river city right in the heart of the Amazon. 'Last year we only lost 6,500 sq km.' However, that is still an area more than four times the size of Greater London.

7 | D |

His grandfather had been among the first of his tribe to be contacted and his own sons were wearing football shirts; his eldest was training to be a guide. He put it like this: the Amazon matters because right now it is where humanity is making its biggest decisions – actualities that have an impact first on the lives of his children, but eventually on the lives of ours too. To have no view, I realised as I left, amounted to much the same as being a hypocrite.

A It is important to acknowledge though, that not everything is getting worse. Some of the campaigning in the past 20 years has worked and there are cautious grounds for hope. Paulo Adario, a veteran ecologist, is one of the individuals to have done most in the service of conservation, and he is happy to bring me up-to-date.

B There are hundreds of such tribes in the forest – many of them now enmeshed in 'integration projects' or other demoralising fiascos – but those that most often capture international attention are the uncontacted. There is some dispute, however, as to what exactly is meant by the term.

C The best way to think about these few remaining isolated tribes is to imagine a series of concentric circles. There are the tribes that have regular relations with the outside. Then there are a good number of tribes who have very circumscribed dealings with the outside world. Then finally, in the heart of the forest, there are these few remaining peoples with none.

D Time on the river is like time at sea. It's measured in the way the light changes the colour of the water. At dawn, there are mists and the river appears almost milky. By noon it is the colour of cinnamon. And then, in the evening, the low sun shoots streaks of amber and gold before the dusk rises up and everything turns to indigo. One such evening, we visited a fisherman.

E Tribal leaders have even been to London to complain, saying that these dams will force their people from the land and threaten their way of life. There has also recently been an unprecedented operation to destroy the unlawful gold-mining dredgers that are now killing off river habitats by dredging up silt.

F The amount of land that has been covered by concessions for its extraction, together with gas, has increased fivefold in the last ten years – almost 50 percent of the entire Peruvian-owned Amazon. This means that the government has effectively sold off half of the rainforest it owns for this purpose and 75 percent is forecast by 2020.

G One reason we struggle to understand the region is that there is so much to take in. And because there has been some good news on the headline problem – deforestation – it has faded in our collective consciousness in the past few years. So it's worth stepping back and reminding ourselves of some of the fundamentals.

H In other words, it is the incursions and what follows that have the most impact. But now another problem is causing acrimony, fear and dispute. More than 100 new hydroelectric dams are planned across Brazil and Peru, including the most controversial of all – the Belo Monte Project on the Xingu river.

Vocabulary

Word formation: verbs → nouns ending in -ion

1 The suffix -ion when added to a verb refers to a state or process, e.g. operate → operation.

a Find the noun form of these verbs in the text on page 25 and complete the sentences. Discuss the meaning of any words that are unfamiliar.

[handwritten: colonisation   consumption   disruption   extraction]

colonise   consume   disrupt   extract
integrate   isolate

[handwritten: integration   isolation]

1 Over-*consumption*, when we buy or eat more than we need to fulfil our basic needs, will have to be curtailed in order to preserve resources. *[handwritten margin: stop]*

2 It is doubtful whether the *integration* of native tribes into modern society is desirable or beneficial to them.

3 When humans start building roads and bridges in the jungle, this can cause severe *disruption* to the whole ecosystem of the forest.

4 The *colonisation* of Antarctica is unlikely given the difficult living conditions there.

5 Only a few communities nowadays live in complete *isolation* from the modern world.

6 Many multinational mining companies are involved in the *extraction* of gold, copper and diamonds from the world's rainforests.

b The following verbs (1–10) have noun forms ending in -ion. Write the noun form and match the verbs to their meanings (a–j). Where is the stress in the pronunciation of the noun forms?

1 contaminate	contamination	h
2 degrade	degradation ?	g
3 deplete	depletion ?	i
4 deteriorate	deterioration	a
5 devastate	devastation	b
6 implement	implementation	e
7 irrigate	irrigation	j
8 legislate	legislation	f
9 pollinate	pollination	c
10 rehabilitate	rehabilitation	d

[handwritten beside rows 1–3: for physical things   area, land....   forest]

a become worse
b damage sth badly or completely
c enable a plant to produce seeds
d help (a person, an animal) to live a normal life again
e make changes that have been officially decided
f make a law
g make the condition of sth worse
h pollute
i reduce the amount of sth
j water land or crops

c Complete the sentences with an appropriate noun from Exercise 1b.

1 For animals born in captivity, there are some very successful *rehabilitation* programmes whereby they are eventually released back into the wild.

2 *Irrigation* of the land to keep it watered and *pollination* of the crops by insects or the wind are essential for the livelihood of millions of people.

3 Uncontrolled development can often lead to the *contamination* of water supplies by waste chemicals and a *deterioration* in the quality of life of local peoples. Suitable *legislation* and its *implementation* are of the utmost urgency to control the situation.

4 Environmental *degradation* is largely caused by the reduction or *depletion* of the world's natural resources. This also includes the *devastation* of its forests by short-sighted companies hoping to make a quick profit.

Animal sounds – figurative use

2a 🎧 T1.09 Can you identify the following sounds mentioned in the text on page 25? Which type of animal or bird do you think might make them?

1 croak   *frog*   4 chirp   *birds*
2 growl   *tiger*   5 hoot   *owl*
3 screech   *parrot*   6 squawk   *parrot*

b Here are some more animal sounds. Which animals or insects might make these sounds?

1 bark *[dog, seals]*   3 buzz *[bee, mosquito]*   5 howl *[wolf, dog]*   7 roar *[tiger, lion]*
2 bellow *[bull, ox, elephant]*   4 chatter *[parrot, monkey]*   6 hum *[bee, humming bird]*   8 squeak *[mouse, rabbit, hamster]*

c Animal sounds can be used figuratively in our daily language. Circle the verbs that would be most commonly used in the following sentences. Discuss the contexts in which the verbs in Exercises 2a and 2b can be used, giving examples where possible.

1 'Get back to your room!,' Dad screeched / *growled.*

2 'It's such a lovely morning!' she *chirped* / squawked happily.

3 'I've got a really sore throat,' he hooted / *croaked.*

4 'Can you stop squeaking / *screeching* in my ear? You'll deafen me,' she said.

5 The car *roared* / howled off down the road in a cloud of exhaust fumes.

6 He was so cold in the snow his teeth were humming / *chattering.*

7 The coffee shop at Kew Gardens was *buzzing* / bellowing with activity last Saturday morning.

d What do these phrases mean?

1 I don't give a hoot.   *I don't care*

2 He's very chirpy this evening.
   happy
   lively

die down — become less strong
back — lose its leaves
out — stop existing

amount to sth

crack up
down (on sb/sth)
try harder to prevent an illegal activity

Phrasal verbs

3 Read the sentences below. Use your dictionary to find the correct phrasal verbs to complete each gap using the verbs and particles given. Write the phrasal verbs in their correct form.

amount come crack	back down up
cut die hand step	out down on
use wipe	up against to

1 Governments are trying to _crack down on_ the companies that carry out illegal logging and _hand out_ some serious punishments.
2 Environmentalists are warning about the dangers of _using up_ existing water supplies in certain parts of the world.
3 _Cutting down_ areas of forest could effectively _wipe out_ certain species.
4 It is often the case that local peoples _come up against_ impossible odds when they try to protect their immediate environment.
5 Campaigns by the international community against whalers have prevented the blue whale from _dying out_.
6 Her reaction on hearing the news _amounted to_ nothing less than disbelief.
7 The company needs someone who can _step back_ from the immediate problems and consider the situation long-term.

Use of English 1 (Paper 1 Part 3)

Word formation

1a Read the text below quickly. What is the alternative source of power referred to and why is it currently not being used so much?

b Now do the task.

➤ EXPERT STRATEGIES page 167

For questions 1–8, read the text below. Use the word given in CAPITALS at the end of some of the lines to form a word that fits in the gap in the same line. There is an example at the beginning (0).

The power of the tides

In recent years, a lot of international **(0)** _attention_ has focused on the idea that we should be aiming to meet the needs of the present without compromising the ability of future generations to meet theirs. This idea is generally referred to as **(1)** _sustainable_ development, and an integral part of the wider aim is the use of so-called **(2)** _renewable_ sources of energy.	ATTEND SUSTAIN RENEW
Tidal power, the **(3)** _harnessing_ of the movement of the oceanic tides to generate electricity, has a part to play in this, especially given the greater **(4)** _predictability_ of tides compared to other sources of power, such as the wind or the sun. Until recently, however, tidal power has remained a largely **(5)** _untapped_ source of energy, due to the relatively high costs involved. If this issue can be addressed however, tidal power could represent an almost **(6)** _inexhaustible_ source of energy, and recent technological **(7)** _breakthroughs_ are beginning to make this into a more realistic proposition. If costs can be brought down, then electricity produced in this way could compete more **(8)** _effectively_ on the open market.	HARNESS PREDICT TAP EXHAUST BREAK EFFECT

untapped — available but not yet used

exhaustive — including everything possible very thorough or complete

integral part sustainable development oceanic tides
tidal power renewable resource technological breakthrough
future generation untapped source open market
inexhaustible source realistic proposition

Collocations

2 Find at least eight collocations (adjective–noun) in the text in Exercise 1. Make a note of them and discuss their meaning.

3 Have you seen any evidence of renewable energy sources being used in your country? What is your opinion of them?

Listening 1 (Paper 3 Part 1)

Before you listen

1 Discuss the following question.

Look at the photographs. What can we learn from studying these creatures and animal life in general?

Identifying speaker purpose, gist, detail

2 🎧 T1.10 Listen to three short extracts from talks, then answer the question that goes with each extract.

Extract One: listen for speaker purpose
Why does the speaker mention what certain orang-utans do?

Extract Two: listen for gist
What is the point of the new 'smart' collar?

Extract Three: listen for detail
In what ways might bycatch be better controlled?

Multiple-choice questions

➤ EXPERT STRATEGIES page 170

3 🎧 T1.11 Read the strategy, then do the task.

You will hear three different extracts. For questions 1–6, choose the answer (A, B or C) which best fits according to what you hear. There are two questions for each extract.

Extract One

You hear part of an interview with a scientist called Ruth Carter who studies the emotional life of animals.

1 Ruth feels that animals are often not credited with having feelings because of

- A inadequate research to support the idea.
- B false assumptions based on appearance.
- C prejudice against certain species.

2 Why does Ruth mention an incident with a whale?

- A to give weight to her arguments
- B to show how events can be misinterpreted
- C to underline how much research still needs to be done

Extract Two

You hear a zoologist called Liam Evans giving a talk about a species of ape called white-handed gibbons.

3 According to Liam, what is unusual about the gibbons?

- A how they move through their natural habitat
- B similarities between them and some species of frog
- C the way their limbs have adapted to their environment

4 Liam mentions Greek athletes in order to explain how gibbons manage to

- A carry objects when jumping.
- B jump relatively great distances.
- C control their landings after a jump.

Extract Three

You hear a radio report about a man called John Reybridge, who worked as a volunteer at a wildlife rescue centre in Africa.

5 What led John to decide to go to Africa?

- A fear of losing his job in a recession
- B frustration at his poor career prospects
- C loss of motivation for his previous work

6 In Africa, John got most satisfaction from

- A successfully returning animals to the wild.
- B preparing captive animals for life in the wild.
- C rescuing animals that couldn't survive in the wild.

Development and discussion

4 If you were given the opportunity to take a year out to spend studying wildlife or the environment generally, where would you choose to go, and why? Give your reasons and discuss.

{ nothing to do ... 今はやることない
nothing to be done ... なすすべない }

Language development 1

Passive forms

> EXPERT GRAMMAR page 174

Active or passive infinitive?

1 Complete the sentences with the active or passive infinitive.

1 I'm afraid there's nothing *to ~~done~~ be done* (do) since we've tried everything. The new road through the jungle is going ahead.

2 He looked for his binoculars but they were nowhere *to be found* (find).

3 In the end, the police found that no one was *to ~~be blame~~* (blame) for the fire; it was an accident.

4 I've got so much work *to do* (do) to complete this report.

5 The animals are usually *to be fed* (feed) at noon.

6 The reason behind the new government strategy is impossible *to understand* (understand).

Impersonal passive structures

2 Read the grammar reference on impersonal passive structures on page 174.

In pairs, rewrite the following sentences, using an impersonal structure. Compare your answers.

1 I know that his furniture business only uses recycled wood – that's a fact. *It is known that ~*
His furniture business is known to only use recycle wood.

2 They claim that the environmentally-educational board game Ethica is really good.
The environmentally-educational board game Ethica is claimed to be really good.

3 I think that the turtle population is increasing in certain parts of the world.
The turtle population is thought to be increasing in certain ~

4 I believe that the largest deep sea coral is near Norway and covers more than 100 sq km.
It is believed that the largest deep sea coral is near Norway. ~

5 Scientists say that more than 600 new species have been discovered in Madagascar in the last decade.
It is said that

6 Deep-sea fishermen have reported seeing giant squid but they still remain elusive creatures.
Seeing giant squid has been reported but they still ~
Giant squid has been reported to be seen but ~

Currently は 現在形
(完了形では使わない)
後照的な

Other passive forms

3 Rewrite the sentences in the passive. Make any changes that are necessary.

1 They have seen elephants crying.
Elephants *have been seen [~~to~~ crying*].

2 The monkeys loved it when we took their photographs!
having the photographs taken
The monkeys loved *to be taken photographs*.

3 You must finish this report by Monday without fail.
This report *must be finished by Monday without fail*.

4 He explained to us how a herd of elephants behaves. *to us group*
It *was explained how a heard of elephants behaves*.

5 They made us wear hats and heavy boots on our jungle walk.
We *were made to wear hats and heavy boots on our jungle walk*.

6 They suggested that we took part in a new eco-project.
It *was suggested that*.

7 The girl's parents didn't let her keep snakes in the house.
was
The girl *~~were~~ not allowed to keep snakes in the house*.

The passive: mixed tenses

4 Complete the text with the correct form of the passive. More than one answer might be possible.

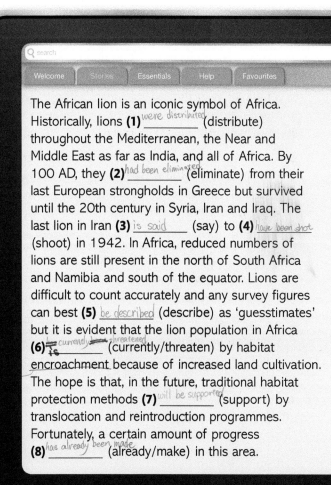

The African lion is an iconic symbol of Africa. Historically, lions **(1)** *were distributed* (distribute) throughout the Mediterranean, the Near and Middle East as far as India, and all of Africa. By 100 AD, they **(2)** *had been eliminated* (eliminate) from their last European strongholds in Greece but survived until the 20th century in Syria, Iran and Iraq. The last lion in Iran **(3)** *is said* (say) to **(4)** *have been shot* (shoot) in 1942. In Africa, reduced numbers of lions are still present in the north of South Africa and Namibia and south of the equator. Lions are difficult to count accurately and any survey figures can best **(5)** *be described* (describe) as 'guesstimates' but it is evident that the lion population in Africa **(6)** *is currently threatened* (currently/threaten) by habitat encroachment because of increased land cultivation. The hope is that, in the future, traditional habitat protection methods **(7)** *will be supported* (support) by translocation and reintroduction programmes. Fortunately, a certain amount of progress **(8)** *has already been made* (already/make) in this area.

[handwritten notes at top: wallow in the defeat / sad /self-pity ← (不好受/得不到认可的) / 自己以为可以享受. だ / wallow in self-pity]

Writing 1 (Paper 2 Part 2: Article)

What makes a good article?

1 Skills for article-writing include:

1 How will you know who your target readers will be?

2 Give examples of types of articles that will require formal and semi-formal language. Can articles include more than one style? Give an example. *[handwritten: to walk proudly with your head up 昂首阔步 闊步する]*

3 Give three examples of how you might organise your writing to be more effective.

4 How can you make your writing more interesting through your choice of vocabulary? Give examples. What grammatical structures should you try to include?

5 In what ways can you make a title stand out? What linguistic tricks can you use in the first paragraph to grab your readers?

2a The following extract is about the Amboseli elephants in Kenya and includes some interesting descriptive language. Complete the gaps with a word from the list below that has a similar meaning to the word given.

daintily	euphoric	grumpy	lavishly	lazily
massive	peacefully	trumpeting	wide-eyed	
wistfully				

3 The extract continues when the writer returns after many years. Discuss the meaning of the verbs in **bold**. How does the use of these verbs add to the effectiveness of the description?

[handwritten: (large animals) lie & roll in water/mud to keep them cool] *[handwritten: to run with long steps, enthusiastic way]*

Nearby, hippos **wallowed**, and bushbuck and oryx **twitched** nervously before **bounding** out of their path, while brightly-coloured crested cranes, the ballet dancers of the bush, **strutted** their stuff. At one point I leaned out of the Land Cruiser to see two huge catfish in the crystal-clear water of a swamp; later I spotted a family of hyenas **skulking** in the elephant grass.

[handwritten: to hide or move around secretly especially when you are planning sth bad]

➤ **EXPERT WRITING** page 191

➤ **EXPERT STRATEGIES** page 169

4 Read the writing task below. Write your article. Try and include some interesting descriptive language.

> An online environmental magazine has asked readers to send in articles about places of natural beauty that they have visited. You decide to write an article describing a place you enjoyed visiting, what you saw there and evaluating its importance as a place of natural beauty.

Amboseli, Kenya:
where elephants have the right of way

A 15-year-old English schoolboy gazes **(1)** wide-eyed (wonderingly) over the lush savannah lands of Kenya's Amboseli Reserve. Large herds of zebra, wildebeest and buffalo are moving **(2)** peacefully (quietly) through a landscape of acacia bushes and elephant grass as giraffe feed **(3)** daintily (delicately) on the elegant, outstretched branches of fever trees. In the background, hovering above a halo of cloud, Kilimanjaro's cone is **(4)** lavishly (thickly) laden with snow.

The young man's eye is caught by a small group of elephants enjoying a mud bath in the Longinye Swamp. The family members, from matriarch to **(5)** grumpy (bad-tempered) adolescent to a crèche of **(6)** trumpeting (noisy) toddlers, bring a **(7)** euphoric (happy) smile to his face. Just a few months before, he had gazed **(8)** wistfully (longingly) at scenes just like this in a book of prints by the wildlife artist David Shepherd.

And now, as the sun drops like a giant blood orange *[handwritten: simile]* in the west, a **(9)** massive (huge) bull elephant with tusks large enough to grace a mammoth wanders **(10)** lazily (slowly) onto the road in front of the vehicle he is travelling in. And stops. Beside him a sign reads *Elephants have right of way*. Neither vehicle nor elephant moves for the next hour.

b Discuss the meaning of any unknown words.

Listening 2 (Paper 3 Part 2)

a tadpole
おたまじゃくし

Before you listen

1 What factors should you consider when planning to keep animals at home? Think about the following:

- shelter
- cost
- feeding
- long-term commitment
- safety
- neighbours
- noise

Sentence completion

2 🎧 T1.12 Listen to this short extract about building chicken coops *鶏小屋* (houses) and complete the gap. What do you notice about the sentence that you have to complete?

According to the speaker, it's important for chickens to have _____ in their coop where they can sit at night.

> EXPERT STRATEGIES page 170

3 🎧 T1.13 Read the strategy, then do the task.

You will hear a writer called Alex Horne talking about keeping chickens as a hobby. For questions 1–9, complete the sentences with a word or short phrase.

KEEPING CHICKENS

A website with the name (1) *chicken world* _____ supplied Alex with all he needed to begin his new hobby.

The section of the chicken house intended to act as the (2) *roof* _____ was the only part that wasn't straight.

Alex found some wire in the shape of a (3) *tunnel ?* _____ , which was designed to keep predators out of the chicken house.

The first (4) *fence* _____ which Alex constructed in his garden was not very effective.

Alex mentions being impressed by how (5) *self-sufficient / happy* _____ the chickens seemed to be.

What Alex calls the chickens' (6) *duties* **sleeping quarters** _____ had to be cleaned on a regular basis.

Alex uses the word (7) *sneaky* _____ to describe the personality of the chicken called Shakira.

Alex describes his garden as a (8) *wilderness ?* _____ to give an idea of what it was like after the chickens had been digging.

Even the traps and (9) *alarms* _____ which Alex bought didn't solve the problem of rats.

> HELP

1 How did the website called *Poultry Plus* help Alex and his wife?

6 How often did Alex have to do his chores?

9 How did Alex try to solve the problem of the rats?

Discussion

4 Discuss the pros and cons of keeping animals as a food source.

5 Check the meaning of these key words and phrases from the audioscript.

> EXPERT WORD CHECK
>
> straightforward   dump   deterrent   teething problem
> scramble (over sth)   solidarity   fret   tweak   sneaky   stalk

Speaking (Paper 4 Part 3)

Lead-in

1a For years, the idea in farming has been that 'bigger is better'. However, things seem to be changing. Look at the pairs of photographs A and B and discuss the differences – from the point of view of the animals, the farmer and the consumer.

b Why are honey bees important in food cultivation?

Vocabulary: food production/environmental issues

2 Complete the fact sheets below with the words and phrases below. There should be only one answer for each gap.

animal pollination   confined space
cost-effective   daylight hours   fungal diseases
lifespan   natural surroundings   nutritional value
roam freely   welfare concerns

A

Factory farming

- greater milk yield (22–30 litres per day)
- cows milked 3/7 (three times a day)
- animal (1) _____ regarding mega-dairies
- cows live up to 5 years
- 1,000–30,000 cows in a barn or shed

Factory-reared meat
- animals are given lots of antibiotics

Organic farming

- smaller milk yield (5 litres per day)
- cows milked 2/7 (twice a day)
- cows in (2) _____ are not stressed
- cows live up to 20 years
- 50–100 cows in a field/barn

BUT
- organic farmers still make a profit by selling high-quality milk direct to the customer
- organic farmers grow their own feed so they don't have to buy expensive processed feed supplements

Organic meat
- animals graze the grass and are fed natural products

Battery/Caged hens

- produce more eggs (?)
- more (3) _____ because they eat less, more control
- eat less

BUT
- are enclosed in a (4) _____
- have health problems, e.g. painful feet
- slaughtered young

Free-range hens

- produce slightly fewer eggs but higher (5) _____ (less cholesterol), taste better
- less easily controlled
- need more food because more active
- (6) _____ , eat insects, etc.
- are happy and healthy (apart from the normal illnesses)
- live out their normal (7) _____

Honey bee collapse

- Almost a third of global farm output depends on (8) _____ , largely by honey bees. Honey bees pollinate 80%–90% of fruit and vegetables consumed globally.
- Bees are in decline. What are the causes? Pesticides seem to be the main culprit. Some pesticides harm the bees' memory; others poison them; yet others reduce their resistance to (9) _____ .

What can be done?
- curb pesticide use during (10) _____ , the time when bees are active
- plant more bee-friendly flowers and shrubs, especially in cities
- give more help and support to bee-keepers

B

C

Part 3 Individual long turn

> **EXPERT STRATEGIES** page 171

5a Work in pairs. Firstly, read the strategy on page 171, then look at the Task cards below. Student A should respond to the question on Task card 1 and talk for about two minutes. ☉ There are some ideas on the card for you to use if you like. Student B should respond briefly to their question.

> **Task card 1**
>
> What steps are being taken to protect the environment?
> • sustainable/alternative technology
> • scientific research
> • animal protection programmes

Question for Student B:
• In what ways can people try to help the environment in their daily lives?

b Student B should respond to the question on Task card 2 and talk for about two minutes. ☉ There are some ideas on the card for you to use if you like. Student A should respond briefly to their question.

> **Task card 2**
>
> What responsibilities does having domestic pets entail?
> • providing adequate exercise, care and attention
> • not leaving them locked up for hours
> • providing the right food and veterinary care

Question for Student A:
• What can be done about the problem of mistreated or abandoned animals?

Part 3 Model answer

3a Look at Task card 1 and the possible points to talk about. Make a note of important points you would mention under each section.

b 🎧 T1.14 Listen to a student doing the task. ☉ Time how long she takes.

> **Task card 1**
>
> How much do these issues concern you?
> • factory farming, battery or caged hens
> • recycling
> • deforestation

c 🎧 T1.14 Now listen again.

1 Add any important points the speaker mentioned to your notes for Exercise 3a. How do your ideas compare?
2 Note down any useful linking structures that were used in the task.

Useful language: structuring your extended contribution/talk

4 You can use the useful language listed on page 206 to help you structure your long turn. Add any phrases you found in Exercise 3b.

Developing the discussion

6 Discuss the following questions.

1 Why are certain animal and plant species in danger of dying out?
2 How can governments be persuaded to change their minds about environmental policies?
3 What are some of the main dangers facing our seas and the creatures that live in them?

Language development 2

Collocational phrases

> EXPERT GRAMMAR page 175

General verb phrases

1a Complete the verb phrases in the sentences with the words below. The verbs are in **bold** text.

at (your) ease   the attention   importance
interest   no signs of   on a whim   thanks to
the needs   up-to-date

put sb at ease
= make sb feel relaxed
catch

1 Their boss always **brings** them _up-to-date_ with the latest developments in the market.
2 The man at the organic farm **put** us quickly _at ease_ and answered all our questions.
3 Don't ever **buy** an animal or bird _on a whim_ because they require an awful lot of looking after.
4 The video of the rehabilitated battery hens **captured** _the attention_ of YouTube viewers.
5 A small city centre flat doesn't really **meet** _the needs_ of farmyard animals.
6 Children often **take** more _interest_ in healthy food if they are taught to grow vegetables themselves.
7 The dolphins **showed** _no signs of_ tiring of their game.
8 Schools these days **place** a lot of _importance_ on educating children about the environment.
9 It **was** _thanks to_ a friend that I got interested in ecological issues.

b Now complete the verb phrases in the following short article using the correct form of the verbs in **bold** in Exercise 1a.

The good life

Some years ago, a meeting of village residents
(1) _took_ **place** in the village where I live. Jan, a friend of mine, **(2)** _was_ ⁽ᵖᵘᵗ⁾ **in charge** of the proceedings. Her idea was that we should work together as a community to grow and then sell our own produce. That way, she said, we would both save money and eat more healthily. I must admit her ideas **(3)** _captured_ **our imagination** and, quite surprisingly, everyone at the meeting agreed. Jan **(4)** _brought_ the meeting **to an end** by handing out some seeds for us to sow which she had **(5)** _bought_ **in bulk** from a local supplier. The aim, she told us, was to be up and running as a business by the following summer.

From the very next day, we **(6)** _put_ **our plans into action** and started digging our gardens! Would you believe it, by the following summer we had **(7)** _met_ ⁽ᵃᶜʰⁱᵉᵛᵉ⁾ **all our goals**, we were producing loads of vegetables and people were phoning from all over the area to **(8)** _place_ **orders**! The business even **(9)** _showed_ **a small profit** in the end so we treated ourselves to a meal out at a country restaurant. On the menu were our vegetables!

Phrases with *have*

2 Complete the sentences with the correct form of a phrase with *have*.

have a major impact on   have the right to
have no say   have access to
have no inclination to   have serious consequences
have strong views on

1 Unfortunately, people often feel that they _have no say_ in the matter of policy-making but that is not always the case. All individuals _have the right to_ put forward their opinion.
2 The inability of countries to reach an agreement could _have serious consequences_ .
3 If you _have strong view on_ ecological issues, there are plenty of societies you can join.
4 The oil spill from the tanker _⁽ʷⁱˡˡ⁾ have a major impact on_ marine life in the area.
5 The group really _have no inclination to_ walk through the jungle at nighttime. _interest_
6 It is crucial for people all over the world to _have access to_ drinkable water.

Prepositional phrases

3a Combine the words and prepositions below to make phrases (e.g. *in other words*) and discuss their meaning. You will need to use some of the prepositions more than once.

by   _in_ _⁽ᵖʳᵒᵇᵃᵇˡʸ⁾_ all likelihood   _out_ of breath
in   _in_ captivity _↔ in the wild_   _in_ other words
on   _by_ chance   _with_ pleasure _sb't accept with pleasure_
out   _with_ ease _- easily_   _in_ sb's/sth's wake
with   _in_ living memory   _out_ (of) tune with _in_
             _on_ occasion
             sometime   _everyone who live in today_

b Work in pairs. Carry on a dialogue using as many of the phrases as possible.

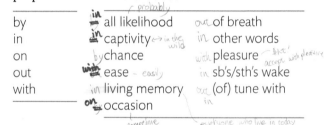

Use of English 2 (Paper 1 Part 2)

Open cloze   **1**   Discuss these points related to recycling:

1 Are there any recycling bins in your local neighbourhood?
2 Are recycled products sold in the supermarkets in your area?
3 What proportion of your household rubbish goes for recycling?

Developing skills: understanding text structure   **2**   It is important to understand why a particular text has been written. Read the text through quickly and answer the questions.

1 What is the author's problem with recycling?
2 Do you think he is being entirely serious? Why/Why not?

➤ EXPERT STRATEGIES page 167   **3**   Read the strategy on page 167, then do the task.

For questions 1–8, read the text below and think of the word which best fits each gap. Use only one word in each gap. There is an example at the beginning (0).

There's more to recycling than meets the eye.

The relationship **(0)** _between_ the modern consumer and their rubbish is a complex one. **(1)** _Getting_ rid of rubbish has come to mean a great deal more than simply consigning breakfast leftovers to a plastic bag. With the advent of recycling, rubbish has now invaded many people's personal lives **(2)** _to_ an unprecedented degree. **(3)** _there_ was a time, in living memory, when rubbish collection was a simple matter – but today's household rubbish, before **(4)** _being_ discarded, has to be filed and sorted into colour-coded containers according to its recycling category.

(5) _What_ is more, we are brought out in a rash of irritation by the suggestion that, if rubbish collections were to become more infrequent, people would then **(6)** _make_ the effort to cut **(7)** _down_ on shopping and recycle more. We might be excused for wondering how this would be possible. Can people realistically buy **(8)** _fewer_ eggs or tubes of toothpaste than their lives require?

Recycling is supposed to be good for us. But for some, it's just a load of rubbish!

Discussion   **4a**   Do you think recycling is 'rubbish'? Why/Why not?

b   Some supermarkets sell products that are 'bio-degradable' or 'eco-friendly'. What type of products might they be? Do you buy them? Why/Why not?

c   How can the government of a country encourage people to follow its policies on recycling?

Writing 2 (Paper 2 Part 2: Article)

Lead-in 1 The photograph is of an organic farm. What would you expect to find there? Discuss and create a list.

Understand the task 2 Read the writing task and note down your answers to the questions. Look back at Writing 1 on page 30 for ideas.

1 What type of writing will you include in your article?
2 What topics will you need to cover in your article?
3 What title will you give it?
4 How will you organise the article?
5 What particular vocabulary will you use?

> You recently spent two weeks working as a volunteer on an organic farm, as part of a project to familiarise young people from the city with country life. You have been asked to write an article for a local environmental newsletter, describing your responsibilities during that time and discussing your experiences.

Plan your article 3 Read the points below about planning your article. Is there anything you would add?

1 Identify the main points you need to cover in the task and brainstorm your ideas around those points.
2 Organise them in a way to make them more interesting and effective.
3 All writing requires a degree of imagination! You don't have to base what you write on your personal experience.
4 Remember that descriptions should go from general to specific.
5 Check that you have an interesting introduction and conclusion.

4 Write your plan for the article. Include any interesting items of vocabulary that you would like to use.

Language and content

5 Complete the phrases with the words below.

common   community   crack   home-made   manual   quiet
self-sufficient   starry   touch

Work experience
- get up at the (1) _crack_ of dawn ~~common~~
- have a sense of working towards a (2) ~~community~~ goal *common*
- have the aim of being (3) ~~common~~ with regard to basics such as vegetables, etc. *self-sufficient*
- experience a sense of (4) ~~self-sufficient~~ *community*
- cook (5) _home-made_ meals
- do hard (6) _manual_ labour

Nature
- get back in (7) _touch_ with nature
- look up at the (8) _starry_ sky at night
- enjoy the peace and (9) _quiet_ of the countryside

6a Here are some different ways of expressing movement that might be useful in the context of the task. Check the meanings of the verbs in a dictionary.

stagger   stride   stroll   tramp   trudge   wade

b Here are some useful adverbs. Check their meanings. Can you think of any others you might need for your article?

hurriedly   painstakingly   pleasantly   thankfully   wearily

pleasantly surprised

c Remember you can use some of the phrases below to describe the conditions.

boiling hot   freezing cold   soaking wet   pouring with rain

Model introduction

7 Read the two introductions for the task in Exercise 2. Discuss and analyse which one you prefer, and why.

A

As I staggered outside sleepily at 6 a.m., the sun was already up and the grass was sparkling with early morning dew. The cows were munching the grass and the sheep were roaming peacefully over a distant hillside. Other than that, there was just peace and quiet. No noise of traffic, no horns blaring, no people rushing to work. Yes, my jobs on the farm were about to start but for now I had five minutes to enjoy the sounds and smells of the natural surroundings.

B

I had decided to take part in a volunteer scheme for young people from the city to live and work on a farm for two weeks in the summer. Farm life had always attracted me and I also belonged to an environmental organisation so I had an interest in the growing of organic vegetables and in keeping livestock. So it was with lots of enthusiasm that we set off for the farm one day early in July. Little did I know what delights were awaiting me!

Write your article

> EXPERT STRATEGIES page 169

8 Now write your article, using the ideas and the language from this section and from Writing 1 (page 30). Write your answer in **280–320** words.

Check your article

> EXPERT WRITING page 191

9 Edit your article, using the checklist on page 191.

Review

1 Complete the sentences with the nouns formed from the verbs below.

---
colonise   consume   destroy   extract
implement   integrate
---

1 A certain amount of environmental _____ will be caused by the proposed high-speed railway line.
2 _____ of too much red meat is generally thought to be not very good for our health.
3 It's quite easy to accept new measures: it's their _____ that causes the most problems.
4 The _____ of oil and other fossil fuels often happens in areas where there are potential problems for the natural surroundings.
5 The _____ of parts of Africa by different European powers took place from the 15th century onwards.
6 Unfortunately, the attempted _____ of indigenous peoples into a different type of culture has often failed.

2 Circle the correct phrasal verb to complete the sentences.

1 Conservationists are doing their best to prevent certain species from being *wiped out / died away*.
2 Governments should *crack down on / wipe out* businesses that keep their animals in inhumane conditions.
3 Sometimes it's important to *step back from / crack down on* the daily problems and take a look at the bigger picture of what's going on in the world.
4 I can't understand why they *cut down / used up* those apple trees just so they could build a house.
5 The sounds of the birds singing gradually *died away / wiped out*.

3 Complete the short text with the missing words.

You might think there is little left **(1)** _____ discover on Earth in the 21st century, yet the deep sea remains almost entirely unknown. Life in the deep, apart from fish and other creatures such as the giant squid, **(2)** _____ found in the form of bacteria, worms and crustaceans, which teem in the abyssal plains that cover vast stretches of the deep. They feed off organic 'snow' that falls from above. Deep below the sea floor, life was **(3)** _____ thought to be possible. But then in 2003, researchers found many unique bacteria 300 metres beneath the Pacific sea floor, feeding on sediments millions of years old. More spectacular are the deep-sea corals, found at depths of up to 6,000 metres in waters as cold as 2°C. These slow-growing animals **(4)** _____ now found from Ireland to New Zealand, and have even **(5)** _____ discovered growing on the legs of oil rigs.

4 Choose the correct word to complete the sentences.

1 I could hear the frogs ___ in the stillness of the night.
   A squawking   B chattering   C croaking
2 All my friends ___ with laughter when I told them I was going to take up gardening.
   A chirped   B hooted   C bellowed
3 Being a farmer entails a lot of ___ labour.
   A manly   B strong   C manual
4 Solar power is a useful ___ of energy in hotter countries.
   A source   B resource   C basis
5 Some animals in danger of extinction are born and raised in ___ .
   A capture   B captivity   C enclosure
6 I have no ___ to go out in the field in the pouring rain and get wet and muddy!
   A preference   B inclination   C tendency

5 Complete the text with the missing prepositions.

Hugh Fearnley-Whittingstall, who has been called an 'eccentric' chef by some, set **(1)** _____ his own organic farm and restaurant in the south-west of England a number of years ago. Thanks **(2)** _____ his dedication to organic farming and a 'back-to-nature' lifestyle, he has had quite an effect **(3)** _____ the way people see food and where it comes from. One thing he places importance **(4)** _____ is a sense of respect **(5)** _____ the animals that provide us with our food. As the years go by, Hugh shows no signs **(6)** _____ relaxing his belief in himself and the issues he finds important. This has led to his involvement **(7)** _____ campaigns **(8)** _____ battery-farming and for sustainable fishing, amongst other things. He is fortunate that he has the ability to speak in front of a camera **(9)** _____ ease, as the many TV shows he has produced prove. Several of these can be watched **(10)** _____ YouTube, if they are unavailable in your area.

3 Surviving and thriving

3A
- **Reading and Use of English:** Multiple matching (Part 7); Word formation (Part 3); Open cloze (Part 2)
- **Listening:** Multiple-choice questions (Part 1); Understanding the main ideas
- **Language development:** Conditionals tense review
- **Writing:** Discursive essay (Part 1); Summarising and evaluating

3B
- **Listening:** Multiple choice (Part 3)
- **Speaking:** Collaborative task (Parts 1 & 2): Ways to relax; Sustaining a conversation
- **Reading and Use of English:** Multiple-choice cloze (Part 1)
- **Language development:** Introductory and emphatic *it* and *there*; Inversion
- **Writing:** Discursive essay (Part 1); Summarising and evaluating

Lead-in

1 Compare two of these cartoons and say what the cartoonist is trying to convey. How do they make you feel?

2 Below are five titles of popular psychology self-help books on the market. Which titles could match the cartoons A–C? Give reasons for your choice.

1 *Brilliant confidence: what confident people know, say and do*
2 *Water off a duck's back: how to deal with frustrating situations, awkward, exasperating and manipulative people and ... keep smiling!*
3 *Working with the enemy: how to survive and thrive with really difficult people*
4 *In sheep's clothing: understanding and dealing with manipulative people*
5 *Feel the fear and do it anyway: how to turn your fear and indecision into confidence and action*

3 If you could choose one of these books to read, which one would you choose, and why?

4 In pairs, think of ideas for cartoons to illustrate the two remaining books.

5 What advice would you give a friend if:

1 someone was trying to manipulate him/her by using threatening language?
2 he/she was giving in to peer pressure to commit a crime?
3 he/she had argued with a good friend and didn't know how to resolve it?

Reading 1 (Paper 1 Part 7)

Before you read **1** Compare the following pairs of sentences. Which pair is similar in meaning, and which pair is different?

1 a This book adopts an essentially objective approach to its subject.
  b The concepts in this book are presented in an informative, non-judgemental manner.
2 a You are presented with a number of practical techniques for achieving your goals in life.
  b The concepts presented offer you practical ways to be more optimistic in your life.

Skimming **2** Read through each review on page 41 quickly. Which book(s) might you recommend for someone who:

1 is suffering from anxiety?
2 has recently experienced a crisis of confidence?
3 is simply interested in the subject of psychology?

Scanning **3** Answer the following questions.

1 Read the questions in Exercise 4, and underline the key words and phrases.
2 Read the reviews and underline the relevant information.
3 Check the questions against the text again. Then complete Exercise 4.

Multiple matching **4** Read the strategy on page 168, then do the task.

➤ EXPERT STRATEGIES page 168

You are going to read some reviews of self-help books. For questions 1–10, choose the best answer from sections A–D. Some of the choices may be required more than once.

About which book is the following stated?

It can be an enjoyable read irrespective of whether you have problems.	1 _____
It presents ideas in language that is accessible to the non-specialist.	2 _____
It examines the evidence to support some of the claims made by exponents of self-help.	3 _____
It offers a step-by-step guide to working through a psychological dilemma.	4 _____
It describes ways in which people can make the most of their unfulfilled potential.	5 _____
It suggests that people may be encouraged to have unrealistic expectations.	6 _____
Many of the suggested therapies are based on a recognised methodology.	7 _____
The quality of writing makes the advice appear more credible.	8 _____
It suggests that we should view one particular negative emotion as something natural.	9 _____
It offers comfort and advice to those frustrated by seemingly straightforward problems.	10 _____

Discussion **5** Discuss. Under what circumstances would you recommend that someone should:

• buy a self-help book?   • consult a professional psychologist?

6 Check the meaning of these key words from the text.

> **EXPERT WORD CHECK**
>
> fallacy   fabrication   advocate   misconception   perspective   jargon
> prose   pronouncement   solace   premise

DIY psychology

Books offering self-help and advice sell in their millions. We take a look at four of the most popular.

A The last self-help book you'll ever need by Paul Pearsall

In this book, Pearsall explores the tendency for proponents of self-help therapy to substitute clichés for serious thought. Hackneyed fallacies like 'be all that you can be', 'live up to your full potential', 'nurture and understand your inner child', are just a few of the arguably silly fabrications that masquerade as legitimate advice, and Pearsall exposes them to the light of scientific scrutiny. Primarily, this book advocates accepting that you may never become a concert pianist or an international footballer, and concentrating on achieving what is within your reach. You can derive more happiness from life, he suggests, when you appreciate your current situation and those around you. Were people less caught up in the misconception that they should be happier and more fulfilled, they probably wouldn't be so discontented. Pearsall sees much of what we might term 'therapeutic culture' as based on rather questionable remedies that over time have gained the status of unassailable truth. He effectively explores the validity of these assertions from a more objective, down-to-earth perspective.

B Instant confidence by Paul McKenna

McKenna puts forward the notion that people who feel they lack confidence are in fact confident – if only in the belief that they have no confidence! He offers techniques to help people develop their hitherto suppressed abilities and apply these to situations in which they may be of use. Many of his suggestions follow well-known coaching concepts familiar to practitioners of neuro-linguistic programming. However, the book is written in a refreshingly down-to-earth style that avoids the almost incomprehensible jargon which some self-help practitioners are prone to! One of McKenna's key ideas is to encourage people to visualise and experience as far as possible what 'the confident you' will be like. He advocates the simple use of a technique which helps to reframe negative 'inner thoughts' in a 'positive' way. Don't expect to develop instant or total confidence as a result of reading this book, but if you follow the suggestions and practise them, you should make some progress.

C Help: How to become slightly happier and get a bit more done by Oliver Burkeman

This is a genuinely useful book; the writer really does want us to become slightly happier and get a bit more done, just as the title promises us. In a winning aside, he says that 'adding an exclamation mark to the title of your book isn't necessarily going to help make it fun. (There are some exceptions.)' And this is an exception, because it is fun, and can be read for pleasure even if you judge your self-management and feelings of personal fulfilment to be in good shape. I like to think that a decent prose style is one of the guarantors of sanity, and Burkeman has a lovely turn of phrase, neither too dry nor too flashy; but a sort of just-rightness that makes his pronouncements sound wholly trustworthy. In short, *Help* is win–win. Should you find yourself prone to those niggling difficulties which, though surmountable, are disproportionately aggravating, then you'll find solace and good counsel here.

D Feel the fear and do it anyway by Susan Jeffers

The subject of this book rests on the following premise: fear is a necessary and essential element of life and pushing through fear is actually less frightening than living with a feeling of helplessness. Susan Jeffers highlights the paradox that whilst we seek the security of a life free of fear, this creates an environment in which we are denied the satisfaction of achievement or development. The result is a no-win situation in which we experience both a fear of change and fear of staying the same. The book introduces a progression of truths which illuminate the crippling effects of fear and build the case for taking action to address the problem. Given that you accept these truths, you can change your attitude and approach. A number of simple models and techniques are engagingly presented through a series of first-hand accounts of people at various stages of succumbing to or addressing their fears. When strung together, these provide a structured programme with which you may set about changing your attitude and raising your self-awareness and self-esteem.

Vocabulary

Compound nouns with *self-*

1a All these nouns can be combined with *self-* to make compound nouns (e.g. *self-help*). Complete the sentences with a suitable compound noun.

awareness   belief   confidence   discipline
discovery   esteem   evaluation   help   knowledge
management   worth

1 _self - management_ skills are very important if you want to make the most of your time.
2 Sometimes in life there are crisis points where you need to go through a period of _self - evaluation_ : a time when you can discover what your strong and weak points are.
3 The journey of life is all about the process of _self - discovery_ .
4 Any course of study requires a certain amount of _self - discipline_ .
5 Children often acquire a sense of their own _self - esteem_ (worth) from their parents.

b In a similar way, discuss the concepts expressed by the remaining compound nouns in Exercise 1a. In what way are they important?

Word formation (1): prefixes (*inter-, mis-, non-*)

2a Adding a prefix can have a radical effect on the meaning of the base word.

- *Inter-* often has the meaning of things being connected in some way (e.g. *interact*).
- *Mis-* usually means things done wrongly or badly (e.g. *mislead*).
- *Non-* usually expresses the opposite of the base word (e.g. *non-aggressive*).

Complete the short extract with words formed from a prefix given, plus a word below.

inter/mis   non   mis   mis
connecting   essential   interpret   use

Company rules

- You are kindly requested to keep your desks clear of any **(1)** non-essential items. A messy office is a sign of a messy mind.
- Any **(2)** misuse of office materials will not be tolerated.
- All **(3)** interconnecting doors between offices should be kept closed because of fire regulations.
- Critical feedback on projects should be given face-to-face whenever possible: feedback by email can often be **(4)** misinterpreted

b Create word formation lists in a vocabulary notebook, using different prefixes and suffixes and add to them as you come across new words. Make a point of revising them each week.

Word formation (2): suffixes (*-ment, -tion, -ness, -sion*)

3a Read the dialogue below quickly. How do Charlie and Jessica's opinions differ with regard to self-help books?

b These words form nouns ending in *-ment, -tion, -ness* or *-sion*. Complete the noun forms, then choose an appropriate word to complete the dialogue.

1	achieve	achievement	unachievable
2	conceive	conception	
3	decide	decision	undecided indecision
4	fulfil	fulfilment	unfulfilled
5	happy	happiness	unhappy
6	helpful	helpfulness	unhelpful
7	inspire	inspiration	uninspire
8	motivate	motivation	unmotivated
9	solve	solution	unsolved
10	weak	weakness	

Charlie: What do you think of self-help books, Jessica?

Jessica: Well, to be honest, I was a bit doubtful about their rather exaggerated claims, you know, about finding an immediate (1) _solution_ to problems, overcoming your (2) _weaknesses_ or achieving (3) ~~happiness~~ fulfilment in your chosen path in life! It all sounded too good to be true. However, after reading one recently, I realised that I'd had no (4) _conception_ of how complicated people's emotions actually are and I felt that I learnt a lot. Also, I drew (5) _inspiration_ from its positive approach and the idea that the (6) _achievement_ of (7) _happiness_ is in our own hands.

Charlie: I agree, although I think their (8) _helpfulness_ is limited in the sense that we all still have to make our own (9) _decision_ in life, no matter how many books we read. There has to be the personal (10) ~~fulfilment~~ motivation to learn and to change, doesn't there?

Jessica: Sure, but this is where this sort of book can sometimes show the way, I feel.

c To which nouns in Exercise 3b, including their derivatives, could you add the prefix *un-*?

d In pairs, discuss the following points, using some of the words from Exercise 3b.

- How far do you think people can change the way they behave through reading books?
- How can psychotherapy help people?

Use of English 1 (Paper 1 Part 3)

Word formation

1a Quickly read the text below. What would you say some of the dangers are of not expressing how you feel?

b Read the strategy on page 167, then do the task.

> EXPERT STRATEGIES page 167

For questions 1–8, read the text below. Use the word given in CAPITALS at the end of some of the lines to form a word that fits in the gap in the same line. There is an example at the beginning (0).

EMOTIONAL AND PHYSICAL HEALTH

To a large extent, problems and difficulties are an **(0)** _unavoidable_ part of everyday life. According to psychologists, however, there is a **(1)** _tendency_ for people in the west to hide negative feelings, such as anger or **(2)** _dissatisfaction_, rather than express them. Furthermore, studies have shown there to be an **(3)** _interdependence_ between physical and emotional health. For example, via the **(4)** _nervous_ system, a person's emotions have a direct effect on heart rate and digestion, and the suppression of strong emotions can have a **(5)** _detrimental_ effect on a person's health.

AVOID

TEND

SATISFY

DEPEND

NERVE

DETRIMENT

Such findings, however, should not be taken to mean that emotions are best expressed in a totally **(6)** _uncontrolled_ manner. On the contrary, the ability to convey feelings in a rational way is widely regarded as evidence of emotional maturity. So the questions people need to ask themselves are: Am I a good **(7)** _communicator_? Is there balance in my relationships with others? Do I show **(8)** _sensitivity_ to others' emotions and moods? If the answer to these questions is 'yes', then they are on the right path.

CONTROL

COMMUNICATE

SENSE

Idioms: animal idioms

2 Animal idioms often illustrate personality types or ways of dealing with difficult situations. Discuss the meaning of the idioms, then choose a suitable idiom to complete the sentences. Suggest situations where the remaining idioms might be used.

as stubborn as a mule   a wolf in sheep's clothing
flog a dead horse   have kittens   let sleeping dogs lie
like water off a duck's back
put the cat among the pigeons   (cause lots of problems)
take the bull by the horns   have a bee in one's bonnet

(annotations: get really worried about sth; don't work; 寝た子を起こす; そっとしておく; 他人に影響されない)

1 I was advised to tell my friend the reasons why her behaviour annoys me. That's certainly going to _put the cat among the pigeons_

2 My attempt to change his mind about the plans for the evening was hopeless: it was like trying to _flog a dead horse_. *It's flogging a dead horse. (telling my mom how to use her phone)*

3 Sarah never takes any notice when other people criticise the way she dresses: it's _like water off a duck's back_ *(not be bothered / not influence on sb)*

4 Jack won't stop going on about that conference he wants me to go to: he's certainly got _a bee in one's bonnet_ about it. *(constantly talking about sth)*

5 Trish can be _as stubborn as a mule_ when she doesn't want to do something.

Discussion

3 If you had to give three pieces of general advice to a friend, what would you tell them? Use phrases that you have learnt in the Vocabulary section.

Listening 1 (Paper 3 Part 1)

Before you listen 1 Discuss the following questions.

1 What does Emotional Intelligence (EI) mean?
2 How would you describe bullying behaviour?

Understanding the main ideas 2 🎧 T1.15 Listen to people speaking about three different topics and answer the questions that go with each extract.

Extract One: bullying in the workplace
1 Where did Emma find help?
2 How did Emma's feelings change after reading about bullying?

Extract Two: dealing with difficult conversations
1 What is James asked to give his opinion about?
2 What problems does he mention?

Extract Three: the importance of Emotional Intelligence
1 According to the speaker, what new system are some employers using?
2 What does the speaker say could be a way to begin the process of acquiring Emotional Intelligence?

Multiple-choice questions 3 🎧 T1.16 Read the strategy, then do the task.

➤ EXPERT STRATEGIES page 170

You will hear the three extracts again. For questions 1–6, choose the answer (A, B or C) which fits best according to what you hear. There are two questions for each extract.

Extract One

You hear part of an interview with a woman called 'Emma Collins', who suffered bullying in the workplace.

1 When she was being bullied, she felt

 A determined to prove her colleague wrong.
 B convinced that her colleague's criticisms were just.
 C indifferent to what her colleague said about her work.

2 What helped her to overcome the problem?

 A sharing her story with other victims
 B coming to terms with the reality of the situation
 C getting her manager to confront the person responsible

Extract Two

You hear an actor called James Milner talking about a book he read as a teenager.

3 Before reading the book, James had been feeling

 A unable to discuss an issue.
 B in need of career guidance.
 C unwilling to listen to advice.

4 James liked the book because it taught him how to

 A develop professional skills.
 B deal with demanding people.
 C express his own feelings calmly.

Extract Three

You hear a psychologist talking about the use of tests of 'emotional intelligence'.

5 What does she suggest about the cosmetics company?

 A It has been slow to experiment with new recruitment procedures.
 B It now looks for a wider range of abilities in prospective employees.
 C It has solved a long-term problem with poor levels of staff retention.

6 Who is her target listener?

 A people who may be looking for a job in the future
 B companies aiming to recruit effective salespeople
 C academics preparing students for the world of work

Development and discussion 4 Assertiveness training is all about expressing what you feel in a non-aggressive way. Read the list of rights below and discuss.

• You have the right to change your mind.
• You have the right to make mistakes – and be responsible for them.
• You have the right to make seemingly illogical decisions.
• You have the right to say, 'I don't care.'

Language development 1

Conditionals tense review

➤ EXPERT GRAMMAR page 176

1   Read the conditional sentences and choose the correct answer. Check your answers and discuss any ones you were not sure about.

1   If it _____ , we could go and play tennis.
    A didn't rain   (B) wasn't raining

2   Susie _____ the topic of conversation if she didn't like it.
    A had changed   (B) could have changed

3   Without her insight into his problems, he _____ got better so fast.
    A would have   (B) wouldn't have

4   I wouldn't have been able to go to the concert if the lecture _____ cancelled.
    (A) hadn't been   B hadn't

5   _____ any later, we would have missed meeting the author.
    (A) Had we arrived   B Should we arrive

6   _____ disagree with their advice, what would their reaction be?
    A Imagine to   (B) Were you to

More constructions with *if*

2   Write conditional sentences that have a similar meaning to the sentence given. Choose one of the following phrases for each sentence: *If it hadn't been for, If you happen to, If* or *Even if.*

1   Have you decided to do a course in psychotherapy? I hope you'll let me know.
    If you have decided to do a course....., please let me know

2   The other students helped me to understand the problem.
    If it hadn't been for other students (help), I wouldn't have understood the problem

3   Sally was so self-confident that when other people criticised her, it was like water off a duck's back!
    Even if other people criticised Sally, she didn't lose her confidence

4   Is there any chance that you'll be in this evening? I'd like to ask your advice about something.
    If you happen to be in this evening, I'd like to ask ~

Alternative conditional phrases

3   Choose one of the following phrases to complete the conditional sentences. There are two extra phrases that don't fit any of the sentences. In which sentences could you also use *if*?

assuming (that)   but for   imagine   in case
on condition that   otherwise   unless   what if
whether or not

1   He would have carried on bullying her _otherwise_ .

2   Jan won't forgive me _unless_ I apologise, something that I'm not prepared to do.

3   I'll give you my honest opinion _on condition that_ you don't get angry.

4   Sometimes I don't know _whether or not_ it would be a good idea to say something.

5   _Assuming that_ everyone here is interested in improving their social skills, let's start off with a few practical exercises.

6   Can I have your phone number _in case_ I need to ring you tomorrow?

7   Please read this book, _otherwise_ you won't know what I'm talking about.

Use of English 2   (Paper 1 Part 2)

Open cloze

1a   Read the extract from a magazine article quickly. In what way is positive psychology different from previous branches of psychology?

b   Read the strategy on page 167, then do the task.

➤ EXPERT STRATEGIES page 167

For questions 1–8, read the text below and think of the word which best fits each gap. Use only one word in each gap. There is an example at the beginning (0).

POSITIVE PSYCHOLOGY

For anyone involved in the field, the term 'positive psychology' has **(0)** _become_ a familiar one in recent years. The term is attached to a movement which seeks to restore **(1)** _what_ are regarded as 'positive' features of human nature, such as happiness, virtues, personal strengths and altruism, **(2)** _to_ their rightful place within the field of psychology. The movement can be seen as a reaction to a perceived over-emphasis on mental illness, **(3)** _at_ the expense of mental health, in the study of psychology. **(4)** _Although_ the term positive psychology was actually coined by humanistic psychologist Abraham Maslow as **(5)** _far_ back as 1964, neither the term nor the intellectual approach surrounding it really took **(6)** _place off_ until Martin Seligman made it the centrepiece of his presidency of the American Psychological Association in 1998. **(7)** _Since_ then the movement has **(8)** _gained been_ ground across the USA and beyond, with popular authors, like former New York Times writer Daniel Goleman, playing a major role in fuelling its widespread appeal.

Discussion

restore sb/sth to sth
gain ground (to become more powerful or successful)

2   Imagine you could choose to do anything you liked or live anywhere you liked in the world. What or where would you choose, and why?

Writing 1 (Paper 2 Part 1: Essay)

Summarising and evaluating

1 Read the exam task and texts below, then answer the following questions.

1 What is positive psychology?
2 What kind of person is a defensive pessimist?
3 Do you regard yourself as an optimist or a pessimist? Why?

Write an essay summarising and evaluating the key points from both texts. Use your own words throughout as far as possible, and include your own ideas in your answer.
You should write **240–280** words.

1 Get happy with positive psychology

No more saying, 'I should and I would if I could.' Positive psychology turns the focus away from how and why things go wrong and towards how and why things go right.

Critics of the movement say it is akin to the sort of frivolous self-help advice that tells people to smile more and they'll feel better. However, scientifically speaking, positive psychology views the development of happiness from an evolutionary standpoint. Happy people are healthier and live longer. They make better mental connections, hence they improve systems and solve problems quicker and in new ways. They have more energy for other people and contribute to the improvement of society.

2 Is positive psychology for everyone?

Psychologist Julie Norem questions the assumption that 'positive psychology is for everyone', presenting us with an illuminating example. If you know someone who drove everyone nuts in school worrying about how he/she would do in exams and who ended up getting A pluses, you probably know a defensive pessimist. For defensive pessimists, worrying about upcoming challenges is a way of life. But it's also a healthy coping strategy that helps them prepare for adversity. Norem has shown that when defensive pessimists are deprived of their pessimism by being forced to look on the bright side of life, their performance in tasks plummets. For defensive pessimists, positive psychology has a decidedly negative side.

2 Which of the following offers the best summary of text 1? Why are the others not suitable?

1 In text 1, positive psychology advocates approaching life from an optimistic perspective, arguing that happier people make more effective members of society.
2 Text 1 makes a case for positive psychology, refuting suggestions that its concept is ineffectual by arguing that having a more optimistic outlook benefits not only the individual but society in general.
3 According to the writer of text 1, positive psychology turns the focus away from how and why things go wrong and turns to face how and why things go right, creating happy people who make better mental decisions and contribute to improving society.

3 Find words or phrases in the summaries in Exercise 2 that mean the following.

1 recommend as being beneficial   3 argue in favour of
2 a positive viewpoint   4 show that an idea is wrong

> EXPERT STRATEGIES page 169

4 Read the strategy on page 169. Using your own words as far as possible, write a brief summary of text 2. Write between 25–35 words.

5 Using information from the summaries of texts 1 and 2, write a paragraph of between **60–70** words.

[handwritten notes:] text 2 mentions that positive psychology doesn't always work for everyone, especially for defensive pessimists, who are regularly apprehensive about future challenges as which attitudes enable them to prepare for difficult situation. could

[handwritten annotation near Ex 3:] advocate (noun) (doing.)   make a case for
[handwritten annotation under Ex 3 item 2:] an optimistic perspective / outlook
[handwritten annotation Ex 3 item 4:] refuting suggestions that its concept is ineffectual

3B Mind and body

Listening 2 (Paper 3 Part 3)

Before you listen

1 Discuss. What are some of the main causes of stress? Is stress increasing in the modern world? Why?

2 Read the task questions below, then discuss the following.

1 What is a laughter club?
2 How might laughter clubs help people with stress-related problems?
3 Underline the words in the question options which give you that impression.

Multiple choice

➤ EXPERT STRATEGIES page 170

3 🎧 T1.17 Read the strategy on page 170, then do the task.

You will hear two alternative practitioners called Stella and Rick McFarland, talking about laughter therapy. For questions 1–5, choose the answer (A, B, C or D) which fits best according to what you hear.

1 What do Stella and Rick see as the <u>main explanation</u> for the popularity of what are called 'laughter clubs'?

A They allow people to share their problems with others.
B They don't require people to make a long-term commitment.
C They are a cost effective way for people to access professional help.
D They appeal to people who may be sceptical about other forms of therapy.

2 Rick feels that <u>the main role of a laughter therapist is</u> to

A ensure that people get sufficient rest and relaxation.
B help people to escape from one pattern of behaviour.
C make people aware of the consequences of depression.
D investigate the causes of people's emotional problems.

3 What does Rick regard as <u>the principal benefit</u> of the laughter therapy sessions he runs?

A They enable people to feel less inhibited. *reticence* *reticent*
B They stop people taking life too seriously.
C They give people a good physical workout.
D They encourage people to form lasting bonds.

4 <u>Rick's interest in laughter therapy initially arose</u> from

A first-hand experience of another method.
B participation in his wife's group sessions.
C a desire to help his clients more effectively.
D his mistrust of other alternative approaches.

5 <u>Why does Rick</u> tell us about a client who had problems giving presentations?

A to suggest an alternative remedy for work-related stress.
B to highlight the way in which essential oils affect the senses.
C to show how stress can affect a person's level of performance.
D to support Stella's point about making time for certain activities.

➤ **HELP**

1 Listen carefully to what both Rick and Stella say before making your choice.
2 What does Rick say the laughter therapist aims to do?

5 Rick begins the story by saying *to give you an example.* An example of what?

4 Check the meaning of these key words and phrases from the audioscript.

benefits
reap = reward
dividends

EXPERT WORD CHECK

practitioner   accessible   intimidating   buy into   knock-on effect
grumpiness   downward spiral   dispel   reticence   reap benefits = *get benefits*
myth
misconception
make it disappear

Discussion

5 Discuss the benefits and drawbacks of the ideas Stella and Rick put forward. Give reasons for your views.

You reap what you sow.

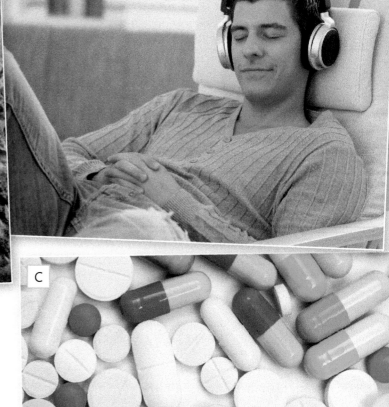

Speaking (Paper 4 Parts 1 & 2)

1 In Part 1 of the Speaking paper, the examiner asks candidates some questions about themselves. Read the following questions, and answer them as fully as you can.

1 What do you do to relax at weekends?
2 Which activity do you feel helps you to relax the most?

Vocabulary: ways to relax

2 Match some of the words below with the photographs. You can use the words more than once.

acupuncture   aromatherapy   meditation
relaxing pastime   emotional comfort   reflexology
medication   pain relief

3a Use the words and phrases below to talk about the positive and negative aspects of using the relaxation methods shown in the photographs.

emotional/physical benefits
drawbacks
beneficial
detrimental
keeps you active
provides you with an interest
can do more harm than good
gives lonely people physical contact
rather exclusive
expensive and so for the privileged few
effective relaxation technique
takes your mind off things
it's emotionally uplifting
helps you unwind
relieves tension

b Complete the statements with the phrases below.

not for everyone   makes me feel frustrated
rather weird   enjoyable pastime
should be seen as a last resort
did me the world of good

1 Personally, I think it's _____ to have your feet massaged. It makes me shiver.
2 OK, I know essential oils can be beneficial, but they're _____ . I mean, I know several people who can't stand strong smells.
3 I spent the afternoon working in the garden, and it _____ . I felt so refreshed afterwards.
4 Quite frankly, having my feet massaged _____ . I can't relax at all.
5 I think taking anti-depressant pills _____ . Try to find other solutions first.
6 Listening to music is a really _____ , and technology has improved the sound quality no end.

4 Use some of the words and phrases from Exercises 2 and 3 to talk about two of the photographs.

D

Part 2 Model answer

5a 🎧 T1.18 Listen to the examiner's instructions for the first section of Paper 4 Part 2, then answer the questions.

1 Which pictures do the candidates have to talk about?

2 How long do they have to speak?

b 🎧 T1.19 Listen to two candidates performing the task, then discuss the following.

1 How well they tackle the task.

2 How successful they are at interacting.

6a 🎧 T1.20 Now listen to the instructions for the second section of the task, then answer the questions.

1 What do the candidates have to do?

2 How long do they have for this section?

b 🎧 T1.21 Listen to the candidates perform the task, then answer the questions.

1 What techniques do they use to develop and sustain the conversation?

2 How do they achieve a balance between them in sharing the conversation?

3 What do you notice about Ariana's performance in this part of the task?

Useful language: discourse markers for sustaining a conversation

7a 🎧 T1.21 Listen to the candidates perform the second part of the task again, then complete the extract below with a word or short phrase.

Ariana: This is a really good way to relax! I like this myself, particularly listening to classical music. It makes me feel calm after a difficult day at work. (1) _____ for many people ... Er, don't you, Jarek?

Jarek: (2) _____ ! I totally agree with you, and I often listen to music on the train going home. It shuts out all the noise of people around me! I also like the idea of a massage, even though it can be expensive. Some big companies offer this service once a fortnight to their employees, and I think this is a really good idea.

Ariana: Yes. I've only had an aromatherapy massage once, and it was very relaxing, but I really like having reflexology. Having your feet massaged is really special. I think that massage is an important relaxation technique, however, even though it is expensive. It's very ... how do you say ... beneficial, I can say. What do you think?

Jarek: (3) _____ , I think gardening is also a very popular way for people to relax. It covers a wide range of people, too, of different ages and social backgrounds. Don't you think?

Ariana: (4) _____ , it's an outdoor activity. So, people are in the fresh air. What about this photo with the pills? I cannot see the reason for that. How do pills help us relax?

Jarek: Mm. (5) _____ because when people are really stressed, they sometimes take pills ... erm ... how are they called? Anti-depressants. This is not a good approach, though. (6) _____ , if you're really depressed, then they might be necessary.

Ariana: (7) _____ , I don't think I like that photo for the article, as we want to emphasise the more positive ways to relax. So, which two photos should we choose?

Jarek: Well, (8) _____ , the pills could be shown as a contrast to the more positive activity of ... say, gardening. After all, the article will probably mention pills, if only to criticise them.

b Which of the expressions in the extract mean the same as the following?

1 definitely   3 actually

2 apart from that   4 this is the case

Part 2 Collaborative task

> **EXPERT STRATEGIES** page 171

8 In pairs, look at the photographs on page 204, then do the tasks below. Use the strategies to help you.

1 First, look at photographs A and C and talk about how beneficial these activities are for the individual. ⏱ You have about a minute for this.

2 Then, look at all the photographs. Imagine you are promoting a TV programme on popular leisure activities today. Discuss how popular each activity is, and then decide which two should act as the focus of the advertisement for the programme.

Task analysis

9 Discuss the following questions.

1 Did you use examples or personal experiences to illustrate your points?

2 Were you able to respond to your partner's points in a natural way?

3 How many of the discourse markers from Exercise 7a did you use together?

Language development 2

Introductory and emphatic *it* and *there*

> EXPERT GRAMMAR page 177

1a Complete the sentences with *there* or *it*.

1 ___it___ 's possible that he's just gone for a walk.
2 Is ___there___ any likelihood that he's left the country?
3 ___There___ isn't much point in phoning him, I suppose.
4 ___It/There___ 's no use asking Sally to help! She hates him!
5 ___There___ appears to be no relation between the theft and his disappearance.
6 ___It___ could be that he's depressed about Celia leaving.
7 ___There___ 's no harm in checking his room.
8 ___It___ might also be an idea to check the hospitals in the area.

b Complete the passage by adding *it* where appropriate.

'I'm quite a private person at heart, and prefer **(1)** _____ people phoning before they visit. ~~something comes to your space~~ So, I consider **(2)** ___it___ an ~~intrusion~~ to have my neighbour popping in whenever she feels like **(3)** ___it___ . I've tried telling her that I'm busy, but **(4)** ___it___ makes no difference. She always manages to keep me talking for ages. And just when I decide to be ~~blunt~~, ~~speak very directly @ bluntness~~ she'll do something extra nice, like bringing me a cake. So, **(5)** ___it___ doesn't seem appropriate to tell her to get lost. Honestly, I can't stand **(6)** _____ hiding, but I've started sneaking around the house and not answering the door when she calls. I can't take **(7)** ___it___ much longer. I tell you, if **(8)** ___it___ weren't for my psychotherapist, I'd have gone out of my mind by now ...'

2 What would you say in response to someone who said the following to you? Use the phrases in brackets to help you.

1 The conference room is ready for you, and the team's waiting there. (this is it)
2 I'm not coming to the party. I just don't feel up to it. (it's a pity) *you can come whenever you feel like it*
3 Which is more beneficial, a massage or reflexology? (it's a matter of) *your body*
4 So, should I tell him to get lost, or not? (it makes no difference) *to me what you do*
5 Who told Mr Jones the truth about that fire? (it was) *his neighbour*
6 Gina really helped me get through that difficult period with my father. (if it hadn't been for) *her, you wouldn't be like now*

Inversion

3 Circle the most suitable words in *italics* to complete the sentences.

1 Only after *he had left / had he left* did they relax.
2 On no condition *you should / should you take* these pills without consulting your doctor first.
3 Little *she realised / did she realise* that the treatment would be so expensive.
4 Not until *I'd had / had I had* a massage did I realise how stressed out I'd been.
5 No sooner *I'd started / had I started* the yoga class than I began to feel better.
6 *Hadn't it been / Had it not been* for Berthold's help, we wouldn't have got home that night.

4a Rewrite the sentences without inverted phrases. Make any changes necessary.

1 Not only did Mandy do a course in aromatherapy but she became a professional too.
2 So unable to cope was she after losing her husband that she sought professional help.
3 At no time during your acupuncture treatment should you move your body.
4 Hardly had she got back from the hospital when she fell down the stairs and broke her leg!
5 Should you see Hannah, tell her to phone me.
6 Such was the response to the Laughter Club's advertisement that they had to create three classes.

b Rewrite the sentences using inverted phrases.

1 I didn't seek psychological help for my depression at any time.
2 I'd only just got out of hospital when I was involved in a car accident.
3 I didn't realise it would be so hard to cope with all the extra work.
4 I only began to relax once the unwanted visitors had left.
5 She didn't feel happy until she had left her job.

Use of English 3 (Paper 1 Part 1)

1 Discuss the following questions.

1 What sort of music, if any, do you like dancing to?
2 How does dancing make you feel? Can you explain this?

Developing skills: words often confused

2 Choose the correct word to complete the following sentence. A thesaurus will tell you that they all mean *supported*. You need to examine the whole sentence to see which one fits.

Dr Schneider has long ___ the use of alternative treatments for stress-related problems.

A believed in   B advocated   C engaged in   D subscribed to

Multiple-choice cloze

➤ EXPERT STRATEGIES page 167

3 Complete the task below. Use the Help notes for support.

For questions 1–8, read the text below and decide which answer (A, B, C or D) best fits each gap. There is an example at the beginning (0).

The origins of dance therapy

Dance therapy gained professional **(0)** _B_ during the 1940s. It was the inspiration of Marian Chace, who began teaching dance after her own dancing career **(1)** ___ to an end in 1930. She noticed that some of her students were more **(2)** ___ in the emotions they experienced while dancing than in technique. Intrigued by this, Chace encouraged them to explore this aspect, and **(3)** ___ developing classes that emphasised **(4)** ___ of expression through music.

(5) ___ , local doctors started sending her patients, including anti-social children and people with mobility problems. Later, Chace joined the staff at St Elizabeth's Hospital, where she worked with emotionally troubled patients, some of whom were suffering from **(6)** ___ stress disorders. Success for these patients meant being able to move rhythmically in **(7)** ___ with others in their class. Chace went on to study Psychiatry, and the fact that the first dance therapy interns began learning and teaching dance therapy in the 1950s is **(8)** ___ to her tireless dedication.

➤ **HELP**

1 Which word completes the fixed expression with 'an end'?
2 Choose the word which can be followed by the preposition *in*.
4 You are looking for a word which usually collocates with *expression*.

0	A standing	B status	C level	D mode
1	A got	B reached	C came	D arrived
2	A absorbed	B captivated	C preoccupied	D enthralled
3	A made off	B set about	C took up	D turned over
4	A licence	B freedom	C openness	D liberty
5	A Eventually	B Frequently	C Specifically	D Effectively
6	A harsh	B oppressive	C austere	D severe
7	A symmetry	B balance	C unison	D relation
8	A evidence	B witness	C proof	D testimony

Task analysis

4 Which questions required knowledge of:

1 collocations?
2 differences in the use of words of similar meaning?

Discussion

5 In pairs, practise giving each other advice on taking up one of the following activities.

dance   aerobics   football   swimming   T'ai Chi   yoga

You should mention:

• its physical benefits
• any emotional benefits it may have
• any drawbacks, such as money, time needed, etc.

Writing 2 (Paper 2 Part 1: Essay)

Lead-in

1a Discuss. Do you exercise regularly? What kind of exercise do you do?

b Which of the following techniques for stress relief do you think is the most/ least helpful? Why?

deep breathing exercises
meditation yoga massage
guided imagery technique
drinking a cup of tea/coffee
listening to music
working out in a gym

Understand the task

2 Read the question below. What must you remember to do when answering it?

Read the two texts. Write an essay summarising and evaluating the key points from both texts. Use your own words throughout as far as possible, and include your own ideas in your answer.
You should write **240–280** words.

1 Relax with a nice cup of tea!

How many of us look forward to a soothing cup of hot tea at the end of the working day? Why is it that in so many countries tea is drunk not only to refresh us, but also to help us calm down after a stressful experience? The truth is that tea contains chemicals that induce a feeling of well-being. Research has shown that green and white tea, in particular, are conducive to relaxation due to their low levels of caffeine. They contain the amino acid L-theanine, which evokes a sense of calm in the brain, yet without a feeling of drowsiness.

2 Yoga for stress relief

Should you crave solitude, solo relaxation techniques such as meditation will give you the tools to quieten your mind. If, however, you lack the self-discipline to maintain a regular programme, a class setting may help you to stay motivated. It would be better to avoid power yoga, with its physically demanding poses and focus on fitness, as classes that emphasise slow, steady movement and gentle stretching are best for chronic stress relief. Consider your level of fitness and any medical issues before joining. There are many yoga classes for different needs. If in doubt, consult a specialist.

3 Make a note of the key points in each text.

4 Look back at your summary of the texts in Writing 1, on page 46. Then compare the two texts above, and make a note of the similarities between them. What is the main difference?

Plan your essay

5a T1.22 Listen to some students discussing how to organise their answer to the task in Exercise 2. Complete the plan below, based on what they decide to do.

Paragraph 1: Introduction   Paragraph 3: _____
Paragraph 2: _____   Paragraph 4: Conclusion

> EXPERT STRATEGIES page 169

b Do you agree with their decision? Why/Why not?

Language and content

invigorate

render

1/24 Iain

a class environment

preferable

profitable

6a Choose the most suitable word to replace each of the following words from text 1.

1 soothing
  (A) calming   B gentle
2 refresh
  A renew   (B) invigorate
3 induce
  A encourage   (B) cause
4 are conducive to
  (A) lead to   B boost
5 evoke
  (A) produce   B render
6 drowsiness
  A weakness   (B) sleepiness

b Write a sentence that summarises the information below. You should be able to reduce the number of words by 50 percent. Begin with the words given.

1

Should you crave solitude, solo relaxation techniques such as meditation will give you the tools to quieten your mind. If, however, you lack the self-discipline to maintain a regular programme, a class setting may help you stay motivated.

For people who find it difficult to _keep their motivations to do solo relaxation programmes regularly, which is helpful to soothe yourself, it would be_

2 _better to participate in a class._

It would be better to avoid power yoga, with its physically demanding poses and focus on fitness, as classes that emphasise slow, steady movement and gentle stretching are best for stress relief. Consider your level of fitness and any medical issues before joining. There are many yoga classes for different needs. If in doubt, consult a specialist.

Think carefully about your health before _____ .

7 Complete the summary of the two texts above with the correct form of the words below.

while   need   benefit   caution   highlight   advocate   however
means

As their titles suggest, both texts focus on ways of helping people to relax. The first text describes the emotional **(1)** _benefit_ of drinking a cup of tea, **(2)** _highlighting_ the properties found in green and white teas which make them especially suitable, **(3)** _while_ the second text **(4)** _advocates_ taking up yoga as a physical **(5)** _means_ of relieving the long-term effects of stress. **(6)** _However_ , it advises **(7)** _caution_ in choosing the right type of yoga to suit your **(8)** _need_ , as slow, gentle exercise is preferable for dealing with chronic stress.

8 🎧 T1.23 Listen to Sukhi and Enrique discussing ideas to include in the evaluation stage of their essay. What points do they make?
Sukhi: _____
Enrique: _____

9 In pairs, discuss how far you agree with Sukhi and Enrique, and add your own ideas for evaluation of the two texts.

Write your essay

➤ EXPERT STRATEGIES page 169

10 Now write your essay, using the ideas and some of the language you have already discussed. Write your answer in **240–280** words.

Check your essay

➤ EXPERT WRITING page 191

11 Edit your essay, using the checklist on page 191.

Review

1 Complete the idioms with the missing words.

1 Whatever I said to Alex about her attitude, she couldn't have cared less! It was like water off a _duck_'s back!

2 Your parents will have _kittens_ when they hear you want to emigrate to Australia!

3 Poppy can be as stubborn as a _mule_ when she has set her mind on something.

4 I'm trying to finish this essay for tomorrow but I haven't got any more ideas: I feel like I'm flogging a dead _horse_ !

5 There's no alternative but to take the _bull_ by the horns and explain what the problem is. There's no point in running away from it.

6 Oh I don't know, if the problem isn't serious then I think you should let sleeping _dogs_ lie and pretend you know nothing about it.

7 Asking for time off work to go on an assertiveness training course has really put the _cat_ among the pigeons – everyone else wants to go now!

8 Kevin has got a _bee_ in his bonnet about punctuality this month: woe betide you if you're more than five minutes late for his classes!

2 Complete the second sentence so that it has a similar meaning to the first sentence. Use between three and eight words.

1 If you see Mary, ask her to demonstrate that new relaxation technique. (**happen**)
If _you happen to see_ Mary, ask her to demonstrate that new relaxation technique.

2 If I disagreed with Tom, how would he react? (**were**) _Tom's reaction be it I were / Tom think_
What would _were I_ to disagree with him?

3 I may need to leave early, so could I have the car keys? (**give**)
Could _you give me the car keys in_ case I need to leave early?

4 They would have ended up fighting, but for Mark's intervention. (**for**)
If _it had not been for Mark's intervention_, they would have ended up fighting.

5 Only thanks to the counselling, have I been able to go back to work. (**not**)
Had _it not been for the counselling_, I would not have been able to go back to work.

6 John will only do the gardening if the sun shines. (**unwilling**)
John _is unwilling to do anything but the gardening if_ the sun shines.

7 She only got over her feeling of shame because her neighbours were so kind. (**but**)
She would never have _got over her feeling of shame but for_ the kindness of her neighbours.

8 As soon as the infuriating couple left, Mark got on the phone to his therapist. (**had**)
No sooner _had the infuriating couple left_ than Mark called his therapist.

3 Complete the sentences with the correct form of the words in brackets.

1 That film was very _uninspiring_ (inspire): just the same old plot full of clichés. _uninspired_

2 I'm _indecisive_ (decide) about my plans for next year as yet: let's hope I'll be able to clarify things soon. _undecided_

3 Sometimes other people's _thoughtfulness_ (thought) is very heartwarming.

4 If you can respond calmly and _non-aggressively_ (aggressive), then I think that would be the best way forward.

5 One thing I really enjoy about academic life is the _exchange_ (change) of ideas and opinions.

6 I think Katie is deservedly proud of her _accomplishment_ (accomplish).

7 I'm afraid there's been a _misunderstanding_ (understand): the meeting was due to start at 2 p.m., not at 3 p.m.

8 Some people get very annoyed when others try to use their gifts of _persuasion_ (persuade) to try to get them to change their mind. It doesn't often work!

4 Complete the text with the words below. There are two extra words you don't need.

assertiveness   circulation   derive   effective
effects   holistic   manage   negative   optimistic
self-confidence   technique   therapeutic

The benefits of yoga, many of whose poses originate from the observation of animals and of nature generally, seem to be endless. Apart from being particularly (1) _holistic_ in reducing stress levels as a relaxation (2) _technique_ , it also improves balance, flexibility and strength. As a form of exercise, it is (3) _effective_ for your mental health, since it helps to combat negative emotions, makes you more (4) _optimistic_ and gives a boost to your (5) _self-confidence_ Millions of people all over the world (6) _derive_ a lot of satisfaction from this (7) _therapeutic_ system of mind and body fitness which has been in existence for over 5,000 years. T'ai Chi, a martial art which is several hundred years old, is likewise reputed to be a form of exercise that has beneficial (8) _effects_ on the mind and body, by improving (9) _assertiveness_ and mental concentration. T'ai Chi has also been very effectively integrated into (10) _____ training and stress management courses in modern-day society.

4A
- ➤ **Reading and Use of English:** Gapped text (Part 6); Open cloze (Part 2)
- ➤ **Listening:** Multiple-choice questions (Part 1)
- ➤ **Language development:** Modals 1: Obligation, necessity, advice and criticism
- ➤ **Writing:** Report (Part 2); Presenting factual information

4B
- ➤ **Listening:** Multiple choice (Part 3)
- ➤ **Speaking:** Individual long turn (Part 3): News and information
- ➤ **Reading and Use of English:** Key word transformations (Part 4); Word formation (Part 3)
- ➤ **Language development:** Modals 2: Ability, possibility, probability and deduction
- ➤ **Writing:** Report (Part 2)

Lead-in

Look at the three photographs and the words and phrases below. Use them to discuss the following questions.

multi-tasking	access information	visual stimuli	interactive	digital organiser
exciting challenges	chat rooms			

1 Why do you think people become addicted to the following, and how might such a dependency affect their daily life?
- digital media
- computer games
- social networking

2 How do computers help people enjoy life?
- escapism
- convenience
- work

Reading 1 (Paper 1 Part 6)

Before you read

1 Look at the photograph and the article heading on page 57.

1 What do you do if you have a 'detox'?
2 What kind of 'detox' might you usually have?
3 What does the use of the word suggest about the writer?

Skimming

> EXPERT STRATEGIES page 168

2 Read the main article and find out what the writer did to get a 'detox'. Don't worry about the missing paragraphs for now.

3 Do you think people will change their digital habits as a result of reading this article?

Gapped text

4 Read the article again. Seven paragraphs have been removed. Using the strategy on page 168 to help you, choose from the paragraphs A–H the one which fits each gap (1–7). There is one extra paragraph which you do not need to use.

> **HELP**

1 What do you normally do to capture a special moment on holiday? Which paragraph A–H reflects that reaction?

3 Which paragraph A–H highlights how technology affects our daily routine?

5 Look for evidence to support the point made in the previous paragraph.

Task analysis

5 Look at the following phrases from the text again. Who or what do they refer to? How did they help you link the paragraphs in the text?

1 That weekend, however (para 2)
2 Like me, he is a true believer (para D)
3 What did strike me though (para G)
4 What's more, the hustle they develop (para H)

Discussion

6 Discuss the following questions.

1 Do you think the couple will change their everyday digital habits?
2 How do your digital habits compare with those of the couple?
3 How do you think digital dependency will change within the next five years?

7 Check the meaning of these key words from the text.

> **EXPERT WORD CHECK**
>
> crouch   blessed   obsession   permeate   impulse   reinforcement
> erode   fallible   mundane   take precedence

My digital detox

Spending a weekend without access to communications technology was an eye-opener.

We were brushing through wet grass in the early morning when we saw it – a flash of white drifting behind a small patch of trees, backlit by the sun. Crouching down next to Artley, our twenty-one-month-old son, my partner Will and I watched the unmistakable shape of a barn owl until it disappeared into the wood. The look on Artley's face was part of a brief moment of magic, the kind of memory that we live for. Ordinarily, my next thought would have been to pull out my phone, take a photo or video and send a message. Connecting is something I do unconsciously now, and sharing such moments has become second nature.

1 F

That weekend, however, the three of us were, by our own choice, offline. We were camping at a rural site called Swallowtail Hill in southern England, which offers visitors the option of leaving all their electronic devices in the safe keeping of the owner for the duration of their stay – a kind of digital detox, you might say. We had been inspired by William Powers' book *Hamlet's BlackBerry*, an imaginative and thoughtful work that explores reactions to new technologies throughout history and the lessons we should have learnt from them. Blessed with two days of good weather and some delicious local food, I barely noticed I wasn't online.

2 G

I take equal responsibility for our digital obsession – magnetically drawn, as I am, to any screen that can feed my addiction. Nonetheless, any objections of mine to this specific vice are usually swiftly defended by an explanation of the importance of dealing with whatever it is now, though it never seems anything that couldn't wait half an hour. Suddenly, however, we had his full attention – well almost. There was a moment when he was distracted by a buzzing sensation and automatically reached for his phone, before realising it was a bee.

3 B

By breaking away from my connected life, however, I came to appreciate just how much it had permeated my way of being. So-called 'early adopters', the heavy technology users who throw themselves at every new device and service, will admit to an uncontrollable impulse to check their email accounts or social networking sites. Researchers have called this 'variable interval reinforcement schedule'. Such people have in effect been drawn into digital-message addiction because the most exciting rewards are unpredictable.

4 H

A study by the University of California concluded that such constant multi-tasking gradually erodes short-term memory. It also discovered that interruptions to any task requiring concentration are a massive problem, as it takes us much longer to get back into them than it does to deal with the interruption itself.

5 C

In other words, what was once exterior and faraway is now easily accessible and this carries a sense of obligation or duty. He sees the feeling that we should be reaching out, or be available to be reached out to as tied to the self-affirmation that the internet, and all that goes with it, provides us with.

6 D

One practical suggestion, for example, is to use paper as a more efficient way of organising our thoughts. The theory of 'embodied interaction' asserts that physical objects free our minds to think because our hands and fingers can do much of the work, unlike screens where our brains are constantly in demand.

7 E

As we left Swallowtail Hill, we seemed to have achieved that. The real work was just starting, however, trying to put this and other ideas into regular practice in an attempt to balance work and home life. Powers also talks about 'vanishing family trick', where a seemingly sociable family gradually dissolves away to screens in different corners of the house. It's clearly a situation to be avoided. Our digital detox had been something of a wake-up call. And guess what? When the owner handed back our phones, we didn't have a missed call or message between us.

A At home, those concerns about my digital addiction are most acute when I catch my son looking at me while I'm checking a screen. It's reinforcing how much more important the screen is than him, as if I'm teaching him that obeying these machines is what he needs to do.

B In truth, he wasn't alone in such lapses. Without our hand-held devices, neither of us had much idea what the time was. Then, I reached for mine when I wondered about local shopping facilities and whether it is normal to see a barn owl during the day. And the magical moment when Artley was being read his bedtime story in front of an open fire, I've had to try and commit to my own fallible memory.

C For those of us compelled to check email every few minutes, that finding accounts for those days which seem to pass so quickly with so little getting done. And this is part of a wider trend. 'The more we connect, the more our thoughts lean outward,' Powers writes. 'There's a preoccupation with what's going on "out there" in the bustling otherworld, rather than "in here" with yourself and those right around you.'

D Like me, he is a true believer in the value and potential of digital technologies. He concludes, however, that we need to find the discipline to restore control by reintroducing a little disconnectedness.

E More radical still is the idea of banning the internet at weekends on the grounds that being away from it on a regular basis allows us to grasp its utility and value more fully. Hopefully, it also brings about a shift to a slower, less restless way of thinking, where you can just be in one place, doing one particular thing, and enjoy it.

F The meaningful and the mundane have thus merged into one, all dutifully and habitually recorded – my enjoyment split between that technological impulse and the more delicate human need to be in the moment. This is how we live these days.

G What did strike me though was the change in Will's behaviour. If my worst habit is incessant messaging, his is allowing his phone to take precedence over everything else. Country walks, dinner, bathing our son – no moment is safe from the seemingly irresistible ringing, vibrating, nagging phone, that demands – and wins – his attention when he should be enjoying the moment with us.

H What's more, the hustle they develop as they struggle to keep up with the pace of all that incoming information has produced a restless, anxious way of engaging with the world. Desperate for efficiency, this seeps into people's physical lives. Perhaps that's why I feel compelled to tidy while on the phone, to fold the washing while brushing my teeth, and no single job has my undivided attention.

Vocabulary

1   Discuss the statement above. Say whether you agree with it or not.

Use of metaphors

2a The following sentences come from the text on page 57. Discuss how the underlined words are normally used, and how they are used in the sentences below.

1   'We were <u>brushing through</u> wet grass in the early morning when we saw it.' (main text, line 1)
2   'no moment is safe from the ... <u>nagging phone</u>, that demands – and wins – his attention' (para G, line 4)
3   'Desperate for efficiency, this [restless, anxious way of engaging with the world] <u>seeps into</u> people's physical lives. (para H, line 3)

b Work in pairs. Discuss how the following metaphors are used every day in connection with the computer.

search engine	shopping cart/basket	chat rooms
mouse file inbox recycle bin outbox folder		

c The writer of the reading text on page 57 refers to a book called *Hamlet's BlackBerry*. Its author draws parallels between present day technology and the Elizabethan equivalent, the 'writing table'. Discuss the use of the BlackBerry as a metaphor here. Look at paragraph 5 in the main text on page 57 to help you.

Collocations

Many new words and phrases are now part of our everyday language due to computer technology.

3a Match the words in column A with an item from column B to form a collocation.

A		B	
1	download _a_	a	publishing
2	update your _c_	b	wall
3	add new _e_	c	profile
4	blog the latest _f_	d	files
5	post on someone's _b_	e	contacts
6	desktop _a_	f	news

b Complete the sentences with phrases from Exercise 3a.

1   The good thing about this networking site is that I can _add new_ contacts and create job opportunities.
2   Anna, why don't you add some recent photos and update your _profile_ ?
3   Professor Brown's saved all the lecture notes, and you can download the _file_ from the webpage.
4   Some critics argue that while the advent of _desktop_ publishing may have rendered publishing more accessible, it has also led to a decline in quality.
5   Kevin, I've posted details of the meeting on your _wall_ ~~publishing~~ , so check it when you log on this evening.
6   One advantage of reading newspapers online is that journalists _blog the latest_ news, and you can learn about events much faster.

Word formation: words with multiple suffixes

4a Form at least two adjectives from each of the stems below using the following suffixes. Make any necessary changes to the stems.

-ative	-ful	-ed	-ing	-able	-less	-ent -sive
-sory	-ational					

compulsory
compulsive

1   compel _-ed -sive -ing -sory_   4   represent _-ed -ing -ative -ational_
2   meaning _-ful -less_   5   depend _-ent -ing -able -ed_
3   control _-able -ing -ed_   6   inform _-ational -ative -ing -ed_

b Discuss the meaning of each word you formed in Exercise 4a, and complete the sentences below with some of them.

1   Kevin has created incredibly realistic _representational_ ~~compelling~~ graphics for his short animated film.
2   Gregor's mother is worried because he is a _compulsive_ ~~dependent~~ computer gamer, and plays up to 12 hours a day.
3   The seminar was extremely _informative_, and the students felt they'd learned a lot about the latest technology.
4   The survey must be conducted in a _controlled_ environment, to ensure we gain objective results.
5   Computer security is _dependent_ on sophisticated anti-virus software.
6   With the right kind of strategy, seemingly _meaningless_ videos manage to go viral on sites like YouTube.

[handwritten top margin: back down = surrender / give up / compromise   set down: wright sth down / stop and allow sb to get off   put down to = attribute]

Prepositional phrases

[handwritten: let up : stop doing sth / less strong]

5 Complete the short extract with suitable prepositions.

Worried you may be suffering from information overload? Recent studies suggest that what could be **(1)** _at_ fault is people's uncontrollable need to stay **(2)** _in_ touch, either with the latest news, or with activity at the office while on holiday. And thanks **(3)** _to_ developments in wireless technology, they can satisfy this need, even when they're on the beach. However, unlimited access **(4)** _to_ the internet via laptops, cell phones and iPads means that they can never truly escape or relax. With regard **(5)** _to_ work, they are seen as constantly available, and may be expected to reply to emails or messages **(6)** _without_ delay. For those concerned that their job might be **(7)** _on_ the line, this adds extra pressure to stay connected. The problem is, the quality of their holiday, not to mention their relationship with the people they are sharing it with, gets lost **(8)** _in_ the process. So, if you are concerned that this is happening, it may be time to take control.

Phrasal verbs with *up* and *down*

6a Form phrasal verbs by adding *up* or *down* to the verbs below. Some verbs can be combined with both, and some can take a second preposition/ particle after them. *[handwritten: catch up / cause problems / = meeting]*

back _up/down_ set _up/down_ break _up/down_ make _up_ let _up/down_ play _up/down_ follow _up on_ catch _up with_ put _up with/down_ *[handwritten: try to make sth seem less important / criticise]*

b Replace the words in *italics* in the sentences with the correct form of phrasal verbs from Exercise 6a.

1 Georgia felt really *hurt and disappointed* by her sister's lack of interest in her achievement. *[let down]*

2 Felix had to call out the technician after his computer suddenly *crashed*. *[broke down]*

3 The bank tried to *say that* the problem with their computer system *wasn't serious* so as not to cause panic among investors. *[play down]*

4 Make sure you *copy* all your working files onto a memory stick in case your PC crashes. *[back up]*

5 Dan couldn't get a signal for his mobile, which he *decided was caused by* the high mountains blocking transmission. *[put down to]*

Compound words

7a Phrasal verbs can sometimes form compound nouns, e.g. *break up* becomes *breakup*. In pairs, make compounds from some of the phrasal verbs in Exercises 6a and b, then look back at the main reading text on page 57 and highlight any compound words you can find. *[handwritten: eg raining all day]*

[handwritten bottom margin: setup = how sth is organised / the way of organising sth   letup = no break   putup   putdown = making fun of sth]

b Complete the sentences with compound words from Exercise 7a.

1 As a result of the recent **breakdown** in communication, the company has decided not to go ahead with the proposal.

2 Apart from occasionally listening to her **voicemail** and checking for messages, Kelly kept her mobile switched off for most of the weekend.

3 Paul now conducts most transactions and does 80 percent of his shopping _online_, and feels he saves time and money by avoiding the town centre.

4 Sometimes work _overload_ and ineffective time management can lead to exhaustion and depression.

5 Do you have a _backup_ system for saving your work in case your computer crashes?

Use of English 1 (Paper 1 Part 2)

Open cloze

1 For questions 1–8, read the text below and think of the word which best fits each gap. Use only one word in each gap. There is an example at the beginning (0).

Kenya's mobile banking revolution

In recent years, an economic revolution has been **(0)** _taking_ place in Kenya, and a company called Safaricom has been at the centre of it. The company was **(1)** _set_ up in 1997, initially as a mobile-phone business catering **(2)** _to_ the millions of Africans who until **(3)** _then_ had never even had a land line. **(4)** _What_ this meant in effect was that, for the first time, suppliers and customers in rural areas could communicate directly with each other, and the effects were astounding. The company's phone-credit transfer service was **(5)** _of_ even greater significance, however. This was designed so that users **(6)** _could_ buy phone time for relatives living in the bush.

But **(7)** _when_ people began using the facility as currency, paying for taxi rides and other things with cell-phone credit, Safaricom saw a golden opportunity for a mobile money-transfer service, and M-PESA was born. Today, users can pay bills and get money out of ATMs **(8)** _without_ having a conventional bank account or pin number – all they need is a mobile phone.

Discussion

2a Discuss the following statement in relation to your own and your friends' experience:

'I can survive without my laptop for a week, but please don't take away my mobile phone!'

b Write an account of your own relationship with a digital gadget.

Listening 1 (Paper 3 Part 1)

Before you listen

1 Look at the cartoon, and speculate what you might hear in extract 1 which follows.

Listening: understanding the questions

> EXPERT STRATEGIES page 170

2 Read questions 1 and 2 in Exercise 3. Underline the key words that help you to answer the question correctly.

Multiple-choice questions

3 🎧 T1.24 Read the strategy on page 170, then do the task.

You will hear three different extracts. For questions 1–6, choose the answer (A, B or C) which fits best according to what you hear. There are two questions for each extract.

Extract One

You hear two friends discussing a talk they've just been to about a computer game.

1 What does the man think of the speaker's suggestion?

A It underestimates the skill needed to play well.

B It misunderstands the motivation of gamers.

C It overcomplicates a simple problem.

2 The woman thinks the game would generate useful ideas if

A it formed part of a wider educational activity.

B it could be promoted in an imaginative way.

C it was designed by teenagers themselves.

Extract Two

You hear a businessman talking about managing a company's online reputation.

3 What is his opinion of the software he mentions?

A It's not as reliable as has been suggested.

B It needs to be part of a co-ordinated policy.

C It works best when criticisms are unfounded.

4 When he talks about his own company's policy, he is

A proposing a procedure that should be adopted.

B explaining why its rivals have followed its lead.

C describing an initiative that has proved effective.

Extract Three

You hear part of a discussion programme about graduate recruitment.

5 What point does the woman make about corporate use of the internet?

A Usual codes of business conduct may not always apply online.

B Processing the volume of data poses a problem for business users.

C Businesses are inclined to reveal more about themselves these days.

6 What is the man doing?

A warning students to exercise caution online

B criticising the attitude of certain employers

C regretting his own youthful indiscretions

Task analysis

4 🎧 T1.24 Listen to Extract One again, then discuss your answers to questions 1 and 2. Explain why you rejected the other two options in each case.

Discussion

5 Discuss the following statements, explaining whether you agree or disagree with them, and why.

1 'As far as I'm concerned, online games are a great way of learning to perform problem-solving tasks of all kinds.'

2 'Personally, I can't see the point of all these social networking sites, with people cluttering your page with meaningless comments all the time.'

3 'Social networking sites help to expose unfair commercial practices, and warn people against them.'

Language development 1

Modals 1: obligation, necessity, advice and criticism

> EXPERT GRAMMAR page 177

Obligation and necessity

1 Explain whether the obligation in the following sentences comes from the speaker (internal) or someone else (external).

1 It's late. I really must be going. *(in)*
2 I have to wear a shirt and tie to work every day. *(ex)*
3 We had to shut down the system after someone hacked into our network. *(ex)*
4 You mustn't tell him that I told you! *(in)*
5 I resent having to switch off my mobile when I go into the college building. *(ex)*
6 The hotel must have WiFi facilities, or else I'm not going! *(in)*

2a Explain the difference in meaning between the following sentences.

1 You mustn't keep texting her.
2 You needn't go to the club tonight.

b Rewrite the phrases in *italics* with a suitable form of *need*. Make any other changes necessary.

1 *It was not necessary for them* to buy tickets because Beatrice's father had already bought them. *They didn't need to / needn't have bought*
2 You tidied up *but it wasn't necessary*. I could have done it later. *You needn't have (done it) / you didn't need to*
3 You *don't have to* call. Just come when you like. *don't need to / needn't*
4 *It's not necessary for him* to do any shopping, as we're fully stocked. *He doesn't need to / needn't do*

Advice and criticism

3a In pairs, discuss which of the following can be used to give advice, and which can be used to express criticism. Some may be used for both.

should(n't)   would(n't)   could   might
should(n't) have   might have

b Complete the sentences with a suitable form of the modals in Exercise 3a. There may be more than one possibility.

1 You *shouldn't have* uploaded that video on YouTube! Everyone's laughing at me!
2 I *wouldn't* do that, if I were you. You might lose all your files.
3 One thing you *could /might/should* do is to search the Web for universities that offer that kind of course.
4 I think he *might* *should* talk to his course tutor and tell her about the problem.
5 You *should* *might/could* ask Simone for help. She usually knows what to do in these situations.
6 You *might have* *should've/could've* told me you hadn't a clue about computers! That's another morning wasted!

might've ← (with annoying!) more annoyed than could've/should've

Other ways of expressing obligation, necessity and advice

4 Complete the sentences with the words below.

up   ought   had   would   onus   duty
obligation   your

1 It's your *duty* to tell your tutor when you can't make it for a lesson.
2 It's *up* to you to explain to him why you don't want to go to Brussels.
3 Social networking sites have a(n) *obligation* */duty* to warn members of the dangers of revealing too much personal information online.
4 The *onus* is on Daniel to apologise for the mistake.
5 It's *your* responsibility to check that you are buying from a secure site when purchasing products over the internet.
6 You *had* better not play Pro all night again!
7 You *would* be better off uploading your short film onto YouTube if you want to get some feedback on it.
8 We *ought* to send Karen an email about the change of plan.

5 For questions 1–8, fill the gaps with one suitable word from Exercises 3 and 4.

I don't believe it! You **(1)** *might* have told me you didn't need the results until tomorrow! I **(2)** *wouldn't* *needn't* have stayed up half the night working! You'd **(3)** *better* make sure you back up the file, since we don't want to run the risk of losing all that data. Remember, the **(4)** *onus* is on you to explain to the boss exactly how we conducted the experiment, so I think that perhaps you **(5)** *should* prepare what you're going to say to her. We absolutely **(6)** *have* to make sure she gives us the funding for further research. As it's **(7)** *your* responsibility to convince her, I **(8)** *would* wear a shirt and tie, if I were you.

Writing 1 (Paper 2 Part 2: Report)

1   Read the following writing task, then underline the key words that help you to answer the question.

> You have been asked by your course tutor to produce a report on the positive and negative effects of internet use on the individual. You should examine its effects on the individual's social, intellectual and physical development, and make recommendations for encouraging appropriate use.
>
> Write your report. Write **280–320** words.

Presenting factual information

2   Read one candidate's answer below. Does it answer the question fully?

Report on the effects of internet use on the individual

Introduction

This report **(1)** _presents_ / _illustrates_ the **(i)** findings of research into the effects, both positive and negative, of internet use on the individual, and makes some recommendations for improvement. *[describe]* *[results outcomes]*

A _Impact on social lives_
Generally **(2)** _talking_ / _speaking_, the internet's **(ii)** effect on an individual's social behaviour is not all negative. **(3)** _Once_ / _When_ used sensibly, social networking sites actively **(iii)** enhance people's ability to make new friends, and chat rooms and instant messaging **(iv)** facilities allow them to keep in touch with friends after school or work, replacing the phone in this respect. The **(v)** threat of cyber bullying is very real, **(4)** _moreover_ / _however,_ and young people in particular tend to expose themselves to this by uploading too much personal information onto webpages. *[impact influence]* *[increase strengthen]* *[improve update]* *[services platforms]* *[danger]*

B _Intellectual growth_
Increasingly, people are making use of the internet to search for information for school or work projects and study. The wealth of information available encourages them to analyse and assess what they read. **(vi)** Furthermore, online games are interactive, and many involve problem-solving or strategic activities. So, **(5)** _far_ / _apart_ from being mindless, some games are intellectually challenging. The main area for **(6)** _concern_ / _consideration_ is that these games are so attractive that they can become addictive, and there are cases where compulsive use leads to a decline in work performance and anti-social behaviour. *[In addition, moreover, besides, this]*

C _Health impacts_
It cannot be **(7)** _argued_ / _denied_ that some people often spend time on the computer **(vii)** to the detriment of physical activities like sport. Online gaming can **(8)** _lead_ / _result_ to a loss of interest in such activities, and studies suggest a **(viii)** link between excessive internet use and the rise in obesity. *[too or the expense of]* *[connection]*

Recommendations

To encourage responsible use of the internet, schools and colleges ought to include lessons in internet awareness, while internet cafés should display notices warning their customers of the dangers involved in spending too much time playing online.

3   Choose the word in _italics_ (1–8) which best fits in the context.

4   Find suitable synonyms to replace the underlined words (i–viii) in the model answer.

Paragraph organisation

5   It is useful to organise your report into sections with headings. Choose a suitable heading for paragraphs A, B and C in the model answer.

6   In pairs, read the writing task below, then turn to page 200.

Imagine that one of you is the counsellor and one a college student. The counsellor asks the college student questions relating to the points to be addressed in the writing task. The college student gives answers based on his/her personal experience. The counsellor could take notes. The counsellor from each pair should report to the rest of the class on what they have learned, and make some recommendations.

> The Principal has asked you to write a report on the effects of social networking sites on college students, with reference to the time spent online, their involvement in social activities and their academic performance. You should make recommendations for addressing problem areas.
>
> Write your report in **280–320** words.

7   Work in pairs. Decide how many paragraphs you need to answer the task in Exercise 6, then think of a suitable heading for each one.

8a   The verbs _suggest, recommend_ and _propose_ can be used for making recommendations. Rewrite the following sentences, using the words indicated.

   1 I think you should check your computer for viruses.
      I suggest you _____ .
   2 It'd be good to create a blog for the chess club.
      I propose we _____ .
   3 It might be a good idea to update your profile.
      I recommend that _____ .
   4 Let's set up a local Freecycle website.
      I propose _____ .
   5 He should cancel his subscription, in my opinion.
      I suggest _____ .
   6 Why doesn't she join the LinkedIn network?
      I recommend _____ .

> EXPERT GRAMMAR page 178

b   Write a paragraph of **50–60** words outlining problematic aspects of social networking sites and making recommendations for addressing them.

Listening 2 (Paper 3 Part 3)

Before you listen

1 Discuss the meaning of the following proverbs. In what circumstances do you think they are true?

1 Two heads are better than one.
2 A problem shared is a problem halved. *decrease by half*

Multiple choice

> EXPERT STRATEGIES page 171

2 Read the task questions and options below, then answer the following.

1 What is the subject of the discussion?
2 Do the questions focus on factual information or the speakers' opinion?

3 🎧 T1.25 Listen and complete the task below.

You will hear an interview with a scientist called Alicia Graham and an amateur science enthusiast called Jeremy Ingles, who are talking about public participation in scientific research. For questions 1–5, choose the answer (A, B, C or D) which fits best according to what you hear.

1 Alicia and Jeremy agree that rivalries between scientists *competition between two people*

A may impede progress in some areas.
B create a valuable impetus for researchers.
C are the direct cause of certain dishonest practices.
D should be respected by those advocating co-operation.

2 Alicia and Jeremy disagree about the extent to which supporters of open science

A have to provide alternative sources of funding for researchers.
B can ensure that the contribution of individuals is recognised.
C might benefit from the way blogs and forums operate.
D should consider the needs of commercial sponsors.

3 Jeremy's interest in open science arose from

A participation in an online discussion.
B listening to Alicia talk on the subject.
C conducting experiments in his own home.
D research done whilst studying at university.

4 How does Alicia feel about the contribution of amateur scientists?

A She thinks they can reveal weaknesses in existing theories.
B She believes they cast new light on the research process.
C She would like them to be less isolated from each other.
D She actively encourages them to ask for advice online.

5 Jeremy mentions the Polymath project in order to

A show how amateur scientists approach the process of research.
B explain how open science generates enthusiasm and co-operation.
C illustrate Alicia's point about how effective online collaboration can be.
D give an example of a professional seeking the help of non-professionals.

Task analysis

4 Did working out the focus of each question help you find the answer?

5 Check the meaning of these key words and phrases from the audioscript.

> **EXPERT WORD CHECK**
>
> initiative   be up to speed with (sth)   collaboration   sponsor
> think 'outside the box'   constraints   tinkerer   stifle   diehard   barrier

Discussion

6 What other ways of sharing ideas and information over the internet may be beneficial? Discuss among other benefits:

• time   • the subject   • imagination

'Retailers in Britain are hoping the relaxation could provide them with a much needed boost in sales of around £220 million.

'This will be a fantastic opportunity to showcase, not just London, but the whole of the country to the rest of the world and provide a boost for the economy, sales and employment.

'This generation of youngsters have spent most of their shopping lives post the 1994 Sunday Trading introduction and have grown up accustomed to unrestricted trading hours on other days of the week.

'The research shows that the younger generation of shoppers are less conservative than their parents and less attached to the idea of keeping Sunday special.'

Share 108 Facebook 81 Twitter 21 LinkedIn

47 comments

PollyGee
2 minutes ago

Not many pub and restaurant owners would agree with you there, as some of them do most of their business on a Sunday!

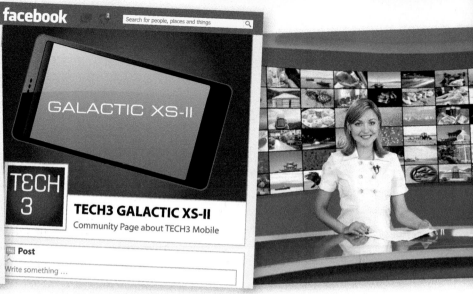

Speaking (Paper 4 Part 3)

Vocabulary: news and information

1a Discuss the sources of information that are illustrated in the photographs. What purposes might each type of media serve?

b The words below can be used to talk about news and the media. Use some of them to discuss the effectiveness of one of the sources illustrated in informing the public of the news. ☺ Talk for one minute. Your teacher will time you.

comment   censorship   restrict   criticise   expose   controversy   bias   objectivity

2a Choose the correct word to complete the sentences.

1 The question of how much information should be revealed to the public is an extremely _____ issue.
A doubtful   B controversial   C questionable

2 The journalist won an award for his _____ of the company's illicit arms deal.
A exposure   B article   C report

3 Do you think the internet should be subject to _____ ?
A censorship   B approval   C examination

4 It is impossible for newspapers to be completely _____ in their portrayal of current affairs.
A biased   B objective   C thoughtful

5 The validity of a lot of information posted on the Web is open to

_____ .
A doubt   B consideration   C question

6 The movie star's comments to the press _____ a heated online response from readers yesterday.
A influenced   B provoked   C followed

b Make sentences using the other options from each question.

Model answer   **3**   🎧 T1.26 Read Egon's card, listen to him perform the task, then answer the questions.

1 How well does he tackle the task?
2 What techniques does he use to develop and sustain his talk?

What effects has the internet had on the way we receive news and information?
• newspapers/TV/radio
• bias
• objectivity

Useful language: comparing

4a 🎧 T1.26 **Listen to Egon again. Complete his statements below with a word or short phrase, according to what you hear.**

1 The _____ tabloids, and even with broadsheet newspapers, is that they cannot avoid some kind of bias coming through.

2 _____ , newspaper websites get round this by presenting their contents on the home page, making it easier for readers to choose an article they are interested in.

3 With _____ the TV and radio, news programmes are restricted by time .

4 But I'm _____ that online articles are more objective in themselves, or that the quality of writing is any better.

5 What _____ online is that readers are able to post comments immediately after an article, and generate discussion.

6 And I _____ , I sometimes find the comment section more interesting than the article that inspired it!

b Which of the expressions you used to answer Exercise 4a could be replaced with the following?

| I must admit | I don't mean | As for | On the other hand |

5a Read the question card and complete the beginning of an answer with the words below.

> What are some of the consequences of sharing information openly online?
> • personal information
> • research
> • exposure to abuse

| the value of this | the thing about | find | rather than | depends |
| in order to |

Isabel: Yes, well, I think (1) _____ sharing information online is that it (2) _____ on what kind of information you're talking about. People share personal information on social networking sites, usually (3) _____ make new friends. I think (4) _____ is that you may meet someone online who will become important in your life. Some people (5) _____ it easier to express themselves via the internet, (6) _____ when they're standing in a group, you know? The Net acts as a vehicle for introductions, if you like. For me, the Web makes me feel …

b Complete the answer with your own views. Use the following words and phrases to help you.

| One of the dangers is | run the risk of | leave themselves exposed to |
| could end up regretting | it is wise to | it is best to |

Individual long turn

➤ EXPERT STRATEGIES page 171

6 Work in pairs. Student A, read Task card 1 on page 205, and Student B, read card 2 on page 205. Using the strategy to help you, practise performing the task for Part 3 of the Speaking test. Remember to use some of the discourse markers from Exercises 4 and 5 in your talk. ⏱ **Time yourselves.**

Task analysis

7 Discuss the following questions.

1 Did you use examples or personal experiences to illustrate your points?

2 Were you able to link your points in a natural way?

3 How many of the phrases from Exercises 4 and 5 did you use?

Language development 2

Modals 2: ability, possibility, probability and deduction

> EXPERT GRAMMAR page 178

[handwritten note box:]
For Modals → always followed by INFINITIVE
...n of *can,*
...n take two

MODAL + INFINITIVE + P.P.

He must have eaten
He could have suffered.

The 3rd person (-S) it is not applied in here.
[FUTURE PERFECT]
(will have finished by ...)
Modal + INF + PP.

...e been ✓
...bed ✓
... make ✓
...really
...Don't
...tes
...led

lecture. Our next project is to research an aspect of cell mutation, but we **(4)** _won't be able to_ access the *[X]* instructions for that until tomorrow. Also, Sara says she's tried several times but **(5)** _couldn't_ *[hasn't been able to]* reach you on your mobile. Have you had it *[X]* switched off? Give her a call, if you **(6)** _can_ ✓. She's been worried about you. I'll try and pop in tomorrow on my way to class. Take care, and get well soon!

Bye for now,

Guppy

Possibility and probability

2 Discuss the difference in meaning between the following sentences.

1 I could join LinkedIn in order to make new business contacts.
2 I should join LinkedIn in order to make new business contacts.
3 I might join LinkedIn in order to make new business contacts.

3 Complete the sentences with the correct form of the modals *can, could, should* and *might* and the verbs in brackets.

✓1 I _might join_ (join) Facebook or MySpace but I'm not sure yet.
✗2 I'm working on your computer right now, so I _should finish_ (finish) fixing it by late this afternoon.
✗3 It _might be_ (be) Josh you saw on YouTube, as he wasn't even at the party!
✓4 The weather _can be_ (be) quite changeable in this area, so make sure you bring a coat.
✓5 It's fairly easy to find your way round the website, so you _should_ (have) any difficulty. _not have_

Deduction

4 Correct the mistake in each of the sentences below. Look carefully at the context!

✓1 I can't access that link Gianni sent me. He can't _could not_ have made a mistake. _(must has made is better)_ *[might has mad...]*
✗2 Jules hasn't phoned home once since she left for college. She must ~~have been~~ having a good time! _be_
✓3 The results must be wrong! I checked them three times! _can't_
✓4 Paola hasn't been online all day. She should have been feeling ~~better.~~ _worse_ _might_ _(must too)_
5 Karen can't access her Facebook account? She can forget her password again. _can't Karen_ _might has forgotten_

Use of English 2 (Paper 1 Part 4)

Key word transformations

1 For questions 1–6, complete the second sentence so that it has a similar meaning to the first sentence, using the word given. Do not change the word given. You must use between three and eight words, including the word given. Here is an example (0).

0 I can't understand why Kyle didn't know about the change of plan, as I texted him earlier.
(known)
I texted Kyle earlier about the change of plan, _so he should have known_ about it.

1 David finally managed to solve the problem after 6 hours' hard work.
(was)
Only after working hard for 6 hours _was David able to_ solve the problem.

2 I think people who reveal personal information on networking sites really crave attention.
(post)
People who _post about_ want to get noticed. _personal information on networking sites must_

✗3 I'd like to drop by and discuss the design of my new website, if that's alright.
(if)
I wonder _if it could be_ and discuss the design of my new website? _I could drop by possible to drop being dropped by_ _would_

✓4 You must be joking about emailing the American President!
(serious)
You _can't be serious_ the American President! _about emailing_

✗5 Right, I've checked the hard drive, so I don't think you'll have any more problems.
(help)
Right, you _should have had_ , as I've checked the hard drive. _should need anymore help_

✗6 I'm certain Kevin is still in the building, as his car keys and BlackBerry are still on his desk.
(have)
Kevin's car keys and BlackBerry are still on his desk, so _he can't have_ the building. _left_

Use of English 3 (Paper 1 Part 3)

Lead-in

1 Discuss the following questions.

1 How many online contacts do you have?
2 How easy is it to find old friends or family that you have lost touch with over the internet?
3 Do you think the Facebook trend is here to stay or just another passing fad?

Developing skills: identifying the part of speech

➤ EXPERT STRATEGIES page 167

2 Read through the extract below and consider the following.

• Which part of speech – noun, verb, adjective, etc. – do you need to fill each gap?
• Is it negative or positive?
• Is it singular or plural?

Word formation

3 Read the strategy on page 167, then do the task.

For questions 1–8, read the text below. Use the word given in CAPITALS at the end of some of the lines to form a word that fits in the gap in the same line. There is an example at the beginning (0).

The **SIX** degrees of separation

The idea that we live in a web of communications and that you're

(0) _effectively_ only six steps away from direct contact with your **EFFECT**

favourite film star is not a new one. Indeed, it **(1)** _updates_ the PREDATES **DATE**

internet and mobile telephony by several decades. In the 1960s,

Stanley Milgram established that it was **(2)** _surprisingly_ easy to ✓ **SURPRISE**

contact anyone in the USA via the postal system, even if their address

was **(3)** _unknown_ to you. However, his findings were deemed **KNOW**

(4) _unconcluded_ since some messages never reached their target. INCONCLUSIVE **CONCLUDE**

Interest in the idea was revived by John Guare's play *Six degrees*

of separation in the 1990s, and then **(5)** _popularized_ by an online ✓ **POPULAR**

game **(6)** _entitled_ the Six degrees of Kevin Bacon, in which ✓ **TITLE**

players link any actor to Kevin Bacon in as few steps as possible.

More recently, people have tested out the theory using social

networking sites like Facebook. There are still questions about how

(7) _representative_ the results are, but the latest technology lends ✓ **REPRESENT**

considerable weight to the underlying **(8)** _unfeasible_ of the theory. FEASIB- **FEASIBLE**
ILITY

Task analysis

4 Discuss the following questions.

1 For which gaps did you find the task strategy useful?
2 What other points do you need to consider when doing this task?

Discussion

5a How successful do you think the Six degrees of separation experiment will be?

b Play your own version of the Six degrees of Kevin Bacon game. Your teacher will give you instructions.

Writing 2 (Paper 2 Part 2: Report)

Lead-in **1** Look at the photograph and discuss the following questions.

1 When do you use your mobile phone?
2 Do you ever switch it off?
3 When do you consider it inappropriate/impolite to use a mobile phone?

Understand the task **2** Read the following writing task and answer these questions.

1 What is the purpose of the report?
2 Who is the target reader?
3 What information do you need to include in your report?

> Your tutor has asked you to write a report <u>on the positive and negative effects of mobile phone use in public places</u> such as shops, bars and restaurants and public transport. You must consider <u>its effects on the individual's ability to relax and interact socially</u>, and also its effects <u>on other people</u>. Make <u>recommendations for encouraging people to restrict their use of mobile phones.</u>
>
> Write your report. Write **280–320** words.

Plan your report **3** Read and compare the two plans below. What do you like and dislike about them? Read the strategy on page 169.

> ➤ EXPERT STRATEGIES page 169

Plan 1
1 Introduction
2 Effects of the mobile phone in shops, bars and restaurants
3 Effects of the mobile phone on public transport
4 Recommendations
5 Effects of the mobile phone on a person's ability to relax and interact socially
6 Recommendations

Plan 2
1 Aim of report + areas of research covered
2 Positive and negative effects on the individual's ability to relax and interact socially
3 Effects on the people around the individual
4 Recommendations – the potential impact of my suggestions

4 Make your own paragraph plan with suitable headings.

Language and content: ensuring your answer is relevant

5a Are the following phrases normally used in:

• Introduction (I)?   • Current situation (C)?   • Recommendations (R)?

This report presents/outlines/examines …	
It is based on …	
At present …	
The current situation suggests that …	
According to some students/tutors …	
Comments have been made about the lack of …	
Generally speaking, …	
Overall, …	
One reason for this could be …	
In view of this, it would be advisable to …	
In the light of the present situation …	
The following measures could improve …	

b Make sentences with at least one phrase from each group that you could include in your report.

6 The following paragraph makes recommendations for improvements to an internet café. Complete the paragraph with the words and phrases below.

appeal   could   premises   in this way   suggestion   in the light of

> **(1)** _____ the information gathered, it is believed that the Alpha internet café **(2)** _____ be improved in several ways. One **(3)** _____ is to redecorate the **(4)** _____ in brighter shades. Creating a coffee bar at the front of the shop instead of the back would also enhance its **(5)** _____ as a meeting place. **(6)** _____ , the café would be able to satisfy all its customers' needs.

7a Several other complaints were made about the internet café. Read them and make recommendations for improvement. Begin your sentences with the words given, and use suitable modals where appropriate.

> 'We need a separate area for group gaming.'
> 'I can't concentrate on updating my CV with all the noise coming from those games.'
> **1** PC terminals could also _____ .
> **2** Gamers _____ .
> **3** Meanwhile, job-seekers and people wanting to use email facilities _____ .

b Rewrite the paragraph from Exercise 6, including the recommendations you made in Exercise 7a.

Write your report

> ➤ EXPERT STRATEGIES page 169

8 Now write your report in answer to the question in Exercise 2. Write your answers in **280–320** words, using some of the language above where appropriate.

Check your report

> ➤ EXPERT WRITING page 191

9 Edit your report, using the checklist on page 191.

Review

needn't have → what you did. In the end, was not actually necessary.

1 Circle the correct words to complete the sentences.

1 You *had* / *would* be better off creating a new file for all that information.

2 'Hannah thinks you're incompetent.' 'She *would* / *might* say that! She can't stand me.'

3 Oh no! We're terribly late! Andreas *won't* / *can't* have waited for us, I just know it!

4 Sorry Ellie, I'd already done it, so you *didn't need to send* / *needn't have sent* me the attachment, after all.

5 I've spent all morning uploading these images onto the website! You *could* / *would* have told me you'd changed your mind!

6 It's your *onus* / *duty* to check through the report before sending it to head office. *(The onus is on you)*

7 You *should* / *might* find it useful to ask tech support for help in the matter, but it's only a suggestion.

6/8

8 Dan's angry with me, so he *must* / *should* have seen that comment I posted on his Facebook wall!

2 Add a suitable suffix to the words in brackets to complete the sentences. Make any other changes necessary.

compulsive

1 Wanda is a _compelled_ (compel) gamer. She plays computer games for up to 8 hours a day.

2 If you want to have _meaningful_ (meaning) relationships, don't rely on Facebook to make friends.
uncontrollable

3 I have this _controlling_ (control) urge to check my emails all the time. I just can't stop myself!

4 We have a talk from science enthusiast, Joseph Jackson _represented_ (represent) the Open Science movement. *representing*

5 Your success is _dependent_ (depend) on whether you can present your artwork effectively in a blog.

6 Dr Nimble is a highly _informed_ (inform) Professor of Chemistry.

7 *The Secret Scripture* tells the _compelling_ (compel) story of a psychiatrist's fascination with the mystery surrounding one of his patients.

8 Fortunately, we have an extremely _dependable_ (depend) young computer technician at the office, who is able to answer all my queries.

COMPEL
(v)
compulsive
compelling
compelled
compulsory

3 Complete the sentences with the correct form of a suitable phrasal verb with *up* or *down*.

1 I can't see you properly, because the image on the screen keeps _breaking_ ! up

2 The problem with his emails was _put down_ to the fact that the server had been overloaded that day.

3 Could you help me with _setting up_ Skype on my new computer? I'm not sure how to do it.

4 I'd like this complaint dealt with immediately, and then _followed_ up by an investigation.

5 I use online chat rooms mainly to _catch up_ on the latest news with friends that I'm unable to see during the week.

6 Simon said he'd show me how to use AutoCAD but didn't turn up. I hate being _let down_ like this!

7 Melanie's a games designer, and spends all day _making up_ new computer games for people like me to play! *thinking up / dreaming up …*

8 I tried to get him to admit he was wrong, but he refused to _back down_ , and continued arguing.

4 Circle the correct word to complete the text.

Managing information

In our desire to appear well **(1)** *informative* / *informed* in all things relating to our working life, we have come to rely on email, RSS feeds and social network sites to keep us **(2)** *upgraded* / *updated* on all the latest news and information, and no matter whether we are in a meeting or in the company of friends, messages sent to our BlackBerry seem too **(3)** *compelling* / *compulsory* to ignore. Research has shown that up to a third of these messages are unnecessary, and that time at work spent sifting through emails can reduce our creative **(4)** *output* / *production*. Therefore, when processing all the information we receive, we need to focus on what is truly **(5)** *relevant* / *meaningful* to our needs. There are solutions available. With respect to emails, it is now possible to prioritise messages by importance of subject history, or sender. Furthermore, aside from filters which isolate items of **(6)** *questionable* / *contentious* content, software tools are being designed to weed out whatever does not appear to be **(7)** *representative* / *representational* of our interests. The **(8)** *question* / *concern* is, how far do we want such tools to control what we read?

5

Language and literature

Overview

5A
- **Reading and Use of English:** Multiple choice (Part 5); Word formation (Part 3)
- **Listening:** Sentence completion (Part 2)
- **Language development:** Words with a similar meaning; Confusable words; Homophones
- **Writing:** Review (Part 2): Language for different types of reviews

5B
- **Listening:** Multiple matching (Part 4)
- **Speaking:** Collaborative task (Parts 1 & 2): Careers and language use
- **Reading and Use of English:** Multiple-choice cloze (Part 1)
- **Language development:** Cleft sentences; Nominal relative clauses; Noun collocations + *of*
- **Writing:** Review (Part 2): Organising your ideas; Useful phrases for describing and evaluating

Lead-in

1 The English language is a mixture of different influences that have accumulated and merged over the years. Look at the timeline below and match the words to the different periods.

The history of the English language: timeline

Celts 500BC–43BC
just a few place names

Romans 43BC–c.450AD
used by merchants and soldiers

Anglo Saxons from 449AD
basic everyday words

St Augustine 597AD
religious words and words for gardening

Vikings 789AD
words derived from Norse – animals and food

Normans 1066
French is the language of the invader

100 Years' War 1337–1450s
after the war, literacy in English improves

Renaissance 1476–1650
printing press introduced, explorers travel

Industrial Revolution 1760–1800s
science, industry, expanding cities

1900s–present day
computer technology, slang, globalisation

1 mods and rockers, cappuccino, cybercafés

2 London, Dover, the river Thames

3 magazine, yoghurt, potato

4 wine, candle, belt

5 history, library, genius

6 earth, house, sleep

7 school, monk, spade

8 biology, chromosome, claustrophobia

9 cake, reindeer, egg

10 chess, banquet, castle

2 Discuss the following questions.
1 Can you think of any other words used in English that have come from other cultures?
2 What influences from other languages are evident in your language?
3 What is the most difficult aspect of learning English: vocabulary or grammar?

Reading (Paper 1 Part 5)

Before you read   **1** Books are the written form of language. They are living proof of the ways in which languages change throughout the centuries.

     1 Do you see this continuing in the same way?
     2 How do you think your language will evolve in the future?

   2 What do you read in English other than your books for study? What sources do you find most useful for language learning?

Skimming   **3** Read the article quickly and find what the author thinks about the question below. Do you agree?

     Will the home library survive the surge of the e-book?

Multiple choice   **4** You are going to read an article about books in the home. For questions 1–6, choose the answer (A, B, C or D) which you think fits best according to the text. Use the strategies on page 168 to help you.

➤ EXPERT STRATEGIES page 168

Task analysis   **5** In pairs, discuss your answers to the questions, underlining the parts of the text where you found your answers.

Discussion   **6a** How important are your books to you? Where do you display your books and which do you display? Are you happy with where they are in your home?

   b Which is the better way to relieve boredom: watching TV or reading a book?

   7 Check the meaning of these key words from the text.

EXPERT WORD CHECK

abound   ensue   speculation   stack   deem   tangible   relegate
deploy   odds   kudos

At home with books

In an age when literature is increasingly going digital, books hold a curious role in some people's homes. There are few purchases which, once used, are placed on proud display and carted round as families move from place to place. And yet that's precisely what sometimes happens with books, despite the existence of a digital equivalent. After all, both the music industry and other aspects of the print media have felt the heat of virtual competition – why not books? Part of the explanation for this may lie in the fact that, when it comes to the crunch, nosing around someone's bookshelves is interesting. 'You can tell a lot about someone by their collection of books,' says Doug Jeffers, owner of a London bookstore.

It's not just the quantity of titles on display, however, that speaks volumes; generation, occupation, political leanings, leisure pursuits (even where they go on holiday) – clues to all of these abound, if you care to analyse the contents of someone's bookshelves, and even casual visitors aren't slow to form judgements. Evidence of this manifested itself when the President of the USA made an informal call on the English Prime minister at home recently, and for some reason the pair posed for photos in the kitchen. One of the snapshots was subsequently released to the press, and widely published. There then ensued much speculation as to how the complete works of Shakespeare had ended up on the shelf in the background rather than a cookery book.

Household stylist Abigail Hall agrees. 'I often style houses for sale and you'd be amazed how important the contents of the bookcase can be.' Apparently, people use such clues to form judgements about the type of person who lives in a property that's up for sale, and this may affect how they feel about going ahead with the purchase. Perhaps we all seek out others whose tastes in such matters match our own, and we can imagine living happily in a space that like-minded people have made homely. And even if we're not thinking of putting our home on the market, instinct tells us that however much they were enjoyed, paperbacks read on the beach might be better put away in a cupboard, whilst the unopened classics are destined for display.

For the interior designer, however, the art of reputation-management-via-bookshelf is not the only issue. Books can also become an interactive display tool. 'They can almost be sculptural in that they offer a physical presence,' explains Abigail Hall. 'It's not just about stacking them on a bookcase, it's how you stack them. I've seen books arranged by colour, stacked on top of each other. Once I saw a load of coffee-table books piled up to become a coffee table in themselves. Books define a space, if you have some books and a comfy chair, you've immediately created an area.' It's a trick of which countless hotels, cafés and waiting rooms for fee-paying clients are only too aware. Placing a few carefully-chosen books atop coffee tables is about creating an ambiance. No one actually engages with the content.

And this principle can be transferred to the home 'I've not actually read any of them. I just love the bindings.' So said the actress, Davinia Taylor, earlier this year when she decided to put her house on the market – complete with its carefully-sourced collection of classic books. Rarely removed from their perch on a bookcase in the living room, their primary purpose was to disguise Taylor's walk-in fridge. And so, with the fridge no longer destined to be a feature in her life, the books were deemed redundant.

Perhaps, then, the future of books lies in this. With more and more being bought in the undeniably handier digital format, the first casualties of the tangible variety are likely to be the beach-read paperbacks – the ones that, if you invite Abigail Hall around, would be relegated to the garage anyway. But given the uses to which we put our other tomes – whether they're deployed to show off, look pretty, or create an atmosphere – the odds of them hanging around look good. The kudos of great work is still there, and there's nothing like being, and being seen to be, in possession of the real thing.

1 In the first paragraph, the writer is
   A outlining the reasons for changing priorities.
   B drawing our attention to an ongoing process.
   C seeking to account for a seemingly illogical attitude.
   D questioning our assumptions about people's behaviour.

2 What does the mention of political figures in the second paragraph serve to illustrate?
   A the public's curiosity about celebrity lifestyles
   B the importance of background detail in photography
   C the extent to which books tend to attract people's attention
   D the false impression that can be gained from books on display

3 Abigail Hall's experience suggests that the books on show in a house for sale
   A may not be as representative of the owners' taste as people assume.
   B can create an affinity between sellers and prospective buyers.
   C might help buyers to assess how keen the owners are to sell.
   D could mislead people into buying an unsuitable property.

4 What is implied about interior designers in the fourth paragraph?
   A They regard books as little more than additional pieces of furniture.
   B They are likely to underestimate the impact of the content of books.
   C They sometimes show a lack of respect for the true function of books.
   D They understand the effect of books on the users of spaces they create.

5 Davinia Taylor no longer wants her books because
   A she has no use for them beyond their current purpose.
   B she accepts that they don't reflect her taste in reading.
   C she realises she selected the titles for the wrong reasons.
   D she feels they are an integral part of the house she's selling.

6 In the final paragraph, the writer expresses
   A a personal preference for books in digital format.
   B optimism regarding the future of non-digital books.
   C regret that the content of all books is not more valued.
   D a hope that attitudes towards books will be different in the future.

Vocabulary

Literary devices

1a Various literary devices are used in writing and in speech. Match the devices below with their meanings. Can you find any more examples in the text on page 73?

1 cliché
2 idiom
3 irony
4 metaphor
5 onomatopoeia
6 personification
7 pun
8 rhetorical question
9 simile

a an expression that has acquired a special meaning which is different from the normal meaning of the individual words, e.g. *She's an absolute angel!*

b a question you ask as a way of making a statement, without expecting an answer, e.g. *Will the digital revolution change that?*

c a way of describing sth as if it were sth else, e.g. *I gave him a piece of my mind.*

d an amusing use of a word or phrase that has two meanings or that sounds similar to another word, e.g. *A gossip is someone with a sense of rumour.*

e a comparison that uses *like* or *as*, e.g. *That car goes like a dream.*

f a phrase that has been over-used and has lost its meaning, e.g. *I thank you from the bottom of my heart.*

g when you use words that are the opposite of what you mean, often to be amusing or sarcastic, e.g. *Are you feeling tired after all that studying you've been doing? Why don't you have a rest – again!*

h when sth that is not human is given human-like qualities, e.g. *The sun smiled down from the sky.*

i a word that sounds like what it means, e.g. *I heard a huge CRACK as the ice broke.*

b Identify the different literary devices in the text below. Discuss their meaning and how effective they are here.

Expressions using *brain*, *face*, *head*, *mind* and *wits*

2a Complete the phrases with *brain*, *face*, *head*, *mind* or *wits*. Discuss the meaning of the phrases.

1 (say sth) off the top of your _____
2 be a load off your _____
3 be at your _____' end
4 be the _____ behind sth
5 come _____ to _____ with (sb/sth)
6 cross (sb's) _____
7 give (sb) a piece of your _____
8 go to (sb's) _____
9 have a good _____ to (do sth)
10 have a _____ of its own
11 keep a straight _____
12 keep your _____ about you
13 bang your _____ against a (brick) wall
14 lose/save _____
15 put your _____ to (sth)
16 rack your _____

b Complete the sentences with a suitable phrase from Exercise 2a. In pairs, make sentences to illustrate the other phrases.

1 When he made a funny remark, it was difficult for her to _____ .

2 When I lost my passport in Japan, I tried to _____ . It would have been helpful to speak the language, though!

3 I've been _____ for hours but I simply can't remember his name!

4 This flat is in a disgusting mess. I'm going to give Tracy _____ when she gets back.

5 _____ , I'd say that his autobiography came out last year, but I'm not sure.

The night was as black as ink. As Detective Rowley trudged through the forest, the wind howled and the trees threw their branches around madly, as if threatening to slap him round the head. 'Where was that cabin?' Rowley asked himself as he peered into the blanket of darkness around him. Normally he had a good eye for spotting things – being a detective – but that night he couldn't see in front of his nose! Suddenly, a piercing scream cut through the wind and darkness like a knife. Detective Rowley snapped his head around and stared in the direction it had come from. Glowing in the darkness was a tiny pinprick of light – the cabin!

Phrases from Shakespeare

3a Quotes from Shakespeare have entered the English language without most of us realising it.

1 Look at the underlined phrases in the text. Discuss their meaning.
2 What other phrases come from Shakespeare? Discuss their meaning.

On quoting Shakespeare

If you cannot understand my argument, and declare 'It's Greek to me', you are quoting Shakespeare; if your lost property has vanished into thin air, you are quoting Shakespeare; if you have ever refused to budge an inch, if you have been tongue-tied or a tower of strength, if you have insisted on fair play, slept not one wink, or had too much of a good thing – why, the more fool you, for it is a foregone conclusion that you are quoting Shakespeare; if you think it is high time and that that is the long and short of it, if you believe that the game is up, if you lie low till the crack of doom because you suspect foul play, then – if the truth were known, you are quoting Shakespeare; even if you bid me good riddance and send me packing, if you wish I was dead as a door-nail, if you think I am a laughing stock, then – Tut tut! For goodness' sake! – it is all one to me, for you are quoting Shakespeare.

b Write the next paragraph from the detective story in Exercise 1b. Include examples of the language in Exercises 1a, 2a and 3a.

Word formation: multiple affixation

4a Many words are formed by adding both a prefix and a suffix to the base word, e.g.

prefix base word suffix

↓ ↓ ↓

un + remark + able = unremarkable

Look at the following word families.

1 Say whether each word is a noun, verb, adjective or adverb. There may be more than one possibility for each word.

understand → understanding → misunderstand → misunderstanding → misunderstood

believe → belief → disbelief → disbelieving → believable → unbelievable → unbelievably

comprehend → comprehension → comprehensible → comprehensive → incomprehensible

2 Explain the difference in meaning for the words highlighted in yellow and give examples. Use your dictionary to help you.

b Make your own word families for the following words. Try to do something similar with new items of vocabulary that you learn.

1 conceive (v) 2 doubt (v) 3 suit (v)

---

budge an inch → You do not want to change/move.

Use of English 1 (Paper 1 Part 3)

Word formation

1 Words and language can be manipulated to suit your purpose. Think of at least three ways in which you can use language more effectively.

2 Read the strategy on page 167, then do the task.

For questions 1–8, read the text below. Use the word given in CAPITALS at the end of some of the lines to form a word that fits in the gap in the same line. There is an example at the beginning (0).

➤ EXPERT STRATEGIES page 167

Word power

Using language **(0)** _effectively_ involves more than simply stringing together a series of words. The power of words lies in knowing how to use them to create **(1)** _subtlety_ (N) of meaning and communicate a clear point of view. This means thinking about the **(2)** _suitability_ (N) _____ of the words themselves and the linguistic context in which they are used. What's called communicative **(3)** _competence_ (N) _____ is the knack of saying what you mean succinctly, yet clearly enough to avoid your being **(4)** mis_understood_ (adj.)

EFFECT

SUBTLE

SUITABLE

COMPETENT

UNDERSTAND

What's more, word power is also a skill that can be used to your advantage. For example, if you want to make your target audience sit up and think, one way of **(5)** _ensuring_ (N)(V) this is to force them to view reality from a slightly different, and possibly **(6)** _humorous_ (adj.) perspective. This can be done through the use of words that are relatively **(7)** _unexpected_ (adj.), and so make an impression.

The **(8)** _inclusion_ (N) of more sophisticated vocabulary in your lexicon also provides the potential for creative language use that is playful rather than simply rule-bound.

SURE

HUMOUR

EXPECT

INCLUDE

Conceive (v)
– conceivable/ unconceivable, conceptual
– unconceiving – concept
– conceivably / conception,
– misconceive / misconception

doubt (v)
– undoubted
– undoubtedly
– doubtable
– doubtfully
– doubtless
– doubtful

– suitor suit (v) – suitability
– suited/ unsuited – suitable / – unsuitable / suitably

Listening 1 (Paper 3 Part 2)

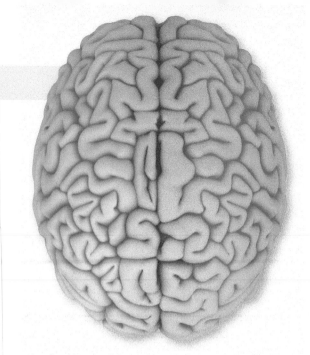

Handwritten notes:

Desinterested → IMPARTIAL
↳ NOT GAINING FROM SOMETHING

Uninterested → Lack of interest
Exhausted → Tired
Exhaustive → very comprehensive.
Thoroughly. / Full-Thorough
Exhaustive search
↳ Look for everything
Historical → relating to the past
Historic → Important event
Inaustrial → related to industry
Industrious → very hard-working
Personal → relating to one person /
Personnel → Private
↳ Staff of a company

1 a Look at the image of a brain. Which of the functions below belong to the right side of the brain and which to the left? Do you find any of them surprising?

- analytic thought
- art and music
- holistic thought (where a person tends to see the 'big picture' rather than the detail)
- language
- science and maths
- creativity
- intuition
- logic

b Which of the above areas do parents tend to encourage more in their young children? How do they go about doing this?

c Which of the above areas do you devote a lot of your time to? Are there any ways in which you might develop your brain more? Brainstorm a few ideas.

Sentence completion

> EXPERT STRATEGIES page 170

2 🎧 T1.27 Read the strategy on page 170, then do the task.

You will hear a researcher called Clive Thomas talking about the world's endangered small languages. For questions 1–9, complete the sentences with a word or short phrase.

ENDANGERED LANGUAGES

✓ • Clive studied [anthropology] **1** as the subject of his first degree.

✗ • Clive has been working as part of a project with the name [~~project~~ *enduring voices*] **2**

✓ • Clive quotes a figure of [6,500] **3** languages that are as yet undocumented.

✓ • Clive uses the word [random] **4** to describe how he selected a language to document.

✓ • Clive's attempt to write a [grammar] **5** of the language he documented was abandoned.

✓ • Clive gives [education] **6** as the main reason for the decline of many minority languages.

✓ • Clive points to a link between [biological diversity] **7** and the survival of many small languages in an area.

✓ • Clive uses the term [folklore] **8** to describe the cultural content of the recordings he makes.

✗ • Clive gives the example of [~~irish and scotish~~ *welsh*] **9** as a minority language which is now becoming more widely spoken.

(7/9)

Discussion

3 How important do you think it is to preserve languages that are only spoken by a small number of people? Are there any such languages in your country or in the place where you are studying? Exchange your ideas and experience.

[Handwritten notes at top:]
Refrain from → You stop yourself to do something.
Entails → is required, MUST.
Fowl → Aves.
Foul → Really Bad.
Fazed → *Dis*Concerned
Ascent → ↗ (ascender) ↳
Assent → Permiso/Consentimiento.
Stationery → Papelería

Lan

Words
words;

▸ EXPERT

Words

1a Complete the sentences with the correct form of one of the words given.

1 entail / contain / enclose
This document _contains_ ~~entails~~ the whole outline of the new book.

2 differentiate / discern / separate
People with dyslexia sometimes have a problem _~~discerning~~_ *differentiating* between the letters *b* and *p* or *d* and *q*.

3 discrepancy / difference
What's the _difference_ between prose and poetry?

4 associate / compare
The new science museum has been _compared_ to something out of a futuristic novel.

5 possibility / opportunity / potential
A creative writer has to learn to tap into the _potential_ of their imaginative powers.

6 rare / scarce
Emma's husband specialises in the buying and selling of _rare_ books.

7 refuse / reject / refrain
Jill _refrained_ from making a comment about his bad grammar while she was reading his essay.

8 match / similarity
Adam was surprised at the lack of _similarity_ between the sisters.

b Use your dictionary to find example sentences using the remaining words in Exercise 1a.

Confusable words

2 Choose the correct word from each pair to complete the short dialogue.

~~disinterested~~ / ~~uninterested~~   exhausted / exhaustive
~~historical~~ / historic   accept / except
industrial / ~~industrious~~   personal / ~~personnel~~

Ben: Look, I can (1) _accept_ ✓ that I'm not the most (2) _industrious_ of people but even so, this research that all the (3) _personnel_ have been asked to do is a bit much, isn't it? 'The (4) _historical_ background and derivation of the word *gobbledygook*' – I wonder who thought *that* one up? *You cannot understand it bc does not make sense. (NOT FORMAL)*

Dana: I know but it's for that new TV quiz and we've got to get it done by the end of today. The research has got to be (5) ~~distinct~~ ✗ *exhaustive* ~~tested~~ otherwise the boss will kill us.

Ben: Never mind, I'm (6) _exhausted_ and with all due respect, I'm totally (7) _____ in all of this. I'm going home! _uninterested_ ✓

Dana: Ben! Come back! What about *gobbledygook*?

Homophones

3 We all know the difference between *break* and *brake* but what makes those two words homophones? Can you think of any other homophones you have come across?

a Identify the homophones (14) in the following sentences and correct the spelling.

1 Despite the fowl weather, they swam out to the red plastic boy and back again. Afterwards, they felt very virtuous! *foel FOUL* *BUOY* ✓

2 All the guests were extremely complementary about the food – the principle dishes were chicken curry and rice or fillet stake with an avocado salad. *complimentary* ✓ *Principal* ✓ *steak* ✓

3 The children were told off for playing hide-and-seek amongst the stationery vehicles. *STATIONARY* ✓

4 'It's rather stuffy in here – can we open a window to get some heir?', a student asked, waiting for the teacher's ascent. *AIR* ✓ *ASSENT*

5 Finally it was time for him to hand over the rains of his company to his sun. *son* ✓ *reins*

6 Sally wasn't at all phased by the news that she was going to be working abroad for a year. *fazed FAZED*

7 I'd really like to know what the sauce of that rumour is. *Gorillas prey SOURCE* ✓

8 Guerillas don't pray on smaller animals: they only eat leaves, fruit and a few insects.

b Can you think of any homophones for these words? Compare your findings and try to put the words you find in a context.

1 aloud *allowed*
2 bite *byte*
3 feet *feat (achievable)*
4 insure *ensure (to make sure)*
5 lent *leant*
6 lesson *lessen (to make sth smaller)*
7 pause *paws*
8 scent *sent*
9 sees *seaze (take it all) "seaze the day"*
10 serial *cereal (and enjoy it)*
11 sight *site*
12 sort *sought (p.p. of seek)*
13 source *sauce*
14 wine *whine (whining)*

Writing 1 (Paper 2 Part 2: Review)

What makes a good review?

- A good review is an interesting and informative one. Remember that, based on what you say, your readers will either go and see that film, read that book, go to that restaurant, or not!
- A review is likely to include narrative, descriptive, explanatory and evaluative language.

1 Stages of review-writing

1 Read the rubric carefully. Who is going to read your review?
2 Think of sub-topics or key points connected with the subject of the review.
3 Plan your review and decide how to order your points.
4 Think of core topic vocabulary.
5 Think of appropriate adjectives (+ adverbs, if desired) to express praise or criticism.
6 Give your review a title.

2 Read the extracts from the two exam rubrics below. Who are the target readers in each case? What type of language will you use?

> 1 Your local town council has organised a competition to encourage people to eat out more often at local restaurants. To win the prize, a free meal at a restaurant of your choice, you must write a review for a tourist brochure of a visit to a restaurant near where you live ...
>
> 2 An online literary magazine has requested reviews of children's fiction. You decide to submit a review of a children's novel ...

3a Look at the sub-topics below. To which type of review might they belong – a review of a restaurant (R), a concert (C), a film (F) or a book (B)? Some may belong in more than one category.

- acting
- atmosphere
- atmosphere/ambiance
- camerawork/lighting
- cast
- characterisation
- choice of music (programme)
- cost/price
- décor
- historical/factual accuracy
- interest level
- length of programme
- location
- location/setting
- plot/storyline
- quality of food/service
- standard of players
- theme music

b Now think of three or four sub-topics for a review of an exhibition and a magazine.

4 In pairs, think of at least five words as core topic vocabulary or core ideas for each type of review mentioned in Exercises 3a and b.

5 Discuss the meaning of these adjectives.

acclaimed   clichéd   exceptional   gripping
hi tech   legendary   mediocre   (un)memorable
over-hyped   over-priced   over-the-top
sophisticated   superb   thriving   true-to-life
up-to-scratch   world-renowned

1 In which type of review (film, book, concert, restaurant, exhibition, magazine) would you most commonly find them?
2 Would you classify them as positive, negative or neutral? Explain your answers.

6a Read the writing task below. Make the plan for your review. Use the notes on this page.

> Your local film society has invited reviews of a recent film based on a book to include in their quarterly magazine. You have decided to write about a film you saw a few weeks ago. Write your review, giving your opinion on the acting, the scenery and the storyline, and stating how far it remained true to the book.

Introduction: _____
Para 1: _____
Para 2: _____
Para 3: _____
Conclusion/Recommendation: _____

b Write your review. Write between **280–320** words.

➤ EXPERT STRATEGIES page 169

Listening 2 (Paper 3 Part 4)

Before you listen

1a How many different types of literature can you think of?

b Which type of book would you take with you to read on holiday, and why? Is there a particular genre you prefer?

c What features make a book a good book?

Multiple matching

2 🎧 T2.01 Read the strategy on page 171, then do the task.

➤ **EXPERT STRATEGIES** page 171

You will hear five short extracts in which different people are talking about books that made an impression on them.

Task One
For questions **1–5**, choose from the list (**A–H**) what led each speaker to read their book.

Task Two
For questions **6–10**, choose from the list (**A–H**) why each speaker particularly appreciated their book.

You will hear the recording twice. While you listen, you must complete both tasks.

A receiving it as a gift	1
B a family member recommending it	
C getting hold of a copy cheaply	2
D reading a review	3
E seeing the film version	
F doing a course of study	4
G buying it on an impulse	5
H being part of an interest group	

A the novelty of a new medium	6
B the fast-moving storyline	
C the underlying message	7
D the light-hearted look at life	8
E the insight into a particular culture	
F the link between landscape and literature	9
G the perceptive characterisation	10
H the use of language	

Discussion

3 Check your partner's tastes in reading and then choose a book you might recommend for him/her. Talk about the book for one minute, saying what you particularly liked about it.

4 Check the meaning of these key words and phrases from the audioscript.

> **EXPERT WORD CHECK**
>
> unfolding   keep (sb) on tenterhooks   quirky   daunting   blow (sb) away
> intricate   browse   eclectic   eye-opener   human endeavour

Speaking (Paper 4 Parts 1 & 2)

Vocabulary: careers and language use

1a Different careers require different skills in language use. What specific language skills do you think would be required in the jobs in the photos?

A politician requires skills of persuasion, explanation, emphasising.

b Here are some requirements of the jobs in Exercise 1a, plus some of the personal challenges. Work in pairs. Choose a job and categorise the points below for that job. Compare your findings.

24/7 availability
can involve being in dangerous circumstances
can suffer from writer's block
creative imagination
dependent on public opinion
good command of the language
has to come up with new and inventive slogans
huge responsibility
involves a lot of travel and time spent away from home
needs to convince the public
potential for high income from sales
requires good oratorical skills
should be able to deal with emergencies
should be sympathetic and well-organised
should describe ongoing situations with the aid of background knowledge
should have good personal skills
should respond calmly to difficult situations
solitary occupation
uncertain future
works under a lot of pressure

1 politician: _____
2 author: _____
3 advertising agent: _____
4 news correspondent: _____
5 holiday/tour rep: _____

c Can you think of any other jobs where the use of language plays a major role? Do they appeal to you at all? Why/Why not?

Useful language: concluding your turn and moving on

2 Here are some ways of concluding what you say and then inviting the other person to speak. Try to use some of them in the tasks below.

Concluding your turn	Moving on
That's about it, I think.	How about you?
That's my personal opinion.	What do you think?
That's how I see things.	How do you feel about that?
That's basically where I'm at on this.	What's your opinion?

Part 1

> EXPERT STRATEGIES page 171

3 Work in pairs. Discuss the following questions, then report back to the class.

1 What foreign languages can you speak? Why do you think it is important to learn foreign languages in today's world?
2 Do you keep a blog or a diary? Do you think it is a good idea to keep a record of your thoughts and experiences?

Useful language: adding points and expressing contrast

4 Here are some ways of adding information and expressing contrast. Try to use some of them in the tasks below.

Adding information	Expressing contrast
On top of that, ...	But in fact, ...
What's more, ...	In reality, ...
And another thing is that ...	The fact of the matter is ...
Not only that, but ...	But actually, ...
	X, on the other hand, ...
	X, meanwhile, ...
	When it comes to X, however, ...

Part 2 Collaborative task

5a Look at photographs A and B. Talk together about what opinion people have of these jobs in your country. ⊕ You have about one minute to talk about this.

b Look at all the photographs. Imagine that your college is organising a careers conference. These photographs show some of the careers. Talk together about the different qualities and responsibilities required for each job. Then decide which photograph would attract most people to the conference. ⊕ You have about three minutes to talk about this.

> EXPERT STRATEGIES page 171

Task analysis

6 Did you:
• express your opinion clearly and concisely?
• say what you wanted to say within the time limit?

Language de[velopment]

More emphatic str[uctures;]
clauses; noun coll[ocations]

> EXPERT GRAMMAR page[…]

More emphatic str[uctures]

1a Compare the pair[s…]
the emphasis chan[…]
relevant phrases.

1 a I like the fact [… her]
   opinions. ✓
   b What I like about her is that she is honest
   about her opinions.
2 a I've always wanted to travel more than anything.
   ✓ b All I've ever wanted is to travel.
3 a I know quite a lot about most things.
   ✓ b There isn't a lot I don't know.
4 a It was a sign of status to have a library.
   b To have/Having a library was a sign of status.

b Rewrite these sentences more emphatically with
the options below.

| All …/The (only) thing … | What … | The reason why … |
| The person who … | There is/isn't … | To … /-ing |

1 I've come to discuss my project with you.
2 You need to see Mr Evans about that.
3 I can't do a lot about the problem, I'm afraid.
4 It would be a pity to give up the course now.
5 I just want to pass my exams.
6 I like the fact that you always try hard!

Handwritten note (top, circled 3a):
- The language of love ✓
- The ~~train~~ point of no return ✓
- The centre of attention ✓
- The price of success ✓
- The crack of dawn ✓
- The balance ~~of year~~ (the) power ✗
- The choice of career ✓
- The matter of principle ✓
- The sign of power
- The ~~life~~ cause of action ✗
- The train of thought ✓
- The time of leisure ✗
- The ~~course~~ of trouble sign ✗

[Participle?] relative clauses

… what (= the thing that) we've been doing with

[th]e way in which) you stack the books …

[… pla]ces where (= the places where) they go on

… when (= the time when) they did their formative

[… n]inal relative clauses, the relative pronoun
[… combin]e a noun + a relative pronoun together.
[… Compl]ete the sentences in any logical way, with the
[… pronouns below. Compare your answers.

| how | what | whatever | when | where |
| wherever | who | why |

1 I completely understand why you told me that
2 You take your thoughts with you whatever are you
3 I really don't know who are you talking about
4 I'll do what you ask me to do
5 Can you remember how did we get here?
6 Does he know when (are) we are moving?
7 I can't remember where I put my keys.

Noun collocations + of

3a Choose a noun from each list and make a
collocation using *of*.

(the) cost of living

| balance | centre | choice | ~~cost~~ | course | crack |
| language | life | matter | point | price | sign | time |
| train |

action	dawn	success	no return	leisure	~~living~~
attention	thought	trouble	power	principle
year	career	love

b Complete the sentences with an appropriate
collocation from Exercise 3a. Then write your
own sentences to illustrate the remaining
collocations.

✗1 I'm afraid that phone call made me completely
lose my train of thought centre of attention .
✓2 Unfortunately, the failure of Serena's relationship
was the point of no return for her.
✓3 At the crack of dawn , they broke camp
and set off for the distant mountains.
✓4 I refuse to throw books away in the rubbish as a
matter of principle .
✓5 French is the language of love , they say.
✓6 According to the news reports, there was no
sign of trouble after the football match.

Stratford-Upon-Avon is where Shakespeare was born.

✓1) The reason why I've come is to discuss my
project with you
✓2) The person who you need to see is Mr. Evans (about that)
✓3) There isn't a lot that I can do about the problem, I'm afraid.
✓4) Giving up the course now it would be a pity.
✓5) The only thing I want is to pass my exams.
✓6) What I like about you is the fact that you always try hard. (to do)

Use of English 2 (Paper 1 Part 1)

Lead-in

1a What qualities do you think you would need in order to write books for children? Discuss your ideas and rank them in order of importance. Use the ideas below as a starting-point.

- a plot that has a 'magical' element to it ④
- ability to use humour effectively ③
- creative use of illustrative material ⑤
- imaginative choice of vocabulary ①
- lovable and appealing characters ②

b What makes a great writer? In pairs, decide on at least three qualities. Are any of them the same as you found for Exercise 1a?
Having a nown style of writing. Picturing the escene with words.

Multiple-choice cloze

➤ **EXPERT STRATEGIES** page 167

2 Read the strategy on page 167, then complete the task.

For questions 1–8, read the text below and decide which answer (A, B, C or D) best fits each gap. There is an example at the beginning (0).

The JOY of words

Cressida Cowell is the author of the **(0)** _A_ -praised *How To Train Your Dragon* series of children's books. She spent her own childhood holidays on a remote island, where she was left very much to her own **(1)** _D_. As a result, she became an avid reader, entertaining herself with books and developing a fervent imagination. She even **(2)** _B_ up her own secret languages.

Cowell believes that today's children still have a real ear for language, even though their attention **(3)** _C_ may not be as great as in her day, **(4)** _C_ them less tolerant of long descriptive passages in stories. Her books are outlandish and exciting, with vivid imagery, cliffhangers and eye-catching illustrations. Dragons seem to **(5)** _A_ to children of all nationalities, who also seem to **(6)** _C_ with her protagonist, Hiccup, quite easily. Hiccup's a boy who battles his way through life's problems, often against the **(7)** _A_ .

Cowell is currently planning an illustrated book for teenagers. In her own words, she enjoys breaking the **(8)** _B_ and finds that kids are open-minded enough to accept this.

0	**A** widely	**B** deeply	**C** greatly	**D** entirely
1	**A** entertainments	**B** pastimes	**C** hobbies	**D** devices ✓
2	**A** created	**B** dreamt ✓	**C** imagined	**D** invented
3	**A** period	**B** time	**C** span ✓	**D** length
4	**A** meaning	**B** resulting	**C** making ✓	**D** causing
5	**A** appeal ✓	**B** engage	**C** entice	**D** attract
x 6	**A** respond	**B** warm	**C** relate (to)	**D** identify
7	**A** odds ✓	**B** hardships	**C** downsides	**D** worries
8	**A** barrier	**B** mould ✓	**C** boundary	**D** limit

7/8

Discussion

3a Which books do you remember from your childhood? What made them special for you?

b Do you have a favourite author now? Do you prefer to read all the works by a particular author or read a variety of authors? Discuss and compare ideas.

Writing 2 (Paper 2 Part 2: Review)

Lead-in 1 Discuss the following questions.

1 If you could request a book as a present, regardless of price, which would it be? Why?
2 What do you think of giving books as presents? Is there anything else that you would prefer to give and/or receive?

Understand the task 2 Read the task below and think about your answers to the questions.

1 What type of writing will you include in your review?
2 What topics will you need to cover in your review?
3 What title will you give?
4 How will you organise the review?
5 What particular vocabulary should you use?

An online book club which makes reading recommendations has requested reviews of books that readers have liked and given as presents. You have decided to write about a book you recently bought as a birthday present for a member of your family. In your review, explain why you bought that particular book, what was special about it and why it was a suitable choice for that person.

Plan your review

3 Before you start writing, you need to organise your ideas. Use the points below to help you do this.

1 Identify the main points you need to cover in the task:
  • what book did you buy?
  • what was special about it?
  • why was it a suitable gift?
2 Brainstorm your ideas around those points:
  • type of book/special features:
    hardback or paperback?
    fiction or non-fiction?
    a 'coffee table book'? (i.e. one with lots of glossy illustrations in it which is meant more for display)
    a first edition/collector's item/rare book?
  • reason for buying:
    recommended by someone else?
    happened to find it while browsing in a bookshop or surfing the Net
    you had already read it
  • suitability:
    you knew the other person would be interested in it (hobby, favourite TV personality, favourite author, etc.)
3 Decide on the main vocabulary items you wish to use in your review. Look back at the sub-topics in Writing 1 (page 78).
4 Write your plan.

Language and content

4 Complete the phrases with the word(s) below.

complex   detail   down to   pleasantly   realism   set   strongest
up to   vivid   worth

Useful phrases for describing
it had some very (1) _____ descriptions of …
it went into great (2) _____ when describing …
it is (3) _____ in/based on …
a mixture of (4) _____ and fantasy
emotionally (5) _____ characters
fantastic illustrations/photography
packed with …
convincing, well-rounded, likeable characters

Useful phrases for evaluating
it was really (6) _____ reading / buying
its weakest/(7) _____ point was
it was lacking in …
I found it unputdownable!
it totally lived (8) _____ my expectations
I was captivated by …
very readable
I was (9) _____ surprised by …
there were some interesting insights into …
it would suit me (10) _____ the ground

Write your review

➤ EXPERT STRATEGIES page 169

5 Now write your review, using the ideas and the language from this section and from Writing 1, page 78. Write your answer in **280–320 words**.

Check your review

➤ EXPERT WRITING page 191

6 Edit your review, using the checklist on page 191.

Review

1 Complete the sentences with the missing word, *brains, face, head, mind* or *wits*.

1 It's difficult to control this electric drill – it seems to have a _mind_ of its own!

2 And who was the _head_ behind this clever little scheme then? *brains*

3 I tried to convince my sister that she was wrong but it was like banging my _head_ against a brick wall.

4 Peer approval is very important for young people and they don't want to lose _wits_ by being criticised in front of others. *face*

5 If you put your _face_ *mind* to something and really want to succeed, then you'll often find that obstacles tend to melt away.

6 So many people let success go to their _brains_ *head* and then they think they are the bee's knees!

7 If anything goes wrong on the journey, keep your _wits_ *mind* about you and don't panic!

8 As I turned the corner, I came _wits_ to _face_ with my worst enemy. *face*

2 Complete the text with a suitable relative pronoun.

Learning a foreign language isn't easy, **(1)** _some_ *whatever* people might say. For example, let's say you've been learning a language and you eventually get to visit the country **(2)** _where_ ✓ people speak that language. **(3)** _How_ well do you understand the people once you've stepped off the plane? **(4)** _When_ *Meanwhile* you're on the bus from the airport to your hotel or place of residence, you may try to surreptitiously listen in on the conversations of people **(5)** _who_ ✓ are sitting around you – not to really listen, if you know **(6)** _what_ ✓ I mean, but simply to see if you can get the hang of **(7)** _what_ ✓ they're talking about. And the sad conclusion is usually in the negative. You may, if you're lucky, catch a few words here and there but **(8)** _nothing/either_ *(what)* you hear seems to be an unending string of noises all joined together with very little break in the middle! And **(9)** _white_ *wherever* you go, much the same thing happens! **(10)** _why_ , oh **(11)** _why_ should this be the case after so many years of study, you might ask? All I can say is – don't give up! Give your ear time to adjust and you'll soon find things settle down. After a couple of days, you might at least manage to formulate a few intelligible sentences and you will be cheered by your hosts telling you **(12)** _how_ ✓ wonderfully you speak the language!

6/12

3 Choose the correct word to complete the sentences.

1 Writing the dissertation for my degree will _____ a lot of hard work.
A include B entail C contain D enclose

2 I'm afraid there's a _____ between the figures in the book and the amount in the till.
A divergence B disagreement
C differentiation D discrepancy

3 In her autobiography, the author described her wartime childhood when food was very _____ .
A rare B infrequent C scarce D occasional

4 I trust her advice – she'll be able to _____ what the best way forward should be.
A discriminate B separate C distinguish
D discern

5 Louise _____ my offer of help so it's up to her now to produce the goods.
A rejected B refrained C excluded
D prohibited

6 I really love the _____ city of Bath with its Roman baths and lovely buildings.
A antique B historical C historic D ruined

7 I think the number of _____ working for the security firm has increased recently.
A personal B personnel C workforce
D staffing

8 You're being very _____ this evening – have you got a deadline to meet for tomorrow?
A tireless B industrious C persevering
D industrial

5/8

4 Circle the correct word to complete the sentences.

1 Collecting books can be an expensive *pursuit* / *recreation*.

2 A *retrospective* / *rhetorical* question is one to which you don't expect an answer.

3 Really, his rudeness was quite *disbelieving* / *unbelievable*.

4 Do you fancy a nice juicy *stake* / *steak* for dinner tonight?

5 The stunning *location* / *ambiance* for that film was in the west of Ireland.

6 Have you decided on a possible course of *activity* / *action*?

7 The book I've just read gave some fascinating *inserts* / *insights* into the Native American way of life.

8 I presume you all have a pretty good *command* / *expertise* of the language by now.

9 There was a high level of *fictional* / *factual* accuracy in the film, which was quite surprising.

10 To gather information for her biography, the author visited all the *sights* / *sites* in Paris where the artist had lived.

6/10

6 Travel

6A
- ➤ **Reading and Use of English:** Multiple matching (Part 7); Open cloze (Part 2)
- ➤ **Listening:** Sentence completion (Part 2)
- ➤ **Language development:** Present subjunctive; Past subjunctive and unreal past
- ➤ **Writing:** Discursive essay (Part 1); Evaluating input material

6B
- ➤ **Listening:** Multiple choice (Part 3)
- ➤ **Speaking:** Individual long turn (Part 3): Travel choices
- ➤ **Reading and Use of English:** Key word transformations (Part 4); Word formation (Part 3)
- ➤ **Language development:** Emphatic phrases with *however, whatever, no matter what/how*
- ➤ **Writing:** Discursive essay (Part 1); Summarising and evaluating

Lead-in

1a Some of the adjectives in column A form collocations with words in column B. Match them to form descriptive phrases. Some words in A may go with more than one option in B.

A	B
1 mountainous	a climate
2 dense	b with life
3 humid	c vegetation
4 quaint	d terrain
5 barren	e landscape
6 bustling	f village
7 pristine	g undergrowth
8 lush	h wilderness

b Compare and contrast the photographs, using some of the collocations in Exercise 1a.

2 Discuss the following question.

What can affect people's appreciation of such places when they visit them?
- atmosphere
- facilities
- self-fulfilment

6A Sense of adventure

Reading 1 (Paper 1 Part 7)

Before you read

1 Do you own any of these? Do you take them everywhere? Which of them would you take on holiday?

- mobile phone/smartphone
- MP3 player
- e-reader
- global positioning system
- laptop/iPad

Skimming

2a Look at the title of the text on page 89. Quickly read through the text. Which writer's opinion most closely matches your own?

b Do all the writers think the travel experience has been destroyed by technology?

Multiple matching

> EXPERT STRATEGIES page 168

3 Read through the questions in Exercise 4, then underline the key words in each.

4 Read the strategy on page 168, then do the task.

You are going to read a text about technology and travel. For questions 1–10, choose the best answer from sections A–E. Some of the choices may be required more than once.

Which writer …

suggests that places retain their essential identity despite the passage of time?	1	B ✓
refers to a tendency for each generation of travellers to look down on the next?	2	E̶ E
expresses a personal feeling of nostalgia for some of the hardships in the past?	3	A ✓
feels that travel can still be spontaneous and unpredictable in the age of the internet?	4	D ✓
explains how even seemingly pointless journeys can have a worthwhile outcome?	5	C ✓
questions the use of a term in relation to one type of traveller?	6	C ✓
reveals a slight sense of guilt in an attitude towards the modern traveller?	7	A ✓
offers a word of caution for those who want to get the most out of a trip?	8	E ✓
mentions valuable insights gained from observing other travellers?	9	D̶ B
insists that modern travellers can do without modern technology if they so desire?	10	D ✓

(8/10)

Task analysis

5 Compare your answers. How successful were you at recognising the key words in each question?

6 Check the meaning of these key words and phrases from the text.

> **EXPERT WORD CHECK**
>
> relish   grimy   privileged officialdom   fraught   allure   hub
> tides of history   (that) old chestnut   a far cry   vagabonding

Discussion

7 Discuss these statements.

1 'He travels fastest who travels alone.' (proverb)
2 'Good company in a journey makes the way seem shorter.' (Izaak Walton)

Has technology robbed travel of its riches?

We asked five experts.

A Jan Morris

I began travelling professionally just after the Second World War, and I travelled mostly in Europe, where famous old cities lay ravaged. Travelling in this disordered region was not easy. Currencies were hard to come by, visas were necessary almost everywhere, food was often scarce, trains were grimy and unreliable and air travel was reserved largely for privileged officialdom. I'm sorry to have to say it, because those times were cruel indeed for many Europeans, but I greatly enjoyed my travelling then. The comfort and safety of modern transport means that while travel is a lot less fraught than it used to be, it has lost some of its allure for me. Partly, I am almost ashamed to admit, this is because everybody else does it too! Travelling abroad is nothing unusual, and even if we haven't actually been to the forests of Borneo or the Amazon jungle, most of us have experienced them via television or the internet.

B Pico Iyer

The world is just as interesting – as unexpected, as unvisited, as diverse – as it ever was, even though the nature of its sights and our experience of them have sometimes changed. I once spent two weeks living in and around Los Angeles airport – that hub of modern travel – and, although it wasn't a peaceful holiday, it offered as curious and rich a glimpse into a new era of crossing cultures as I could imagine. Places are like people for me and, as with people, the wise, rich, deeply rooted places never seem to change too much, even though they might lose some hair or develop wrinkles… Though the tides of history keep washing against a Havana or a Beirut, for instance, their natural spiritedness or resilience or sense of style never seems greatly diminished. My motto as a traveller has always been that old chestnut from the writings of Marcel Proust: 'The real voyage of discovery consists not in seeking new sights, but in seeing with new eyes'.

C Benedict Allen

Now, the world is open to us all. Grab your camera or smartphone and hike! So these couldn't be better times for the average person – we may all share in the privilege. Is it exploration? Well, if it's not advancing knowledge, no. Those who today flog to the Poles are not explorers, they are simply athletes. Yet, exploration isn't entirely about assembling proven fact. Dr David Livingstone made many discoveries in Africa but his biggest role was actually as communicator, giving nineteenth-century Europeans a picture of the continent. Take Ed Stafford's recent walk along the length of the Amazon. Not a greatly significant journey in itself, with two-thousand miles of it along what is essentially a shipping lane. Yet the journey was saved from irrelevance and self-indulgence because along the way he documented the Amazon for his time, which is our time.

D Vicky Baker

Personally, I relish the fact that we can forge new contacts all around the world at the click of a button and a quick email can result in the type of welcome usually reserved for a long lost friend. I also relish the fact that we're less likely to lose touch with those whose paths we cross on the road and that we get to explore places we wouldn't have stumbled across had we left it all to chance. Does all this detract from the experience? I hardly think so. There's nothing to stop you following a random tip you saw on an obscure blog and ending up who knows where. Sure, it's a far cry from what came before, but one day these will be the current generation's 'good old days'. And if you have the time and the money to go off into the back of beyond without so much as a guidebook let alone a smartphone, if haphazard wandering is your thing, those days aren't over either.

E Rolf Potts

Many of the older travellers I met when I first started vagabonding fifteen years ago – some of them veterans of the 1970s hippy trail across Asia – argued that my travel experiences were tainted by luxuries such as email and credit cards. These days I am myself tempted to look at younger travellers and suggest that smartphones and micro-blogging are compromising their road experiences. Any technology that makes travel easier is going to connect aspects of the travel experience to the comforts and habits one might seek back home – and can make travel feel less like travel. There are times when a far-flung post office encounter or directions scribbled onto a scrap of paper can lead a person into the kind of experiences that make travel so surprising and worthwhile. That means 21st-century travellers must be aware of when their gadgets are enhancing new experiences, and when those gadgets are getting in the way.

(handwritten: outward journey → el día que viajas) chartered ⊘ private flight → flight
(handwritten: flight domestic)

Vocabulary *↳ SAME COUNTRY*

Describing places

1 Circle the correct word.

1 Parts of the town were *ravaged / diminished* by the earthquake, and will take time to recover.

2 Berit loves travelling to all the obscure, *diverse / far-flung* corners of the Earth.

3 The slums were *grimy / pristine* and run-down, with litter strewn all over the streets.

4 The rickshaw ride through the centre of Calcutta was rather *fraught / mundane*, and Jane was terrified for most of it.

5 Some veteran travellers believe that the individual character of many old cities has become *glorified / tainted* by modern tourism.

6 Wandering along the *haphazard / bewildered* network of back streets, we were delighted to stumble upon a quaint little tavern where they served the most delicious food I'd ever tasted.

The travel experience

2 Complete the text below with a suitable noun.

nostalgia   spontaneity   cynicism   vagabond
resilience   motto

Musings of a veteran traveller

I was something of a **(1)** vagabond in my youth, and never liked staying in one place for too long. Stifled by the routine of a nine-to-five job, I longed for the **(2)** spontaneity of travelling to distant parts without an itinerary. My **(3)** motto had always been *Carpe Diem*, or 'Seize the day', and I felt I was missing out on life experiences. So, I packed in my job and bought a ticket on the magic bus to see the world.

In retrospect, I was hopelessly romantic and naive but the experiences I had during my travels, though not always pleasant, taught me a lot. I acquired a certain **(4)** resilience, discovering that, more often than not, out of adversity you gain something positive. Now married with kids and living the routine I vowed I would never conform to, I am occasionally filled with **(5)** nostalgia for those times, but am able to say that, thanks to the freedom I had then, I generally feel content and have managed to avoid the **(6)** cynicism that besets so many in middle age. So, I have no regrets!

Travel and transport collocations

3 Circle the words that do NOT collocate with the following. There may be more than one.

1 travel — documents / sickness / *trap* / *agency* / brochure / arrangements

2 flight — chartered / *round* / scheduled / *domestic* / agency / connecting / details

3 trip — *day* / business / boat / *camping* / *documents* / school / *round*

4 tourist — board / *home* / *operator* / information / trap / attraction

5 holiday — resort / *operator* / camp / package / home / season / *tour* / destination

6 journey — tiring / *business* / train / outward / return / *wasted* / *information* / safe / endless

(handwritten: seher = 4 ⑩   soro = 6)

Expressions with *sight*

4 Replace the words in *italics* in the following sentences with the correct form of the phrases below. Make any other changes necessary.

see the sights   be a sight to behold   look a sorry sight
set your sights on   lose sight of   out of sight

1 Tears streaming down her face, Laura kept waving until the train was *no longer visible*. *out of sight*

2 The morning after the raucous wedding party, the hotel conference room *was very untidy*. *looked a sorry sight*

3 Jez and Kalli decided to spend the next day *visiting tourist attractions*. *Seeing the sights*

4 Joanna has *decided she will definitely sail* across the Atlantic single-handed next year. *set her sights on sailing*

5 Set against the backdrop of the Pyrenees, the magnificent hotel *looked fantastic*. *was a sight to behold*

6 Tourist operators often *forget* the fact that local communities depend on them for their livelihood. *lose sight of*

Collocations: describing remote places

5 Complete the phrases with the words below.

beyond   Earth   nowhere   out-of-the-way   track
backwater   far-flung   sticks

1 Jelena loves travelling to the far-flung corners of the Earth, and this year she's decided to visit an aboriginal settlement in the Australian outback.

2 So, there we were, in the middle of nowhere, with nothing around us but miles and miles of mountainous terrain.

3 Fed up with package holidays, we decided to go off the beaten track for a change and went kayaking in Slovenia.

4 Quite frankly, I think Tony's mad, going off to the ends of the Earth, when he's got such a good job here!

✓ 5 Gabriella has moved out of the city. She now lives in a village in the countryside, right out in the __sticks__ .

✗ 6 Hans and Rita live in a rural ~~out of the~~ backwater ~~way~~ that is unaffected by modern social life. out-of-the-way

✗ 7 The hotel was in a remote, ~~beyond~~ _____ spot in the mountains of Andorra la Vella. out-of-the-way

✗ 8 Francesco went off to the back of ~~backwater~~ _____, beyond hiking for a fortnight.

Phrasal verbs with *set*

6a Match the phrasal verbs in the sentences 1–7 with the correct definition a–g.

✓ D 1 Ginny *set out* to arrange transport for everyone to the airport.

✓ E 2 OK, we're in Delhi and we've lost our luggage. So, how do we *set about* finding some clothes and a toothbrush?

✓ A 3 Right, the itinerary says we're going down the Nile on Tuesday, and to see the Pyramids on Wednesday and Thursday. Can some time be *set aside* for shopping in Cairo on Friday?

✓ B 4 What *sets* the islands *apart* from other places is the friendliness of the locals.

✓ F 5 Simon started going on backpacking holidays when he was at university, and has now *set up* a blog offering young people advice on how to get around Europe and Asia.

✓ G 6 While in India, Carl caught malaria, which *set him back* 10 days on his tour.

✓ C 7 Trudi wanted to reach the summit by lunchtime, so she *set off* at 6 a.m.

a to reserve something – time, money, etc. – for a specific purpose

b to make someone or something distinctive, different from others

c to start a journey

d to make plans or intend to do something

e to start dealing with or trying to do something that requires a lot of effort

f to create something, or start a new business or organisation

g to delay the progress or development of something

b Form your own sentences using the phrasal verbs from Exercise 6a.

Verbs of movement

7 Work in pairs. Discuss situations in which the following verbs might be used.

stride   march   negotiate   cross   draw near
wander   stroll   jog   race   pursue

8 Write an account of an outing to a place of interest. Use the verbs from Exercise 7 and other vocabulary items from this section.

Use of English 1 (Paper 1 Part 2)

Open cloze

For questions 1–8, read the text below and think of the word which best fits each gap. Use only ONE word in each gap. There is an example at the beginning (0).

Open-water swimming

Do you feel **(0)** __like__ doing something different this summer? Recently set **(1)** __up__ ✓ by one of the world's great exponents of the sport, Strel Swimming Adventures offers open-water swimming trips in the beautiful lakes region of Slovenia. Other companies offer similar trips but what sets this one **(2)** __apart__ ✓ is the fact that Strel himself is **(3)** __kind__ x something of a celebrity. Renowned **(4)** ~~for as~~ x a long-distance swimmer, he is passionate about preserving the world's lakes and rivers. In **(5)** __order__ ✓ to draw attention to this issue, he swam the length of the River Danube in the year 2000. **(6)** ~~Such so~~ x successful was this trip that he went on to swim other rivers: the Mississippi, the Yangtze and, in his most famous swim to **(7)** ~~achieve~~ date, the Amazon. These days, Strel's main aim is to introduce others to the joys of open-water swimming. If you sign up **(8)** __for__ ✓ one of Strels's courses, you'll find that wetsuits, swimming caps and goggles are all provided. All you need is your swimming costume! 4/8

Listening 1 (Paper 3 Part 2)

Before you listen   **1**   Describe the impression you get of the place shown in the photograph. Use these words to help you.

> desolate   pristine   pure   untouched   wild   isolated   challenging
> mysterious   mountainous   awesome

2   Would you like to go there? Why/Why not? What do you think motivates people to travel to these places?

Sentence completion   **3**   🎧 T2.02 Listen and complete the task below.

You will hear a conservationist called Jane Birch, talking about a recent visit she made to Greenland. For questions 1–9, complete the sentences with a word or short phrase.

Greenland

Jane says that the name of the island was originally chosen as a way of attracting [**1**] to go there.

Jane says that the glacier she went to study is regarded as the most [**2**] in the world.

Jane uses the term [**3**] to underline the importance of the glacier to climatologists and others.

Jane explains how the melting of what's called [**4**] contributes to the greenhouse gases in the atmosphere.

Jane found travelling by [**5**] the most memorable ride during her trip.

By studying what are called the [**6**] on a iceberg, it is possible to predict how likely it is to break up.

Jane learnt that people go close to icebergs in search of [**7**] .

Jane uses the word [**8**] to describe local peoples' reaction to changes in their lifestyle.

Jane gives the image of objects on a [**9**] as symbolising the realities of life in polar regions today.

Task analysis   **4**   Consider the task strategy notes you have been given so far for this task type. See page 170. Decide which strategies help you to complete this task successfully.

Discussion   **5**   The Sermeq Kujalleq glacier was declared a World Heritage site in 2004. This means that while it is to be protected, it will also attract more tourists. Hold a class debate on the following.

'Attracting more tourists to Greenland will greatly improve the island's revenue, and consequently the local way of life.'

Language development 1

Present subjunctive

➤ **EXPERT GRAMMAR** page 181

1a Who might be speaking, and to whom, in the following sentences?

1 '*Far be it from me to tell you what to do*, but I think you'd be mad to give up your job and go travelling.'
2 'I'm going backpacking in India, *no matter what you say!*'
3 'This train's so old and slow!' '*Be that as it may*, it's the only one that will take us across the border.'
4 'If you want to take a year off and go travelling before going to university, *so be it*.'
5 'Why's Jane leaving so suddenly?' '*Suffice it to say*, Mrs Jones, it's not entirely out of choice.'

b Which of the above phrases in *italics* could be replaced by the following?

1 nevertheless
2 go ahead
3 I don't mean to preach
4 put it this way
5 whatever

2 Complete the sentences in your own words.

1 No matter what _____ .
2 This exercise is quite a challenge! Be that as it may, _____ .
3 If we have to _____ .
4 Far be it from me _____ .
5 'Is it difficult to get to Greenland?' 'Suffice it to say _____ .'

3 Complete the second sentence so that it is a more formal version of the first, using the present subjunctive.

1 'The customs official wants you to open your suitcase,' explained the guide.
'The customs official insists that your _____ ,' explained the guide.
2 If you happen to see Joanna in Cairo, say hi from me.
If you _____ my regards.
3 Why don't you go to the market in Istanbul for souvenirs?
I suggest you _____ find souvenirs.
4 I strongly recommend Machu Picchu early in the morning, as it looks more impressive then.
If I _____ early in the morning, as it looks more impressive then.
5 Why don't we cross the desert by camel?
I propose _____ camel.
6 David must follow the guide's instructions while in the jungle.
It is of the utmost importance _____ while in the jungle.

7 Passengers' passports must be ready for inspection.
It is essential _____ to be checked.
8 If they offer her the job, she'll have to move to Madrid.
Should she _____ move to Madrid.

Past subjunctive and unreal past

4 Circle the correct word(s) in *italics* to complete the following sentences.

1 Gerard talks as if he *has / had* never been abroad before but he went to Thailand last May.
2 It's time we*'re packing / packed* our bags and *leaving / left* the hotel.
3 I'd rather you *didn't / won't* speak to the hotel manager.
4 Suppose they *were to / would* follow your advice, and go to Jordan. What would they do next?
5 I see. So, you'd sooner I *wouldn't be / weren't* with you when you speak to the tour rep?
6 *Were / Had* Jane agreed to the plan, she'd have been on her way to Singapore by now.
7 Had you told us you were vegetarian, sir, we would *make / have made* every effort to accommodate you.

5 Complete the email below with a suitable word.

Dear Mr Schwarz,

Thank you for your email. Before you proceed with any legal action, it is essential that you **(1)** _____ certain facts into account with regard to yacht chartering.

It is a standard requirement that at least one member of the crew should **(2)** _____ a recognised yacht master's licence. **(3)** _____ you been able to produce such a document, it would not have been necessary for the boat owner to hire a skipper. Your frustration at not being told that this would involve you paying an extra fee is understandable. Be that as it **(4)** _____ , this information is clearly stated in the Charter Party contract, which you had already signed. In legal terms, therefore, **(5)** _____ it to say, it was your responsibility to read this before signing.

Since the contract is legally binding, **(6)** _____ you to take matters further, I fear the outcome would be unfavourable. For this reason, I strongly recommend that you **(7)** _____ your decision. **(8)** _____ you wish to contact me, I would be happy to discuss an alternative solution.

Yours sincerely,

Helena Vickers

Writing 1 (Paper 2 Part 1: Essay)

Evaluating input material

1 Discuss the following questions.

1 How do you get to work or school? What alternatives are there for you?
2 For people who commute to work, which is the best form of transport for:
   a short distances?   **b** long distances?
   Give reasons for your views.

2 Read the following task and texts, then answer the questions.

1 What is the main point of each text?
2 How far do you agree or disagree with the points they make?

Write an essay summarising and evaluating the key points from both texts. Use your own words throughout as far as possible, and include your own ideas in your answer.
You should write **240–280** words.

1 Commuting by train Increasingly, people are moving to the countryside and commuting to work every day. If you are one of them, there are numerous reasons to choose the train as your mode of transport. Firstly, you avoid the chore of a long drive, coupled with the frustration of sitting in rush hour traffic once you hit the city. Also, the comfort of modern rail facilities means you have space to work if you are on your way to a meeting. Then at the end of the day, you can simply sit back and relax on your way home.	**2 Long-distance commuting: plane, car or train?** Although flying long distances generates more carbon dioxide emissions than going by car, the high price of petrol means that driving from Aberdeen to London, for example, may actually prove more expensive. However, studies suggest that the train produces about half the carbon dioxide emissions of the car. So, despite the recent rise in rail tickets, commuting by train would seem to be the best option in both an environmental and economical sense.

> EXPERT STRATEGIES page 169

3a Discuss the following counter-arguments to travelling by train.

• Trains are subject to delay, particularly in bad weather.
• Rail services are occasionally poorly maintained or insufficient in some areas.
• Rail travel is often expensive.

b List some possible counter-arguments to the points below.

• Travel by car is more convenient.   • _____
• _____   • _____

4 Complete the paragraph with the words and phrases below.

certain   similarly   in fact   while   another point worth   resulting in
with respect to   one of these

(1) _____ the first text makes some strong arguments in favour of travelling by train, there are (2) _____ aspects of rail travel it ignores. (3) _____ is the fact that rail tickets are often expensive. (4) _____ considering is the tendency of rail services to be poorly maintained in some areas, (5) _____ trains being subject to delays. (6) _____ , the second text's argument also has limitations. It makes a convincing case for rail travel as opposed to travelling by car or plane, but this argument is only valid (7) _____ the individual traveller. (8) _____ if four people travel together in the same car, the car not only has a lower negative impact on the environment, but is also cheaper and more convenient than the plane or train.

5 Write an essay in answer to the questions in Exercise 1. Use the work you have done in Exercises 2, 3 and 4 to help you.

Listening 2 (Paper 3 Part 3)

Before you listen

1 Which of the following criteria do you consider when choosing a holiday?
- nightlife
- access to shops
- beach
- convenience of travel

2 What effect do you think these things have on the local community?

Multiple choice

3 🎧 T2.03 Listen and complete the task below.

You will hear a travel journalist called Lucy Marske and a conservationist called Brian Eckers discussing the issue of ethical travel. For questions 1–5, choose the answer (A, B, C or D) which fits best according to what you hear.

1 Lucy and Brian agree that the term 'ethical travel' is most appropriate when

A the profits of tourism are re-invested in the local economy.

B the travel companies source products from within the local area.

C the interests of local people are consistently given a high priority.

D the natural environment of travel destinations remains unaffected.

2 What do Lucy and Brian suggest about the 'green' labels used by tour companies?

A Most of these do not stand up to close examination.

B Travellers should seek proof of claims before booking.

C Rules regarding their misuse are not enforced effectively.

D The regulations governing these need to be more clearly defined.

3 Brian identifies the key aim of the 'slow travel movement' as

A related to the various means of transport used.

B promoting self-catering holidays over other types.

C reducing the distance people cover whilst on holiday.

D addressing people's wider need to relax and enjoy life.

4 Brian explains that on Stradbroke Island, emphasis is placed on preserving

A the lifestyle of a small community.

B a safe environment for visitors.

C the viability of local businesses.

D the integrity of local produce.

5 What reservation does Lucy express regarding Stradbroke Island?

A She's concerned that tourists may find some aspects off-putting.

B She doubts whether all visitors will want so much attention.

C She thinks it might become a victim of its own success.

D She fears that it may attract some negative publicity.

Task analysis

4 Discuss your answers. Why are the other options not suitable?

5 Is Stradbroke Island a place you'd like to visit? Why?

6 Check the meaning of these key words and phrases from the audioscript.

> **EXPERT WORD CHECK**
>
> sustainable travel   underlie   notion   intrinsic   watchdog
> slip through the net   credentials   unwind

Discussion

7 Discuss the following statement. To what extent do you agree or disagree with it?

'We need to restrict the number of tourists visiting such places as Machu Picchu in Peru, and Petra in Jordan, as the volume of visitors is eroding the site.'

Speaking (Paper 4 Part 3)

Vocabulary: travel choices

1a Place the words and phrases in the most suitable category below, according to the context in which we normally use them.

all-inclusive package deal   travel blog   travel agent   holiday brochure
babysitting facilities   sporting activities   newspaper travel section
friends' experiences   proximity to airport   coach tour   weekend break
surfing the Net   backpacking   access to beach/shops

1 Source of information: _____
2 Criteria for choosing: _____
3 Types of travel: _____

b Brainstorm other items to add to each list. Look back through this module to help you.

2a The sentences below can be expressed in different ways. Replace the words in *italics* with one of the words below, and make any other changes necessary. Some sentences have more than one possibility. Discuss the differences in the use of each word.

impact   result   consequences   spin-off   effects   repercussions
outcome   upshot   implications

1 Building an all-inclusive holiday village outside the town may have far-reaching *effects on* the local economy.
2 None of the class could agree on where to go. The *outcome* of this was that they decided not to have a class trip together at all.
3 The *consequences* of increased travel on the Antarctic have yet to be understood.
4 The town council is meeting today to discuss the possibility of building a theme park but it is not yet known what the *result* will be.
5 The decision of the international tour company to take their business to another location has had serious *repercussions* for the island's economy.
6 Staying in fully-equipped luxury tents, known as 'glamping', is an *upshot* of the idea of organised camping.

b Replace the words in *italics* in the following sentences with the correct form of one of the words below. Some sentences have more than one possibility.

promote   advocate   recommend   urge

1 I generally disagree with those who *support* holidays at all-inclusive resorts, as these are often of little benefit to the local community.
2 Gavin *strongly encouraged* Selena to try out the activity holiday, saying it would appeal to her desire for adventure.
3 The restaurant owner *suggested* they try out the Enalion Hotel, on the basis that it was comfortable and reasonably priced.
4 The tour operator has gone to great lengths to *advertise* holidays in Tenerife this year.
5 Their safari guide *advised* caution when photographing the rhinos.

Model answer

3 🎧 T2.04 Look at the Task card on page 205. Listen to a candidate, Jelena, perform the task and answer the questions.

1 Does she address all the points on the card?
2 Does she add anything of her own?
3 Does she finish within the time limit? Does this matter?

Useful language

4 Complete the sentences to express your own ideas in answer to the sample task in Exercise 3.

1 I think it's a matter of personal taste/choice whether you ….
2 Whichever type of holiday you prefer, the cost may affect …
3 As far as freedom of choice is concerned, many people prefer …
4 I feel that it is essential that young families be provided with ….
5 Personally, I'd sooner go …
6 My own holiday decisions are always based on ….

Individual long turn

> EXPERT STRATEGIES page 172

5 Work in pairs. Student A, read Task card 1 on page 205 and Student B, read card 2 on page 205. The main theme is the subject of travel choices. Follow the instructions and perform the task. ⏱ Time yourselves.

a Student A should respond to the question on Task card 1 for about two minutes. ⏱

b Student B, answer the following question. Use the strategy to help you.

Do you usually seek the advice of others when choosing a holiday, or search for information on your own?

c Student B should respond to the question on Task card 2 for about two minutes. ⏱

d Student A, answer the following question. Use the strategy to help you.

What factors influence your choice of holiday?

Task analysis

6a Did you manage to sustain your answer for two minutes?

b In your response to the follow-up question, did you manage to refer to something your partner had said in his/her individual turn?

Discussion

7 Discuss the factors which affect people's ability to travel. Consider the following:

• visa restrictions   • socio-economic status   • fear of flying

Language development 2

Emphatic phrases with *whether, however, whatever, no matter what/how*

▶ EXPERT GRAMMAR page 182

1 Match the sentence beginnings with their endings.

1 Whether you like it …
2 No matter how …
3 Whatever your reasons for …
4 No matter what …
5 Cold though it …
6 However strange it …

a crowded it may be, Calcutta is an amazing city.
b might be at this time of the year, we're going camping in the Scottish highlands.
c may sound, I actually enjoyed the chaotic bus journey from Delhi to Lahore.
d or not, I'm going backpacking with Jeremy round Europe.
e happens at work, I'm taking a holiday next week.
f going to Cape Town may be, I'm not going to stand in your way.

2 Complete the gaps with one suitable word.

The problem with the camera

People travel for various reasons but, **(1)** whatever their tastes may be, there is one item that is rarely missing from their suitcase: the camera. **(2)** Despite they like photography or not, most people feel that a holiday is not complete without a collection of holiday snaps for posterity. And, boring **(3)** as it may seem to others, many delight in displaying photographs of themselves standing in front of famous sites, like the Taj Mahal or Petra.

Be that as it may, I fail to grasp the point of this photographic mania. **(4)** Whenever impressive such pictures may be, I can't help wondering if those people actually remember the experience of being there. Did they allow themselves the luxury of standing still for a moment and soaking up the atmosphere of the place? Did they notice the exquisite detail in the carvings on the wall? Personally, no **(5)** idea matter where I'm going, I never take a camera. Yet, **(6)** if anybody asks me about a place I have visited, I can recall everything from the sounds and smells to the colours of tiles on the floor. This to me is the essence of the travel experience, and it cannot be captured in a frame.

3 Do you agree with the views expressed in the text in Exercise 2? Use the prompts below to make your own statements about holiday photography.

1 Whether you like taking photographs or not, …
2 Personally, wherever I …
3 However strange it may be, …
4 No matter what …
5 Whenever …
6 However, …

Use of English 2 (Paper 1 Part 4)

Key word transformations

For questions 1–6, complete the second sentence so that it has a similar meaning to the first sentence, using the word given. Do not change the word given. You must use between three and eight words, including the word given. Here is an example (0).

0 Our car is in urgent need of a service.
(had)
It's time _we had our car_ serviced.

1 Would you ever consider staying in an underwater hotel?
(entertain)
Would _you ever_ in an underwater hotel?

2 Whatever happens, you can rely on Simon to turn up.
(be)
No matter _what you_ upon to turn up.

3 I have come to a decision about the expedition.
(mind)
My _mind has_ as far as the expedition is concerned.

4 I'm determined not to miss the start of the lecture.
(intention)
Come _with no_ of missing the start of the lecture.

5 If I hadn't ignored Gayle's advice, I wouldn't be in this mess now.
(paid)
Had I _paid_ , I wouldn't be in this mess now.

6 I know it sounds strange, but I've always wanted to explore the Amazon.
(as)
Strange _as it sounds_ , I've always wanted to explore the Amazon.

Use of English 3 (Paper 1 Part 3)

Before you read

1 Which of the following would you like/not like to eat? Why?

• snake • sheep's head • frog's legs • black pudding • haggis
• tripe • head cheese

2a When you visit somewhere new, how adventurous are you with local food?

b There are several popular TV travel programmes that focus on local cuisine. What do you think attracts viewers to such programmes?

Word formation: a noun, but which noun?

3 Some root words can form more than one noun. The example in the text below has two forms: *enthusiasm* (the emotion) and *enthusiast* (the person). Some words can also form compounds. Use a dictionary to find noun derivatives and compounds of the following words.

1 back 2 set 3 work 4 refer 5 life 6 serve

Word formation

4 Read the strategy on page 167, then do the task.

For questions 1–8, read the text below. Use the word given in CAPITALS at the end of some of the lines to form a word that fits in the gap in the same line. There is an example at the beginning (0).

Autumn food festivals

Autumn is the season of food festivals in Europe, giving food **(0)** _enthusiasts_ the world over the chance to combine travel with their favourite pastime. From the Helsinki Baltic Herring Fair to the Living Food Festival in Scotland, different regions celebrate their local produce. Restaurants demonstrate their culinary **(1)** expertise offering visitors tasting sessions at knock-down prices. Some regions even offer cookery **(2)** workshops where people can learn to make some local recipes under the supervision of well-known chefs.

ENTHUSE

EXPERT EXPERTISE
WORK WORKSHOPS

One particularly popular destination is the *Invito a Pranzo* ('Come for lunch') festival held in Friuli, a wonderfully **(3)** unspoiled mountainous region on the Italian border with Slovenia. Against this magnificent **(4)** background twelve local restaurants serve up delicious dishes ranging from river trout to wild boar and venison. Their gastronomic delights are infused with the **(5)** diversity of wild herbs and berries that grow in the surrounding forests. The **(6)** incomparable flavour of the chestnut and porcini soup is not to be missed, and the otherwise simple homemade pasta is **(7)** enriched with nettles. So, if you wish to allow yourself a little **(8)** indulgence this autumn, you could do worse than head for Italy.

SPOIL UNSPOILED
BACK BACKGROUND

DIVERSE DIVERSITY
COMPARE INCOMPARABLE
RICH ENRICHED
INDULGE INDULGENCE

Discussion

5 Why do people hold food festivals? Discuss in relation to your own country or region.

Writing 2 (Paper 2 Part 1: Essay)

Lead-in

1 Discuss the reasons for and against taking photographs on holiday.

2 Look at the photographs on this page. Where do you think they were taken? Why do people like taking these kind of photographs?

3 Are photographs of scenery always successful? What things should you consider before photographing a scene?

Task analysis

4 Read the exam task and texts below, then answer the following questions.

1 What is the overall theme of the input texts?
2 What view does the writer express in each case?
3 How far do you agree with either view?

Write an essay summarising and evaluating the key points from both texts. Use your own words throughout as far as possible, and include your own ideas in your answer.

You should write **240–280** words.

1 Reflections of a travel photographer

The beauty of a travel photograph is perhaps not the moment you first see it, when the memory of taking it is still fresh in your mind. It is that weird moment years down the line, when you come across it in a long-forgotten box, and looking at it evokes a reminiscent glimpse of past travels. You pause for a moment, indulging yourself as memories of sights, smells and sounds flood your brain. In that moment, the photograph isn't just a picture of a scene. It's the whole experience of a journey taken, a place explored and people encountered.

2 Taking good travel photographs

As you arrive at your destination, try to ignore any preconceived ideas about what you will find, and take note of your first impressions. How do you feel as you round that corner and set eyes on the place? What first catches your eye? The colours? The architecture? Sounds? Movement? Whatever it is, keep hold of it, and use it to choose the focus of your photographs. You may find it useful to venture out on initial sojourns without your camera, in order to soak up the atmosphere of the place and consider potential subjects. Then, let your inspiration guide you.

Plan your essay

5 Read the task again and do the following.

1 Summarise the main points of the two texts, to form your introductory paragraph.
2 Brainstorm ideas for evaluating the texts. Discuss the following statements to help you.

> I think it's really important to spend some time just walking around a place before you start clicking away.

> *First impressions of a place can prove to be misguided, especially if your initial reaction is negative.*

> To my mind, photographs without people in them evoke few memories. It is a face that captures my imagination, and not the scene in the background.

> *Photographs are definitely taken for prosperity, and are ultimately very personal.*

> EXPERT STRATEGIES page 169

6 Write a paragraph plan for your answer, and make notes on the points to include in the main body.

Language and content

7 Look back at the vocabulary presented on page 87 and the Vocabulary section on pages 90–91. Decide which words and phrases you can use in your essay.

Evaluating

8 Complete the following statements in your own words. Then choose three to four to help you develop your evaluation of the texts. Look back at Exercises 3 and 4 in Writing 1 on page 94, for extra ideas.

1 The feelings that travel photography can arouse …
2 This is juxtaposed …
3 While the first text examines … , the second text talks about the importance of …
4 According to the second writer, wherever you may find yourself, …
5 Eager though you may be to …
6 Weighing up the points made in the two texts, …
7 The two texts evoke different feelings …
8 It can be argued that …

9 Decide which of the following phrases you could use in your conclusion.

Generally speaking   All in all   Whatever your views   I firmly believe
Ultimately   To my mind   Overall   To sum up

Write your essay
> EXPERT STRATEGIES page 169

10 Now write your essay, using the ideas and some of the language you have already discussed. Write your answer in **240–280** words.

Check your essay
> EXPERT WRITING page 191

11 Edit your essay, using the checklist on page 191.

Review

1 Complete the phrases in the following sentences.

1 The Pyramids at Giza are a sight to _____ !

2 We discovered that the hotel was in the middle of _____ , miles from the nearest village.

3 When travelling across Russia, make sure you have your _____ documents with you at all times.

4 During your trip to Istanbul, try to set _____ some time to visit the Blue Mosque.

5 I'm not interested in going off the _____ track; give me the comfort of a package holiday any day!

6 Marcus has _____ his sights on studying archaeology next year.

7 Their plane arrived late at Gatwick, and they had to run to catch their _____ flight to Glasgow.

8 Although you've only moved to Toronto, it feels like you've gone to the back of _____ to me!

2 Choose the correct word to complete the sentences.

1 We arrived at a picturesque village, with _____ little cottages and cobbled streets.
   A dense B bustling C humid D quaint

2 The company owns several campsites, and _____ eco-holidays in the area.
   A advocates B promotes C urges
   D recommends

3 What sets the Hotel Blue Sky _____ from other resorts is its friendly atmosphere.
   A out B up C apart D off

4 We looked down from the top of the Eiffel Tower on the _____ city below.
   A diverse B lush C sprawling D pristine

5 Due to the drought, the dried up lake looked like a _____ wasteland.
   A haphazard B barren C rugged D vibrant

6 Emil and Uri gazed at the photographs and _____ about the trip they had been on together.
   A reminisced B recounted C reflected
   D recalled

7 In this idyllic country _____ , you can enjoy various outdoor activities.
   A backdrop B setting C landscape
   D vicinity

8 At this riverside restaurant, you can _____ yourself to the local fare.
   A indulge B treat C fill D stuff

3 Complete the sentences by forming a suitable word from the word in CAPITALS.

1 Hans suffered a major _____ when his computer broke down and he lost his files. SET

2 This boomerang is a fine example of Maori _____ . WORK

3 The architecture is _____ of the Greek Doric style. REMINISCE

4 The _____ of two opposing viewpoints in this essay is rather interesting. JUXTAPOSE

5 The _____ unknown workshop where they make statues destined for Madame Tussaud's wax museum is well worth a visit. COMPARE

6 The Taj Mahal is a famous _____ of India. LAND

7 One of the main problems facing monuments around the world is that of _____ due to pollution. ERODE

8 That trip was one of the most _____ I've ever been on. MEMORY

4 Complete the email with a suitable word or short phrase.

To	Mr Arne
Subject	Hotel complaint

Dear Mr Arne,

In reply to your request for further details of my complaint against your hotel, **(1)** _____ to say, I was disappointed with both the service and the facilities. The description on the website is most misleading, and I suggest that you **(2)** _____ it as soon as possible.

Firstly, I discovered the shower in my room was not working, and requested that it **(3)** _____ fixed. The receptionist assured me that someone would be up immediately, but the plumber only arrived four hours later. **(4)** _____ he apologised, I might have accepted the delay, but he was most abrupt. Then, at dinner, I was informed that none of the fish dishes on the menu were available. Obviously, you can't always guarantee the presence of a particular type of fish. **(5)** _____ it may, I would expect a hotel that 'prides itself in its wide range of seafood' to at least be able to provide some of those dishes on any occasion, **(6)** _____ the season. As if that **(7)** _____ not enough, I then decided to use the gym, only to find the door locked and a sign informing me that it was undergoing renovation.

All things considered, I think it fair to request that I **(8)** _____ given some form of compensation.

Yours sincerely,

A. Haslow

7A
> **Reading and Use of English:** Gapped text (Part 6); Word formation (Part 3)
> **Listening:** Multiple-choice questions (Part 1)
> **Language development:** Relative clauses; Reduced relative clauses; Reduced non-defining descriptive clauses
> **Writing:** Letter (Part 2): Varying your language in descriptive writing

7B
> **Listening:** Multiple matching (Part 4)
> **Speaking:** Collaborative task (Parts 1 & 2): Social life
> **Reading and Use of English:** Multiple-choice cloze (Part 1)
> **Language development:** Clauses of time and reason, result, concession
> **Writing:** Letter (Part 2)

Lead-in

1 Discuss. What aspects of the way people live today do the photographs depict? Use the words and phrases below to help you.

meeting place   mall   stress buster   way to unwind   connections   social contact   keep fit
gossip   change of scenery   organic produce   get out of the house

2 Discuss the questions with regard to your neighbours.
1 How well do you know your neighbours?
2 What makes a good neighbour?
3 Are there any committees to address the needs of local residents where you live?

3 Which of the following do you think are important features in a community?

- cafés/bars
- squares
- parks
- gardens/allotments
- cycle lanes
- shopping centres
- street markets
- facilities for children
- neighbourliness

Reading 1 (Paper 1 Part 6)

Before you read   **1**   Discuss the following question.

How do you learn the latest news and gossip?
- internet chat rooms
- meeting friends for coffee
- TV, radio, newspapers, phone

Skimming   **2**   Read through the main text quickly and make notes on the following.

1 What comparison is made between the internet and coffee houses in the seventeenth and eighteenth centuries?
2 What view do coffee drinkers of the past and today's internet users appear to share with regard to information?

Gapped text   **3**   You are going to read an article about the social history of coffee houses. Seven paragraphs have been removed from the extract. Choose from the paragraphs A–H the one which fits each gap (1–7). There is one extra paragraph which you do not need to use.

> EXPERT STRATEGIES page 168

Task analysis   **4a**   Did you check the finished task to see if the text flows naturally?

    b   Why does the extra paragraph not fit?

    5   Check the meaning of these key words and phrases from the text.

EXPERT WORD CHECK

stay abreast of   flit   (political) fermentation   beverage   oscillate
proclamation   public outcry   ambience   invigorating   rein (sth/sb) in

---

Discussion   **6**   Discuss the following questions.

1 The seventeenth-century coffee house shown in the picture is Edward Lloyd's famous coffee house in London, which eventually became the insurance company, Lloyd's of London. How does it illustrate the point the writer makes about the significance of coffee houses at that time?
2 How important are coffee houses today? How has their role changed, and do you think they are still a necessary part of the community?

The internet in a cup

The internet café is not such a new idea – something similar existed back in the seventeenth century.

Where do you go when you want to know the latest news, keep up with celebrity gossip, find out what others think of a new book, or stay abreast of the latest scientific and technological developments? Today, the answer is obvious: you log on to the internet. Three centuries ago, the answer was just as easy: you went to your favourite coffee house.

1 _____

What's more, rumours, news and gossip were often carried between them by their patrons and runners would flit from one to another to report major events. Each establishment was, therefore, an integral part of quite a complex web of contacts. But of even greater importance was their role as centres of scientific education, literary and philosophical speculation, commercial innovation and, sometimes, political fermentation.

2 _____

This reputation accompanied its spread into Europe during the seventeenth century, at first as a medicine, and then as a social beverage in the eastern tradition. It was reflected in the decor of the dedicated coffee houses that began to appear in European cities, London in particular, where they were often adorned with bookshelves, mirrors, gilt-framed pictures and good furniture.

3 _____

There was a new rationalism abroad in the spheres of both philosophy and commerce, and this ethos struck exactly the right note, whilst coffee was the ideal accompaniment. The popularity of the beverage owed much to the growing middle class of information workers – clerks, merchants and businessmen – who did mental work in offices rather than performing physical labour in the open, and found that it sharpened their mental faculties.

4 _____

As with modern websites, the coffee houses an individual or group frequented reflected their interests, for each coffee house attracted a particular clientele, usually by virtue of its location. Though coffee houses were also popular in Paris, Venice and Amsterdam, this characteristic was particularly notable in London, where eighty-two coffee houses had been set up by 1663, and more than five hundred by 1700. For many, coffee houses had become almost an extension of the home.

5 _____

That said, most people frequented several houses for the purpose of furthering their commercial, social or political interests. A merchant, for example, would generally oscillate between a financial house and one specialising in shipping or trade with a particular region. The wide-ranging interests of Robert Hooke, a scientist and polymath, were reflected in his visits to around sixty houses during the 1670s. Not to visit one at all was to invite social exclusion.

6 _____

This is exactly the kind of threat that worries some people today about the power of social-networking sites. Interestingly, a proclamation of 1675 that sought to outlaw the coffee houses of London was met by a public outcry, for they had become central to commercial as well as political life. When it became clear that the proclamation would be ignored, it was toned down and then quietly dropped.

7 _____

But history also provides a cautionary tale for those operators who would charge for access. Coffee houses used to charge for coffee, but gave away access to reading materials. Many coffee shops are now following the same model, which could undermine the prospects for fee-based hotspots. Information, both in the seventeenth century and today, wants to be free – and coffee-drinking customers, it seems, expect it to be.

A According to local custom, social differences were left at the door when you entered such a scholarly space, each of those details contributing to an ambience that fostered sober, respectful behaviour. Indeed, anyone who started a quarrel had to atone for it by buying a coffee for all present. In short, these were calm, well-ordered establishments that promoted polite conversation and discussion.

B But that was a risk some were willing to take, for coffee houses did have their detractors. Coffee itself was held by some to be a harmful substance, although this was never taken particularly seriously. The real opposition came from those who were alarmed at the houses' potential for facilitating political discussion and activity.

C Coffee, the drink that fuelled this vibrant network, originated in the highlands of Ethiopia, where its beans were originally chewed rather than infused for their invigorating effects. Coffee spread into the Islamic world during the fifteenth century, where it came to be regarded as stimulating mental activity and heightening perception.

D In the days before formal addresses or regular postal services were introduced, for example, it became a common practice to use one as a mailing address. Regulars could pop in once or twice a day, hear the latest news, and check to see if any post awaited them.

E Lavish entertainment at home was beyond the means of this social stratum but a few pence a day on coffee could be afforded. What's more, coffee houses provided a forum for education, debate and self-improvement, and were nicknamed 'penny universities' in a contemporary English verse.

F Such kinship was soon underlined by the establishment of so-called 'hotspots'. What's more, from the outset these often provided access in establishments where coffee was also on offer – this can't have been a coincidence.

G The parallels are certainly striking. Originally the province of scientists, the Net also soon grew to become a nexus of commercial, journalistic and political interchange. In discussion groups, gossip passes freely – a little too freely, according to some regulators and governments, which have generally failed in their attempts to rein them in.

H The quality of the coffee wasn't the only factor governing which one this would be, however, for these lively and often unreliable sources of information typically specialised in a particular topic or political viewpoint. They also doubled as outlets for a stream of newsletters and pamphlets that reflected the interests of their particular clientele.

Vocabulary

Collocations

1a Form collocations of the words 1–5 with the items below. You may need to add *of* to some of them.

of one's own   human   spirit   rural   community
pride   belonging   neutral   social   level   centre
security   safe   financial   wellbeing

1 community: _____
2 place: _____
3 ground: _____
4 a sense: _____
5 services: _____

b In pairs, choose words from Exercise 1a that can complete the phrase in the following sentences. For items where more than one option is possible, discuss any differences in meaning.

1 Places like neighbourhood cafés and bars give local people a sense of _____ ; the feeling that they have a place in the community.
2 One thing that struck me about the old people's centre was the community _____ among its members.
3 Natalie works in _____ services as a home help coordinator for the elderly.
4 The statue was given _____ of place in the town square.
5 You'll be on _____ ground discussing this with Julia, as she knows a lot about the subject.
6 It's good to get involved in community _____ when you move to a new area, as it's a way of meeting people.

Expressions with *place*

2a Complete the sentences with the words below.

an advertisement   bets   hopes   importance
restrictions   blame

1 In this company, we place great _____ on community projects.
2 It's early days yet but I'd place _____ on Graham winning a gold medal in the Olympics.
3 Angry residents placed the _____ for the rise in accidents on the council.
4 The community centre placed _____ in the local newspaper for volunteers.
5 Due to cutbacks, the college has had to place _____ on the number of new students it can accept each year.
6 Several rural communities are placing their _____ on receiving government grants.

b Replace the words in *italics* in the following sentences with one of the phrases below.

in place   be going places   a place of her own
out of place   fall into place   there's a time and a place

1 Fiona's staying with her aunt at present but she's hoping to get *her own home* soon.
2 Olivier's doing well in his new job and it seems he will *become successful*.
3 Anna shouldn't have spoken out against the Mayor at the council meeting. *There are certain circumstances* for doing such things.
4 I went along to the meeting at the Town Hall but I felt *I didn't belong* there.
5 Everything seems strange and new to you now but once you settle in, it will soon *become natural*.
6 For the transport scheme to work, certain conditions need to be *ready* first.

Purpose and *intent*

3 The following sentence appears in the paragraph after gap 5 in the text on page 105.

That said, most people frequented several houses for the purpose of furthering their commercial, social or political interests.

Rewrite the sentence using the following phrases.

1 with the intention of
2 intent on

Is there any change in meaning or emphasis?

4a *Intent, intention* and *purpose* have several uses. Using your dictionary to help you, explain the meaning of the words in *italics* in these sentences.

1 The meeting was due to carry on until 4 o'clock but, *to all intents and purposes*, had finished by 3, the most important decisions having been made.
2 Danny claimed he had not hit the old lady *on purpose* but the police didn't believe him, and he was charged with causing grievous bodily harm *with intent*.
3 The protesters all marched to the town council offices *with the intention of* waiting outside until the Mayor agreed to listen to their demands.
4 The council bought and renovated the old double-decker bus *for the purpose of* using it as a mobile library.
5 The Youth Centre *served its purpose* well, becoming not only a meeting place for teenagers, but also a venue for social events and local entertainment.
6 Angry with his rowdy neighbours, George went round, *intent on* having an argument.

b In pairs, form your own sentences with phrases from Exercise 4a. How many can you produce?

Word formation: derivatives of *social* and use of the prefix *inter-*

5a The words *antisocial*, *unsociable* and *unsocial* appear to be closely connected in meaning but have differences in use. Use a dictionary to find out their differences.

b Use derivatives of the word *social* to complete the following sentences:

1 In his role as president of the tennis club, Martin spends a lot of time _____ with members.
2 Five youths were arrested outside a pub last night for _____ behaviour.
3 Gavin is hoping to study _____ at York university next year.
4 School plays a vital role in the _____ of children who have no siblings.
5 Keira is quite outspoken and belongs to the university Debating _____ .
6 Michael is rather _____ , and keeps to himself most weekends.
7 Mark is fed up of working such _____ hours, and is searching for another job.
8 _____ people will love the friendly atmosphere in our town square.

c Make a list of other derivatives of *social*. Include some compound words.

6a Which of the words below can take the prefix *inter-*?

departmental   action   rate   connect   mixed
supportive   city   section   change   social
continental   direct

b Make sentences with each of the words you formed in Exercise 6a.

Use of English 1 (Paper 1 Part 3)

Word formation

1a Look at the photograph of a city square and think of a square in your area. Discuss the following questions.

1 What is the function of the square today?
2 How might life in the community be affected if the square were not there?

b For questions 1–8, read the text below. Use the word given in CAPITALS at the end of some of the lines to form a word that fits in the gap in the same line. There is an example at the beginning (0).

The central square

The central square is a (0) _typical_ feature of the European city. Most cities began as commercial centres, the original (1) settlement ✓ growing up around a marketplace that was a *local* (2) ~~focused~~ ✗ point for the local agricultural community. Even where cities developed for (3) ~~strategical~~ ✗ reasons, like those near castles guarding key routes, the establishment of a market square often heralded truly urban development.	TYPE SETTLE FOCUS STRATEGY
As the city grew and became (4) ~~prospective~~ *prosperous* so the square became the centre of the community, and prominent public buildings and private houses were constructed around it. The physical sense of enclosure helped to give the city its (5) identity, and the square became the obvious meeting place for its citizens. It was where they gathered at festival time, and where they went to protest in times of (6) ~~restness~~ *unrest* .	PROSPER IDENTIFY REST
Today, despite the trend for commercial activities to leave the central area and (7) relocate ✓ in the suburbs, the square remains an important part of a city's identity, in stark contrast to the seeming (8) ~~anonymou~~ *anonymity* of modern suburban development. For this reason, it is still regarded as significant by town planners.	LOCATE ANONYMOUS

3/8

Discussion

2 Discuss the following question.

How important are public meeting places in a neighbourhood?

• squares
• public libraries, community centres
• community spirit

Listening 1 (Paper 3 Part 1)

Before you listen

1 Which of the following social activities do you participate in? Explain what is special about it/them, and what benefits they offer. Can you think of any other activities?

- sports or other social club
- college/school association or committee
- charity work (voluntary)
- other
- online discussion forum

2 Do you enjoy getting involved in social activities at college, work or in your local community? Why/Why not?

3 🎧 T2.05 Before you read questions 1–6 in Exercise 4, listen to the extracts once. What seems to be the attitude of each speaker to the subject they are talking about? Use the following words to help you.

> EXPERT STRATEGIES page 170

enthusiastic   matter-of-fact   optimistic

Multiple-choice questions

4 🎧 T2.05 Read the strategy on page 170, then do the task.

You will hear three different extracts. For questions 1–6, choose the answer (A, B or C) which best fits according to what you hear. There are two questions for each extract.

Extract One

You hear two Australian teachers talking about going to work in a rural area.

1 Initially, they were both impressed by

 A attempts to integrate them into the local community.
 B how welcome they were generally made to feel.
 C the range of leisure activities on offer.

2 What concern did the man have about the teaching before he arrived?

 A He'd find it hard to introduce new ideas.
 B He'd have little access to professional support.
 C He'd find that his methods were inappropriate.

Extract Two

You hear a man talking about a possible solution to a traffic problem in his town.

3 Why has the 'shared space' approach been proposed?

 A to allay the fears of the business community
 B to respond to a suggestion from local residents
 C to allow for savings in the local government budget

4 What is his own view of the approach being proposed?

 A He agrees with those who have expressed doubts.
 B He feels cautiously optimistic about it.
 C He regards it as impractical.

Extract Three

You hear a woman talking about a neighbourhood project.

5 What inspired her to set it up?

 A a personal need
 B her social conscience
 C requests from friends

6 What has particularly impressed her so far?

 A the amount of funding received
 B the range of skills being offered
 C the impact on the local community

Discussion

5 Do you agree with the following statements? Give reasons for your views.

1 'I wouldn't go to live in such a remote area, even if you paid me!'
2 'The idea of a shared space approach to traffic is interesting, but I worry that some drivers may still drive recklessly.'
3 'I know recycling is important, but I simply don't have time to repair and recycle things such as clothes!'

Language development 1

Relative clauses

> EXPERT GRAMMAR page 183

1 Circle the correct word or phrase in *italics* to complete the sentences. Explain your choice.

1 The youth club is a place *to which / where* young people can meet and socialise.
2 Many of the residents, some of *whom / which* live close to the main road, are angry about the new traffic regulations.
3 The new public library, *that / which* was designed by a local architect, was opened by the Mayor yesterday.
4 Tomorrow's meeting might have to be cancelled, *at which point / in which case* we will contact all the members.
5 The coffee shop *that / where* was located in the town centre had a really pleasant atmosphere.
6 Courses in woodwork and dressmaking will be available from September, *at that point / by which time* the new workshops should be ready.

2 Some of the following sentences contain mistakes. Find them and correct them.

1 The talk on sustainable communities was very informative that we heard.
2 The chess club was the place where I met my partner.
3 My girlfriend that has recently got a job in the town council hopes to promote community projects in the area.
4 The village pub which we visited it last night was very cosy and welcoming.
5 The councillor who I spoke this morning assured me the problem would be dealt with.
6 Socialising and meeting new people is something that I've always had difficulty with.

Reduced relative clauses with participles and *to* infinitives

3a The following sentences contain 'reduced' relative clauses. Rewrite them with the full relative clause.

1 Anyone wanting to take part in the carnival parade should write their name on this list.
2 All questions raised at the public meeting will be discussed when the organising committee meets next Tuesday.
3 The person to talk to about the arrangements for the carnival is Carrie Evans.

b Make one sentence with a reduced relative clause from the pairs of sentences 1–5 below. You may need to make several changes in structure.

1 The events chairperson, Carrie Evans, introduced the theme of the carnival. The introduction was considered extremely informative.
2 The headmaster of the local primary school spoke next. He offered some interesting ideas.
3 The headmaster's proposal has been met with widespread approval. He advocates the inclusion of a firework display to conclude the celebrations,
4 We plan to provide entertainment in the square. This still needs a lot of organising.
5 Some people may wish to become involved in the carnival preparations. They should apply to Carrie Evans directly.

Reduced non-defining descriptive clauses

4 Read the examples on page 184, then make a similar sentence with the pairs of sentences below. You will need to make several changes.

1 The youth club has been forced to close. It was affected by cutbacks in local government spending.
2 The Town Hall is undergoing renovation. It is one of the finest examples of Victorian architecture in the north-east.
3 The company is a sustainable business. It supports local farmers' cooperatives. Its net profits go to fund community projects in Africa.

5 Complete the text by adding the correct relative pronoun where necessary. Omit the relative pronoun whenever possible. Other words such as prepositions might also be used.

Margit and Richard Schweger are businesspeople **(1)** _____ a social conscience. They are the driving force behind the Noan Olive Oil company, **(2)** _____ a sustainable business dealing in organic olive oil. The company operates on the premise that business should not ignore its responsibility towards the environment or fair trade. With this in mind, they work closely with farmers in Greece **(3)** _____ grow organic olives. Richard, **(4)** _____ ties with the country stem from family holidays spent in the region, personally oversees oil production every year at a state-of-the-art organic olive press situated in the Pelion region. The end product, **(5)** _____ voted one of the best extra virgin olive oils by *The Gourmet* magazine, is then exported and sold to retailers and restaurants with direct sales to companies and via Noan's online shop, in Austria, Germany, Switzerland, with Scandinavia and the UK to join shortly. Besides ensuring that the farmers, most of **(6)** _____ own independent smallholdings, get a fair price for their produce, the company donates its net profit to community education programmes in the countries where the product is sold as well as to other countries in need. In this way, the Schwegers and their team have managed to create a self-sustaining charity **(7)** _____ generates repetitive investment capital to support educational projects for children and youth in need.

Writing 1 (Paper 2 Part 2: Letter)

Varying your language in descriptive writing

1 Read the task below and underline the key points. Then answer the questions.

> An English language magazine has invited readers to send in letters describing community schemes they either know about or are involved in. You have decided to send in a letter describing a project, explaining why you think it is a good idea for local people, and saying what the project hopes to achieve in the future.

1 Who is the letter to?
2 What kind of letter should you write: a complaint, a description or a letter of advice?
3 What do you have to include in your letter?
4 Should the register be formal or informal?

2 Decide which of the following opening paragraphs is the most suitable way to begin your answer to the task in Exercise 1. Explain why the others are not as suitable.

a Dear Editor,
The project I want to talk about is a garden share project called Growing Together. It was thought up by a couple of university students, who noticed that their garden was going to waste.

b To whom it may concern,
I am writing in answer to your request for descriptions of a community project. I'd like to put forward a suggestion that you include mention of the Growing Together garden share project.

c Dear Sir/Madam,
I read the announcement in your magazine asking readers to send in descriptions of a community project. Although I am not directly involved, I would like to describe a project that I particularly admire. It is called the Growing Together garden share project.

3 In pairs, discuss which project you would write about in reply to the task in Exercise 1.

4 Read a student's notes below. Expand them into two paragraphs describing the community project. Use a variety of relative clauses and reduced clauses where possible, and make any other necessary changes.

1 scheme // university students / Bath / help / residents / allotment space / unused gardens vegetable crops /.
2 many students // rented accommodation / gardens unused.
3 neighbours / interested / gardening / no green space // use students' gardens.
4 the Growing Together Project / students and residents // chance to interact.
5 residents // extremely positive / some of them work with students /.
6 Kate Myers / resident / Oldfield Park / enthusiastic / 'no contact / students before / but / lads / house / nice / grow / potatoes for them.'
7 Caroline Walker and Ming Chan / undergraduates / passionate / gardening / helping Kate / theirs / first successful garden share.
8 grow onions, carrots, potatoes / so far // fresh produce / students.
9 several garden shares / functioning / but / hope // more residents / join.

5 Letters of this kind often end with a recommendation, or hopes for the future. Decide on a suitable ending for the letter in Exercise 4, and write the concluding paragraph.

Listening 2 (Paper 3 Part 4)

Before you listen

1 Discuss the following questions.

1 Why do people use a bicycle?
- to get to work/college
- for pleasure
- to keep fit
- for personal needs, e.g. to go shopping or meet friends
- to take part in competitions

2 Is the bike a luxury item, a fitness tool or a basic means of transport?

2 🎧 T2.06 Listen to the five extracts once only, without looking at the questions in Exercise 3. Quickly note down what each person likes about cycling.

Multiple matching

➤ EXPERT STRATEGIES page 171

3 🎧 T2.07 Read the strategy on page 171, then do the task.

You will hear five short extracts in which different people are talking about cycling.

Task One

For questions **1–5**, choose from the list (**A–H**) what led each speaker to take up cycling.

Task Two

For questions **6–10**, choose from the list (**A–H**) what advice each speaker would give to others thinking of following their example.

You will hear the recording twice. While you listen, you must complete both tasks.

A a wish to lose weight	
B a desire to compete	**1**
C a need to economise	**2**
D feeling under stress	**3**
E environmental awareness	**4**
F peer pressure	
G a transport problem	**5**
H health reasons	

A invest in a good bike	
B don't overstretch yourself	**6**
C avoid organised cycling groups	**7**
D try it out before committing yourself	
E find like-minded companions	**8**
F don't waste money on accessories	**9**
G always keep your options open	
H don't take it too seriously	**10**

Discussion

4 What are the benefits and limitations of using bikes as a basic means of transport? Do you think local governments should do more to encourage people to cycle more around the town? If so, how?

5 Check the meaning of these words and phrases from the audioscript.

EXPERT WORD CHECK

axe   a must   be dead set on (sth)   set (sb) back   go over the top
fraternity   steer clear of (sth)   means to an end   progression
bite off more than (sb) can chew

Speaking (Paper 4 Parts 1 & 2)

Vocabulary: social life

1a Place the words below next to the group of words with similar meaning.

fete   contest   spare time   tournament   activity   scheme   competition   celebration   association   function   society   programme   occasion   pastime   match   group

1 sport, hobby, _____
2 event, festival, fair, _____
3 championship, game, _____
4 project, _____
5 leisure, free time, _____
6 club, organisation, _____

b Make sentences with some of the words in Exercise 1a to describe your own interests and experiences.

2 Use verbs from column A and phrases from column B to form sentences to talk about the value of doing the activity depicted in one of the photographs (A–D). Note that different combinations are possible. Make a list of collocations and practise using them. You will need to add your own words and expand the phrases.

It creates opportunities for people to get involved in local events.

A	B
enhance	a bit of fun
boost	a great way to relax
improve	get you out of the house
stimulate	a chance to meet new people/make new friends
generate	let your hair down
create	enjoy making a fool of yourself
develop	get involved in local events
offer	socialise
allow	build relationships/community spirit
encourage	social awareness of the community we live in

Part 1

> EXPERT STRATEGIES page 171

3 In pairs, practise asking each other and answering the following questions. Try to vary your language. Use some of the phrases from Exercises 1 and 2 to help you.

1 What social activities do you enjoy doing in your leisure time?
2 What is the value of local communities holding celebrations?

Useful language

4a Look at photograph D. Use the prompts below to make sentences about the social value of an activity like this. Try to use a relative clause structure (see page 183) where appropriate.

The benefits of this kind of activity, involving people of all ages, …
The act of replenishing forests benefits the local community on two levels, one of which …
Another reason for promoting such activities is …
Personally, I would like to see more …
Having taken part in a similar project/event, I can say that …
Projects such as these, which not only benefit those involved but also …

b Match the sentences 1–4 below with one of the photographs. Then use some of the following phrases to respond to the statements in Exercise 4a and 1–4 below.

Yes, I totally agree with you on that.   Oh, I wouldn't say that!
But think of the benefits to the local clubs that participate every year!
You're absolutely right.   Yes but isn't it better to hold charity events?

1 'Personally, I can't see the point of karaoke nights. A bunch of people singing badly and making fools of themselves is not my idea of entertainment.'
2 'Quite frankly, I'm not sure of the value of holding a carnival, since it's so expensive to organise.'
3 'I think holding fun sports day events is a great way to relax with other people in your community.'
4 'The carnival is often a good way to generate trade for local retailers with visitors from other towns.'

Part 2 Collaborative task

5a Look at photographs A and C and talk together about the value these activities may have for the community. Use examples from your own experience where possible. ☺ Time yourselves, and remember to allow one minute only.

b Look at all the photographs. Imagine that your local newspaper is producing a special supplement featuring aspects of community life. Photographs (A–D) illustrate some of the aspects to be included. Talk together about the role each activity plays in the life of a community today. Then decide which photograph would be the most suitable to place on the front cover of the supplement.

Task analysis

6 Did you:
• interact naturally with your partner?
• vary your language sufficiently from that of your partner?

Language development 2

Clauses of time and reason, result, concession

> EXPERT GRAMMAR page 184

Time and reason clauses

1a Decide which word can begin each of these sentences.

1 *While / After* waiting for ages for a bus, we decided to take a taxi.
2 *Now that / Once* she has stopped eating meat, she feels much healthier.
3 *While / As soon as* the children are growing up, I want to spend weekends doing things with them.
4 *The moment / Until* the film had finished, Peter left without saying a word.
5 *No sooner / Ever since* she could remember, she'd enjoyed rowing.
6 *Until / After* Nick finishes school this summer, we won't even think about moving house.
7 *On / While* arriving in Paris, she joined a community theatre group.
8 *As soon as / No sooner* he arrived home, he decided to leave his office job and travel.

b Complete the sentences with a suitable word or phrase below. There may be more than one possibility. Discuss the effect on the meaning of the sentence in these cases.

since   seeing   planning on   hoping to   in that   in case

1 He decided to go freelance, _____ have more freedom to choose which kind of work he would do.
2 _____ that there is so much interest, we really ought to set up a chess club in the school.
3 Living in a sustainable community involves making a serious commitment _____ you must adhere to the way of life once you've made the decision.
4 I keep my mobile phone switched on even when I'm at work _____ the babysitter needs to reach me.
5 _____ you've made up your mind to become a digital nomad, I'll give you some contacts in Australia and Indonesia.
6 _____ becoming wine producers, they bought a vineyard in Tuscany.

Result clauses

2 Choose the correct word or phrase (A–D) to complete the sentences.

1 There was enormous traffic congestion in the town centre every lunchtime, ___C___ the council's decision to pedestrianise the area.
A therefore   B such was   C hence   D as a result

2 I need to make some changes to my life, ___B___ I think I'll go mad.
A so that   B otherwise   C in which case
D consequently

3 She organised her work schedule ___A___ she could compete in Tall Ships racing events twice a year.
A In such a way that   B so as   C or else
D resulting in

4 Life in the Australian outback was ___A___ they returned to Sydney.
A So harsh that   B such difficult one that
C one such difficult that
D in such a harsh state that

5 She moved to the country and sold her car and TV, and ___B___ her life has become much less stressful.
A otherwise   B consequently
C in such a way that   D hence

6 You said you're moving to Argentina. ___D___ you won't be needing your Harley. Can I have it?
A In which case,   B So as   C Otherwise
D That being the case,

Concession clauses

3a Match the first half of the sentence (1–6) with the second half (a–f).

1 Much as she hates working on Sundays, d
2 I'm not going to become a volunteer overseas, f
3 Despite being in love with Xavier, b
4 I spend hours playing computer games, a
5 She makes all her own clothes, c
6 Difficult though life on the island sometimes was, e

a even though it's a waste of time.
b she isn't willing to go and live in Brazil.
c in spite of being able to afford to buy them.
d it's sometimes unavoidable.
e they managed to raise a family there.
f although I admire the fact that you want to do it.

b Using the prompts, complete the following concession clauses with reference to your own experience.

1 I've been feeling a bit fed up lately. Nevertheless, _____ .

2 I'm afraid I can't come on that trip with you. All the same, _____ .

3 Living on a remote island is not for me. Even so, _____ .

4 I love the nightlife of the city. However, _____ .

5 A nomadic lifestyle sounds very romantic. All the same, _____ .

6 Living a very active life can be exciting. Be that as it may, _____ .

Use of English 2 (Paper 1 Part 1)

Lead-in

1a The person in the photograph is a 'location-independent professional'. Look at the individual words that make up the phrase. What do you think it means?

b What recent developments (e.g. technological and sociological) are changing the way people work, and in what professions?

Multiple-choice cloze

2 Quickly read through the text below. Do not worry about the gaps. What does it imply about professionals who are not tied to an office?

For questions 1–8, read the text below and decide which answer (A, B, C or D) best fits each gap. There is an example at the beginning (0).

Lifestyle design

The term 'lifestyle design' has been **(0)** _A_ quite recently. It describes a way of radically re-evaluating lifestyle choices by encouraging a **(1)** _A_ ✓ away from the idea that a person's job will by **(2)** _D_ ✓ determine where they live. Advocates of the idea argue that the **(3)** _A B_ of laptops and WiFi has enabled certain types of people to **(4)** _C_ free from the nine-to-five mould and arrange their working timetable around family life. They gain, for example, the chance to get involved in activities they would **(5)** _B_ ✓ miss out on because they were at work. The end result is a greatly enhanced quality of life for the whole family.

A group known as 'location-independent professionals', or LIPs have taken the concept a step further. Digital nomads, with no **(6)** _D_ ✓ abode, they travel to distant places, combining work with other life experiences. Work is conducted from internet cafés, hotel rooms or camper vans, **(7)** _A B_ with regular runs along the beach or sightseeing outings. An idyllic life, it would seem, but perhaps less **(8)** _C_ ✓ to raising a family.

	A	B	C	D
0	A coined	B made	C given	D born
✓ **1**	(A) shift	B change	C route	D swap
✓ **2**	A compulsion	B requirement	C obligation	(D) necessity
✗ **3**	(A) onset	(B) advent	C release	D upshot
✓ **4**	A become	B escape	(C) break	D emerge
✓ **5**	A meanwhile	(B) otherwise	C instead	D thereby
✓ **6**	A definite	B known	C certain	(D) fixed
✗ **7**	(A) interspersed	(B) interwoven	C intersected	D interrupted
✓ **8**	A persuasive	B incentive	(C) conducive	D supportive

6/8

Discussion

3 Which would you prefer, working in an office or being locationally independent, and why?

Writing 2 (Paper 2 Part 2: Letter)

Lead-in 1 Festivals are held all over the world for numerous reasons. Describe a festival you know of, and say whether it is held for any of the following reasons:

- to promote tourism in the region
- to celebrate an industry
- to generate local business
- other
- to promote local culture

Understand the task 2 Read the exam writing task below, then answer these questions.

1 Who are you writing to?
2 Why are you writing – to complain, describe an event, give advice, etc.?
3 What should you include in your letter?
4 Should the letter be formal, semi-formal or informal?
5 How long should the letter be?

> An English-language magazine has invited readers to send in letters describing their experience of a recent festival, either in their own country or abroad. You have decided to write about a festival you recently attended, commenting on the festival, saying what was special about it, and if there was anything you didn't like.
>
> Write your letter in **280–320** words. You do not need to write any postal addresses.

Plan your letter 3a Decide which festival you are going to write about. You may choose one of the following, or something else, if you like.

- a food and wine festival
- a cultural festival
- a festival of a particular industry, such as film, animation, tourism, the arts, etc.

b Plan how your letter will develop. Make notes with the frame below.

Paragraph 1: _____
Paragraph 2: _____
Paragraph 3: _____
Paragraph 4: _____

c Compare your plan with a partner, and discuss any improvements you could both make.

Language and content

4 Read the model answer to the question in Exercise 2 and answer the following questions.

1 Does it cover all the points in the task?
2 Is it well developed?
3 Is the level of language suitable?

Dear Editor,

I want to describe for you a <u>festival</u> I went to recently. It was in a place called Boryeong, in South Korea. It's the Mud Festival, and it's <u>great fun</u>!

The festival started in 1998 in order to advertise the benefits of skin-care <u>products</u>. <u>The products</u> were made with local mud that is rich in minerals. Boryeong has a beach that is 13 kilometres long. So, the mud is transported there, and a Mud Experience Land is created in one section. Tourists come from all over the world, as well as local people, in order to <u>get dirty</u>. There is mud wrestling, mud sliding, mud swimming, massages and a photo contest available. <u>The festival</u> has become very popular, and nowadays over 2 million people come. <u>The festival</u> is held in the summer, and I went with a group of friends this year. We <u>had a really good</u>

<u>time</u>, and got <u>very dirty</u>. It's a <u>great</u> way to meet people, as everyone is laughing, and pushing each other in the mud. Once I got some mud in my eyes and mouth, and this wasn't very nice, but generally I <u>had a good time</u>. You must take a change of clothes with you. There are special lockers where you can leave them, and then go and collect them at the end of the day. <u>The festival</u> goes on for a week, and the night-time entertainment is also good. There are firework displays on the opening and closing nights, and parades and local entertainers performing on the other nights. You can also buy the mud skin products at various stalls in the town.

The only problem was with transport. There were so many people in Boryeong that week, and it was difficult to move in the traffic. I think the authorities should do something to solve the traffic problem for next year.

5 Work in pairs. Brainstorm ideas for improving the letter in Exercise 4. Follow the procedure below.

1 Using the paragraph plan you made in Exercise 3b, organise the candidate's points into more appropriate paragraphs.
2 The underlined words in the text are used repeatedly. Brainstorm ideas for replacing some of them, e.g. *get dirty – become muddy/ messy/slimy/grubby/filthy*, etc.

> EXPERT STRATEGIES page 169

6 Think of ways of making the sentences more varied. Look back at the Language development sections in this module and in the previous ones, and use the structures in brackets () to rewrite the following sentences.

1 I want to describe for you a festival I went to recently. It was in a place called Boryeong, in South Korea. It's the Mud Festival. (a relative clause)
2 The festival has become very popular, and nowadays over 2 million people come. (a time clause)
3 The festival started in 1998. It was held to advertise the benefits of skin-care products. (a relative clause)
4 Once I got some mud in my eyes and mouth, and this wasn't very nice, but generally I had a good time. (a clause of concession)
5 Tourists come from all over the world, as well as local people, in order to get dirty. (inversion)
6 The only problem was with transport. There were so many people in Boryeong that week, and it was difficult to move in the traffic. (cleft sentence + emphatic structure)

7 Work in pairs. Rewrite the model answer. Make any other changes you think necessary.

8 Compare your version with others in the class.

Write your letter

> EXPERT STRATEGIES page 169

9 Now write your own answer to the question in Exercise 2. Remember to use an appropriate form of address, both to open and close the letter. Write your answer in **280–320** words.

Check your letter

> EXPERT WRITING page 191

10 Edit your letter, using the checklist on page 191.

Review

1 Complete the collocations in each sentence.

1 Let's not discuss this at your place. I'd rather meet somewhere on __the__ ground, like in a café, say. *near* *neutral*

2 Katrina's just got a new job in advertising. She's really going __well__ ! *places*

3 We believe that upholding local traditions gives residents a __cup__ of pride in the community. *sense*

4 The council have placed __up__ on parking *restrictions* near the town square, as they want to gradually pedestrianise the area.

5 Darren was caught shoplifting for the third time last week, and has been sentenced to six months' __of__ service. He'll be working at the local *community* home for the elderly.

6 Once the funding is in __place__ , restoration work on the museum can begin.

7 As a result of recent break-ins in the neighbourhood, residents have called in __mind__ services to organise patrols. *security*

8 When he moved to the village, joining the local tennis club gave Mike a sense of __calm__ to the community, as he got to know people quickly. *belonging*

9 When the councillor explained the plan to me, everything fell into __pieces__ and I began to understand the reasons behind the move. *place*

2 Circle the correct phrases to complete the sentences.

1 (Much as) / Despite he likes sport, he doesn't want to join the local sports centre.

2 I really admire what Jill has done for the community. (Hence) / Be that as it may, I wouldn't want to be in her shoes right now.

3 Carmen became a digital nomad or else / (so as to) be more flexible.

4 The council imposed speed restrictions, to no avail. In such a case / (As a result,) they decided to adopt the shared space approach.

5 You should join in some social activities, (otherwise) / in case you're going to feel lonely here.

6 (Although) / In spite of her presence at the meeting was expected, Julie decided not to go.

7 Jorge is under a lot of pressure at work. Even so / (Consequently,) he's had to decline the committee's request that he become chairman.

8 The situation in the village was one such awkward / (such an awkward one) that Gareth resigned his post as councillor.

9 Joe refused to join the community group, (despite) / even though being invited to do so by several members.

3 Complete the sentences by forming a suitable word from the word in CAPITALS.

1 Peter is interested in becoming a __sociologist__, and wants to specialise in indigenous social groups. SOCIAL

2 The Law, History and Social Science faculties have decided to hold an _____ party to encourage social relations throughout the university. DEPARTMENT *interdepartamental* *interdepartmental*

3 It wasn't just a slip of the tongue. You made that remark __intentional to__ ruin my image on the committee! INTENT

4 The schoolyard is __closed__ by rather imposing high stone walls. CLOSE

5 'I will be allowed to speak my mind!' shouted Mrs Briggs __defying__ at the meeting. DEFY *defiantly*

6 The Mayor was __unequivo__ in his view with regard to the proposed demolition of the Town Hall. 'We shall fight it, of course.' EQUIVOCAL

7 Mr Clark is a __represent__ of the community centre, and has come to outline their proposal for a new arts wing. REPRESENT *representative*

8 The words *antisocial* and *unsocial* are __change__ in some contexts. CHANGE *able*

9 Without proper council records or deeds, the rightful owner of the property may be __unidentified__ . IDENTIFY *iable*

4 Complete the text with a suitable preposition.

A family tradition in steam

Your first impression (1) __of__ Roland Meeson and his son, Mark, may well be that, aside (2) __from__ the affectionate banter that flows easily between them, they are two fairly nondescript individuals. However, they share an unusual hobby (3) __but in__ that they both drive steam trains. The impetus (4) __of for__ their interest came from Roland's grandfather, a robust man who had worked (5) __for on__ the railways before becoming involved (6) __with in__ a private steam collection. Roland was barely walking before he was working on the trains, and he passed his passion on to his own son. He is unequivocal about the reason for this: 'Steam is fascinating. It's as though the engine comes alive when the steam starts rising. There's nothing like it.' Judging (7) __by__ the number of people that gather at the little station (8) __from out__ of which they operate each weekend, Richard seems to have a point.

8 Changing fashions

Red Tree, Blue Sky (2008) by Sally Trace

Boulevard Montmartre au printemps (1897) by Camille Pissarro

Lead-in

1a Look at the paintings. Painting 1 is representative of Abstract art and painting 2 of Impressionist art.

   1 Which appeals to you most? Why?
   2 What do you notice about the shapes included in painting 1?
   3 What 'impression' does painting 2 give you?

b When innovations occur in the sciences or the arts, how do people often respond? Can you think of any examples from history?

2 Here are some useful words and phrases to use when describing works of art or particular designs. Use them and any others you know to describe one of the paintings above.

straight line	perpendicular	wavy line	perspective	curved line	depth	height	length
width	symmetry	harmony	pattern	contrasting colours	brush stroke		

8A A question of style

Before you read

1 Discuss the following questions.

1 What do you like or dislike about the village, town or city in which you live? In what way would you change it if you could?
2 With regard to old buildings, do you think the better policy is to pull them down and replace them with modern buildings or spend money on restoring them? Give your reasons.

Scanning: finding and understanding detail

2a Read the text through quickly and identify which two constructions or buildings are discussed there.

b In what way are the places you found in Exercise 2a similar and how has their treatment been different?

Multiple matching

> EXPERT STRATEGIES page 168

3 Do the task below. Read the strategies on page 168 before you start.

You are going to read an article about architecture. For questions 1–10, choose the best answer from sections (A–D). The sections may be chosen more than once.

In which section does the writer mention

the idea that a preservation project can regenerate the surrounding area?	1 _____
why a particular structure stood out amongst its contemporaries?	2 _____
the inescapable need to make compromises when structures find a new use?	3 _____
a successful attempt to halt the total destruction of an obsolete structure?	4 _____
a paradox regarding the work of highly renowned architects?	5 _____
an approach to saving the architectural heritage that cannot always be financed?	6 _____
how an architect made a feature of something which is usually obscured?	7 _____
a disagreement about how a principle should be applied in practice?	8 _____
a structure that embodied the optimism of its time?	9 _____
a feeling that alterations to a structure were justifiable?	10 _____

Discussion

4 Discuss the following questions.

1 What kind of historic buildings are conserved in your country?
2 Do you like visiting places of historical interest? What can people learn from visiting such places?

5 Check the meaning of these key words and phrases from the text.

> **EXPERT WORD CHECK**
>
> fortress   transparency   gut   friction   dismantle   flip side   upheaval   buoyancy   elevated   grass-roots

Locked in time

What are the issues surrounding the preservation of good architecture?

A Emerging from the Lincoln tunnel into midtown Manhattan in New York, a yellow cab from JFK Airport takes you past an architectural masterpiece. Number 510 Fifth Avenue was originally the Manufacturers Hanover Trust Bank and was designed in 1954 as a new kind of banking house, something other than a thick-walled fortress. It was a glass temple of finance, inviting passers-by to step through its cool transparency and be converted to its gleaming vision of the future. Mid-twentieth-century banks were usually mundane but at 510 Fifth Avenue, the vault was displayed behind the glazed façade and the escalators became central to the composition, falling and rising diagonally across the gridded lines like an updated game of snakes and ladders. The upper floor featured a gilded screen by the artist Harry Bertoia.

B But things are changing at 510 Fifth Avenue. As a very carefully-designed and much-admired building, it now finds itself at the frontier between developers and preservationists and it's turning into quite a fight. For if there's one thing in architecture that causes friction, it's that our needs change, and so buildings must evolve and adapt in order to stay useful. Within reason. Vornado Realty Trust, the site's owners and one of New York's largest developers, has made the not unreasonable assumption that this commercial building on the world's primary shopping street should be adapted to suit its new tenant, a retailer of lumberjack-style shirts. For this purpose, the gilded screen has been dismantled, the entrance is to be moved, the escalator reversed and the vault moved. On the basis that the façades remain intact, the Landmarks Preservation Commission approved these changes in April. But in July, a judge halted work after a legal challenge by the Citizens' Emergency Committee to Preserve Preservation, which argues that, given the transparency of the façade, Landmark status must extend to those interior features that contribute to the streetscape. Too late. It is now gutted, the interior features broken from their positions of more than half a century.

C Architects are often feted for designing buildings whose form follows function. And that's reasonable – intelligent design brings intellectual and physical beauty to the world. But architects are no better at predicting the future than the rest of us. Hence, the flip side to architectural masterpieces: the closer a building's form follows its function, the bigger the upheaval when the original purpose no longer needs to be served. Preservation groups are aware that conservation is an expensive business. Arguments to preserve for preservation's sake are weakened when loans are in short supply and the economic buoyancy that might offer a long-term business case for the sensitive commercial usage of old buildings starts to sink. The stronger argument is to update historic places so they can fund themselves. In any repurposing of a historic building, something has to give. And it usually gives in the direction of apartments, shops, restaurants or art galleries. It's a global picture.

D The most exciting new place in New York is the High Line, built as an elevated railway through the Meatpacking District and unused since the 1980s. It was scheduled to be torn down, but local residents started a grass-roots movement in 1999. Three years on, they gained the authorities' support for a radical redevelopment as a city garden, a string of improbable greenery threading through an overlooked quarter that has since spread economic fertiliser in its wake with hotels, boutiques and bars abounding. Back in Fifth Avenue, there's much hand-wringing over the stripped modern icon. Is it too late to hope the perfect tenant will turn up and want to strike a deal? If it's not to change further, who will put it back together, take care of it and run it as … what – an icon?

Vocabulary

Architectural and design features

1a Label the drawings with the features below.

alcove   bay window   beam   dormer window
façade   furnishings   loft   ornament   parquet
porch   screen   skylight   wallpaper   windowsill

b Complete the short dialogues with a word from Exercise 1a.

Sara: Max, where are those old school photos of mine? I'd like to have a look through them again.

Max: Oh, I think they're up in the _____ . I need to go up there anyway to get a suitcase down. Shall I get them for you?

Sara: Oh yes, thanks Max.

Later ...

Max: Sorry Sara, but how many _____ do we *really* need on every surface?

Sara: Well, these were gifts from my mum from her holidays, those over there I've picked up on my travels and these here are ...

Max: OK, OK, sorry I asked!

After lunch ...

Max: Gosh, look at that rain – but I've got to go out and buy some more DIY stuff. Where's that big black umbrella, Sara?

Sara: Oh, I was tidying up yesterday and I put it in the front _____ since it looked like rain!

Phrases from art and architecture

2a Complete the phrases with these words below. Then discuss what the phrases mean.

art   designs   façade   line (x3)   perspective

1 I think it's time to draw a _____ under our misunderstanding and move on.
2 Don't worry too much about it. Try to keep things in _____ .
3 Whatever happens, he always maintains a _____ of self-assurance.
4 There's a fine _____ between being original in your tastes and being a bit eccentric.
5 Over the years, she had got her household management skills down to a fine _____ .
6 The local council has got _____ on the field behind our house to build a new housing development.
7 He's gone along with the open-plan working area but he draws the _____ at including his own office!

b Check in your dictionaries to find more useful phrases with *line*.

Collocations: adjective + noun

3a We are all familiar with phrases such as *take a look* or *make a decision*. But do you know which words collocate with *look* or *decision*?

1 *take a ... look (at sth)*
   Tick which of the following words collocate with *look* in this phrase. Discuss their meaning.

bright   close   fresh   good   hard   humorous
near   nostalgic   strong

2 *make a(n) ... decision (about sth)*
   Tick which of the following words collocate with *decision* in this phrase. Discuss their meaning.

central   crucial   fast   irrevocable   permanent
poor   rash   rough   snap   tough

3 *exert/have a(n) ... influence on (sb/sth)*
   Tick which of the following words collocate with *influence* in this phrase. Discuss their meaning.

artificial   beneficial   civilising   continual   destructive
large   peaceful   significant   stabilising   useful
worthy

b Write a couple of short dialogues using words and phrases from Exercises 1, 2 and 3a. Compare with a partner.

Test yourself: prepositions!

4a Complete the text about interior decorating with the words below.

around	back	by (x3)	for	from	of	on (x4)	
out	in	without	up (x3)				

Interior decorating – on a shoestring

These days, there is a growing band of 'shoestring renovators' who, in a climate where finance is hard to come **(1)** _____ , are scaling **(2)** _____ their refurbishment plans and coming **(3)** _____ with imaginative ways to transform their homes. Extra money is **(4)** _____ short supply so things are done **(5)** _____ the cheap – not in a nasty way but in a way that makes use **(6)** _____ materials that other people don't want. Sarah and her husband are an example of this way of working **(7)** _____ a tight budget: the loan **(8)** _____ an old cottage they bought was reduced **(9)** _____ the bank so they had no choice but to do most of the work themselves. Sarah spent every spare minute for a year painting and decorating. She sourced materials and furniture from eBay and recycled friends' unwanted possessions. Do-It-Yourself, however, is not **(10)** _____ its hazards: Steve, Sarah's husband, knocked himself **(11)** _____ cold for two hours **(12)** _____ hitting his head **(13)** _____ a low beam above the front door. Another time, they only just managed to save their new kitchen furniture **(14)** _____ being ruined after a mains water pipe burst. However, the upside is that the project has opened **(15)** _____ a new avenue for Sarah – people have seen her work and have suggested she start **(16)** _____ her own home-styling business. And the cottage next door is **(17)** _____ sale so more creative furniture sourcing could lie just **(18)** _____ the corner!

b Now highlight all the phrasal verbs you can find in the text in Exercise 4a, together with any useful prepositional phrases. Discuss their meanings.

Open cloze

> **EXPERT STRATEGIES** page 167

1a Quickly read the text below. What was unique about the Arts and Crafts Movement?

b What other styles of art or design have you heard of, apart from the ones you discussed on page 119?

c Now do the task, using the strategies on page 167 to help you.

For questions 1–8, read the text below and think of the word which best fits each gap. Use only one word in each gap. There is an example at the beginning (0).

The Arts and Crafts Movement

The Arts and Crafts Movement is **(0)** _one_ of the most influential developments in the history of design. Its origins can be traced to Britain around 1880 but it wasn't long **(1)** _____ its ideas had spread across Europe and the Americas and Asia. The movement grew **(2)** _____ of concern about industrialisation, and the effect this was **(3)** _____ on traditional skills and the lives of ordinary people.

(4) _____ it did in practice was to establish a new set of principles by **(5)** _____ people could live and work. It advocated seeing the home itself **(6)** _____ a work of art, where the wonderful patterns that are found in nature could be reflected.

The Movement's most influential figures were John Ruskin, who examined the relationship between art, society and labour, and William Morris who **(7)** _____ Ruskin's philosophies into practice. This was a Movement **(8)** _____ any that had gone before. Its pioneering spirit of supporting local craftsmen, and the value it placed on the quality of materials and design, helped shape the modern world.

2 If you could design your ideal home, what would it look like and what features would it have? Compare and support your ideas.

Listening 1 (Paper 3 Part 3)

Before you listen   **1**   Discuss the following questions.

     1 Do you know where the buildings in the photos are? (Clue: one is in the United States and the other in Europe.)
     2 What museums or art galleries have you visited? Did you like them?
     3 Do you know the names of any other well-known museums or art galleries? Which ones would you like to visit? Why?

Multiple choice   **2**   🎧 T2.08 **Read the strategy on page 171, then do the task.**

➤ EXPERT STRATEGIES page 171

You will hear two history of art students called Emily and Scott discussing the relevance of museums today. For questions 1–5, choose the answer (A, B, C or D) which fits best according to what you hear.

1   Emily interprets the statistical information she quotes as

   A   an indication that museums are attracting people of all ages.
   B   evidence of the continuing appeal of permanent exhibitions.
   C   reflecting the particular appeal of travelling exhibitions.
   D   being unrepresentative of museums outside big cities.

2   Scott points out that an impressive museum building

   A   can distract attention from the exhibits.
   B   often presents the exhibits in the best light.
   C   should reflect the historical period of the exhibits.
   D   encourages people to spend longer viewing the exhibits.

3   When asked about tour groups, Emily suggests that

   A   people shouldn't feel prejudiced against them.
   B   few of them give participants a good experience.
   C   they're best avoided if you have a serious interest in art.
   D   it would be good to restrict them to designated time slots.

4   What surprised Scott when he was doing research into why people visited a museum?

   A   how reluctant people were to give him a reason
   B   how keen some people were on particular periods
   C   how most people had few expectations before arriving
   D   how differently people from other cultures viewed the visit

5   Emily and Scott agree that virtual museums

   A   are a good introduction to new art.
   B   are quite time-consuming to access.
   C   reduce the need for traditional ones.
   D   can't replicate the real-life experience.

Discussion   **3**   Discuss the following questions.

     1 What are some of the advantages and disadvantages of viewing paintings or museum exhibits online?
     2 Do you think that museums are dying out? Why/Why not?

Language development 1

-ing form

> **EXPERT GRAMMAR** page 185

Verb + preposition + -ing

1 Complete the sentences with the correct preposition, *from, in* or *on,* and the correct form of the verbs below.

| come   convert   create   demolish   have   move |
| paint   study |

1 They're depending _____ a lot of people _____ to the exhibition.
2 I'm afraid I don't believe _____ _____ beautiful old buildings – it's such a waste!.
3 Fortunately, many charities benefit _____ _____ wealthy patrons!
4 Adam specialises _____ _____ old warehouses into office space.
5 His success as a top yacht designer results _____ _____ very hard for many years.
6 Sophie specialises _____ _____ watercolours of flowers, which are very popular as greetings cards.
7 Everyone complimented the couple _____ _____ a very comfortable living space inside a very small flat!
8 I think they're planning _____ _____ house in the very near future.

Common words and expressions + -ing

2 Choose the correct word or phrase to complete the sentences.

Despite / Instead of
1 _____ having a lot of energy and talent, he never quite made it.

It's worth / It's no good
2 _____ mentioning it to Emma – she won't take your preferences into account at all.

can't stand / can't help
3 I _____ feeling a bit pessimistic – I don't think anyone will want to buy my paintings!

There's no point in / There's no prospect of
4 _____ visiting Paris without going to the Louvre museum.

for the sake of / with the purpose of
5 James visited the ancient Greek temple in the late afternoon _____ watching the sunset.

Through / With a view to
6 _____ using all her skills and imagination, Ceri managed to win the interior design competition.

Phrasal verbs + -ing form

3 Complete the text with the correct form of a phrasal verb and the verbs in brackets.

| burst out   cut down on   end up   feel up to |
| make up for   set about   ~~take up~~ |

Tibbs

One day, Clare, a novelist, decided to **(0)** *take up painting* (paint) – not watercolour painting but painting in oils. So the first thing she did was to **(1)** _____ (gather) all the necessary materials together: paints, canvas, an easel, and so on. She **(2)** _____ her _____ (spend), including little luxuries like weekend trips to the cinema so she could buy good-quality stuff. Finally one afternoon, when she had run out of ideas and didn't **(3)** _____ (work) on her novel, she was ready to start. Tibbs, her fluffy grey cat, loved snoozing on the windowsill, so Clare decided to use her as a model. She had just finished when her friend Paul and his dog, Rex, came for a visit.

Rex took one look at the sleeping Tibbs – and a second Tibbs on the canvas – and went wild! He took a flying leap towards Tibbs, landed on the canvas and **(4)** _____ (get) covered in orange paint. Paul was horrified but Clare **(5)** _____ (laugh). 'To be honest, Paul, I don't think I'm much good at this,' she said. 'My painting of Tibbs made her look like a monster. Do you fancy buying the materials off me? Perhaps you'll be a better artist than I am!'

So Paul paid Clare for her painting equipment and, to **(6)** _____ Rex _____ (ruin) her portrait of Tibbs, he took her out to the cinema.

4 In pairs, carry out a role play between the owner of a house and the architect. The owner has been disappointed with the architect's work. Imagine and continue a dialogue between them. Use the notes below to help you. Use as many phrases and expressions from this page as you can.

- the architect apologises for the mistakes he made on the house
- he tries to suggest a friend of his to design and landscape the garden
- the owner is very dubious

Writing 1 (Paper 2 Part 1: Essay)

Structuring your essay

➤ EXPERT WRITING page 192

As with all discursive essays, you need to express what you want to say clearly, using appropriate discourse markers throughout.

1 Here are some discourse markers for discursive essays. Working in pairs, put them into the correct category below. See Expert writing on page 203 for further categories.

although as a result it may be true (that) moreover certainly consequently even so finally first of all for example for instance furthermore granted however if in my view/opinion in particular in spite of/despite in the first place in addition as well as (that) nevertheless of course on the contrary on the one hand … on the other hand so still then therefore what is more while whereas yet

1 adding: _____
2 concession: _____
3 contrasting: _____
4 giving examples: _____
5 giving your opinion: _____
6 result: _____
7 structuring: _____

2a Read the texts below, which are personal responses to the quotations, A and B. Complete the texts with a word or phrase from Exercise 1. More than one phrase might be possible.

A

'Have nothing in your house that you do not know to be useful, or believe to be beautiful.' (William Morris)

(1) _____ , the idea of having only useful or beautiful items in your house is indeed something we could all aspire to. (2) _____ , how many of us actually manage to live in that way? (3) _____ , we all tend to accumulate a multitude of possessions which, for one reason or another, we are loath to part with. (4) _____ , there's the glass bowl that Aunt Minny gave me a few years ago. Instead of throwing it away, I end up keeping it (5) _____ it's not really useful or beautiful. (6) _____ there are the souvenirs we bought which, (7) _____ seeming a good idea at the time, now don't really fit in with our décor.

B

'Any old place I can hang my hat is home sweet home to me.' (William Jerome)

(8) _____ , we are all free to do whatever we like with the place we live in. If we are fortunate enough to live in a place of our own, then that is where we can express our personality. Interior designers might try to tell us what to do; (9) _____ , I feel strongly that your home is what you yourself make it. (10) _____ , my personal principles would be the following: you should feel comfortable in your own particular 'space', you should only follow general guidelines (11) _____ they suit your particular situation and (12) _____ , you should trust in your own judgement!

➤ EXPERT STRATEGIES page 169

b Now do the task below, using the two texts in Exercise 2a. Try to include discourse markers from Exercise 1 and some of the language from Language development 1 on page 125.

Read the two texts. Write an essay summarising and evaluating the key points from both texts. Use your own words throughout as far as possible, and include your own ideas in your answers. Write your answer in **240–280** words.

Listening 2 (Paper 3 Part 1)

Before you listen

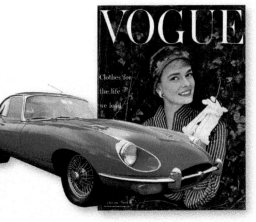

1a Fashions come and go in clothing but also in many other areas of life. What other areas can you think of?

b As fashions change, 'vintage' – things from a previous era – becomes something to be admired or collected. What vintage items can you think of?

c What types of clothes have you worn in the past that you would not consider wearing now? Explain your reasons.

2 Can you describe what the following jobs in the fashion industry might entail? Can you name any others?

visual merchandise designer   costume designer   clothing pattern maker
textile artist   seamstress

Multiple-choice questions

➤ EXPERT STRATEGIES page 170

3 🎧 T2.09 Read the strategy on page 170, then do the task.

You will hear three different extracts. For questions 1–6, choose the answer (A, B or C) which fits best according to what you hear. There are two questions for each extract.

Extract One

You hear an interview with a man who collects vintage cars.

1 What does Harry recommend that potential collectors should do?

A set a budget before beginning the collection

B focus on the particular type of car you're interested in

C be ready to consider whatever opportunities come your way

2 When Harry buys vintage cars,

A the condition is relatively unimportant to him.

B he tends to regard them as a short-term investment.

C he often has to talk their owners into parting with them.

Extract Two

You hear part of an interview with a fashion expert on the subject of sourcing products.

3 How does she feel about the working conditions in clothing factories?

A disappointed with the current situation

B encouraged by ongoing developments

C pessimistic about the coming years

4 When asked about eco-friendly labels, she explains that

A manufacturers regularly mislead the public.

B natural materials do not always carry them.

C the real situation is more complicated than it seems.

Extract Three

You hear a woman giving a talk about her work as a freelance stylist.

5 What does she suggest about it?

A Her contribution goes largely unappreciated.

B Her clients are unreasonably demanding.

C Her role is quite challenging.

6 What is she doing in this part of her talk?

A explaining the process behind a finished product

B encouraging young people to follow her career

C complaining that her work is time-consuming

Development and discussion

4 Discuss the following question.

When you buy an item of clothing, what things do you look for mainly (brand, comfort, cost, durability, etc.)? Compare your ideas with a partner.

5 Check the meaning of these key words and phrases from the audioscript.

> **EXPERT WORD CHECK**
>
> root (sth) out   go with the flow   stash (sth) away   mainstream   turn the corner
> clear-cut   give free rein to   get full credit (for)   wow factor   perseverance

Speaking (Paper 4 Part 3)

Vocabulary: collecting and collectibles

1 Here is a sample of items people collect. Discuss the following questions.

antiques   artwork   autograph books   books   cameras   CDs/DVDs
china ornaments   coins   comic books   entertainment memorabilia
models   porcelain   postcards   posters   radios, etc.   recipes
rocks and minerals / fossils   silver spoons   souvenirs   stamps
teddy bears   vintage clothing   vinyl records/albums

1 Have you collected or do you collect any of these items?
2 Which of the items would increase most in value over the years?
3 Sometimes items are collected or kept for their sentimental value. Which of the items are most likely to fall into this category?

2a The text below gives some tips on collecting. Quickly read the text and identify the two main points the writer makes.

Collecting entertainment memorabilia

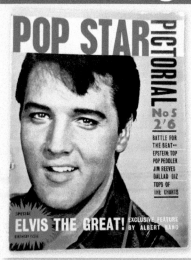

If you are thinking about starting a collection of entertainment memorabilia, there are some important **(1)** *guidelines / plans* to keep in mind. Perhaps the most important thing to remember whether you are collecting for **(2)** *security / investment* purposes or for personal enjoyment is to always buy things you genuinely enjoy. While there are certain **(3)** *styles / trends* in the various collecting markets, it is difficult to consider any of them a sure thing and although the memorabilia market has shown great **(4)** *promise / ability*, there are no guarantees. Collecting pieces you truly find appealing is the best defence against a piece not **(5)** *appreciating / escalating* as much or as quickly as you might have **(6)** *awaited / anticipated*. Another general **(7)** *principle / principal* in collecting is to buy the best pieces within your price **(8)** *limit / range*. Quality vs **(9)** *amount / quantity* should be your mantra. In ten years' time, your collection will **(10)** *command / demand* much more respect if it contains a few really great pieces rather than several average pieces.

b Now circle the correct words in the text, making a note of any useful collocations you find.

Useful language: communication strategies

3 Here are some useful phrases you can use in order to clarify or give further information about what you are saying. Read the extract of spoken language and circle the correct phrase.

I mean   I suppose   in that sense   not only that   so to speak, somehow   sort of   the thing is that   well   when it comes to   you know you see   that's why

Well, I'm not really a person who likes collecting. **(1)** *Somehow / You see*, I have minimalist tendencies which means lots of clean, clear space – uncluttered, **(2)** *so to speak / that's why!* **(3)** *The thing is that / Not only that*, but I like to spend what money I have on travelling: that's my one luxury. **(4)** *When it comes to / Somehow* travelling and holidays have become the thing I work towards every year. **(5)** *When it comes to / In that sense* possessions, I try not to accumulate too many but it's not that easy. **(6)** *The thing is that / In that sense* I grew up in a home where my mother hoarded everything so it's **(7)** *the thing is / sort of* ingrained in me to want to keep things! **(8)** *That's why / Not only that* I have to fight against this tendency all the time.

Individual long turn

> EXPERT STRATEGIES page 171

4a Work in pairs. Student A should respond to the question on Task card 1 (two minutes). Student B should respond briefly to their question (one minute). ⏱ Time yourselves!

Task card 1
What would you say are the most important features of a home?
• décor
• location
• personal possessions

Question for Student B:
• What are the most important features of your home, in your opinion?

b Student B should respond to the question on Task card 2 (two minutes). Student A should respond briefly to their question (one minute). ⏱ Time yourselves!

Task card 2
How does fashion influence our lives?
• clothes
• art and architecture
• collectibles

Question for Student A:
• Do you tend to prefer modern or traditional styles of architecture? Why?

Developing the discussion

5 Discuss the following questions.

1 Do you think changing fashions are a reflection of our consumer society?
2 If you had the money, time and opportunity, what sort of item would you collect?
3 Architects continue to design very high skyscrapers. What is your opinion of such buildings?

forgeries → fake documents (handwritten)

Language development 2

Infinitive or -ing form?

> EXPERT GRAMMAR page 186

-ing form, to + infinitive or infinitive without to?

1 Complete the sentences with the correct form of the verbs below.

~~agree~~ ~~ask~~ ~~be~~ ~~choose~~ ~~go~~ ~~inform~~ postpone
~~sell~~ ~~spend~~ ~~warn~~

1 We were advised *to choose* neutral shades for our living room but I wanted green.
2 I'd rather not *going (go)* to the fashion show, if you don't mind.
3 Steve claims *to be* an expert on 19th-century art.
4 Jenny always avoids *spending* money if she possibly can!
5 I don't really expect you *to agree* with me on this matter.
6 The customers appreciated us *warning* them about the forgeries.
7 Are you contemplating *selling* your book collection online?
8 It really didn't occur to me *to ask* for professional advice.
9 I regret *to inform* you that the museum will be closed tomorrow due to strike action.
10 We'd better *postpone* doing up the living room until next year.

Dependent prepositions + -ing or infinitive?

2 Complete the dialogue with *to*, *at* or *of* and the correct form of the verbs.

Jack: Sally, why don't we take advantage (1) *of* the weather (2) *being* (be) warmer at this time of year and have a five-day break in Florence? It'd be a chance to brush up my Italian and do the round of the art galleries.

Sally: Oh Jack, I'm sorry but I'm committed (3) *to* (4) *organising* (organise) this conference at the moment and I'm really reluctant (5) *at to* (6) *changing/change* (change) anything right now.

Jack: Well, you're a genius (7) *at* (8) *delegating* (delegate) – isn't there anyone who could help out?

Sally: Actually, in addition (9) *to* (10) *being overwhelming/overwhelmed* (overwhelm) at work, I've also got my training for next month's half-marathon …

Jack: OK, Miss Workaholic! So, would you consider the possibility (11) *of* (12) *taking* (take) an autumn break instead?

Sally: OK, let's book right away!

Phrases + -ing form or to + infinitive?

3a How do you feel about your home? Are you fanatically tidy? Are you hopelessly untidy? Using the phrases below, plus some of the phrases from Exercise 2, write a short paragraph about yourself. Make sure you get the right verb form after the preposition!

be (radically) opposed to   be guilty of
have a tendency to   have difficulty in
make up your mind to   take the trouble to

(handwritten) In my room, generally speaking I have a tendency to... be the tidiest person ever. I am radically opposed to my brother, who has difficulty in having the things at their respective? places. I must confess, I am guilty of being a hopelessly tidy person.

b

Ope

> EXP

4

... one word in each gap. There is an example at the beginning (0).

Happy hearts

Born in the Czech Republic, the supermodel Petra Nemcova was scouted walking through Prague (0) *as* a young girl. She worked her (1) *way* up through the ranks, gracing the covers of magazines such as *Vogue*, *Harper's Bazaar*, *Elle* and *Sports Illustrated*, to name but a few. (2) *Although* Petra may be well known for her modelling career, she has also gained public acclaim in recent years (3) *because* of her philanthropic work.

It was the Thailand tsunami of 2004 that (4) *set* ~~brought~~ about this change in Petra's life. (5) *Having* been caught up in the huge wave when on holiday there, she managed to cling onto a palm tree and survive the ordeal. However, the experience (6) *brought/had* a profound effect on Petra, who decided to help children affected by similar natural disasters. The Happy Hearts Fund, a not-for-profit foundation that she (7) *set* up, has been involved in various charitable projects, including the rebuilding of schools in disaster areas. As she says, (8) *whereas* her modelling work brings glamour and beauty to people, helping others brings depth and meaning to her life. (6/8)

Discussion

5 Do you know of any other celebrities who are involved in charity work? What do you think of their involvement in this type of activity?

Use of English 2 (Paper 1 Part 3)

Word formation

Lead-in **1** Discuss the following questions.

1 When you buy something – an item of clothing, an electronic item, etc. – how long do you expect it to last?
2 Have you had personal experience of a reasonably new item not working properly or wearing out fast? What did you do?
3 What would you pay more for: something that will last longer or something that is fashionable?

Developing skills: **2** There are many different ways of forming verbs:
forming verbs
- by adding a prefix, e.g. *dis-*, *en-*, *mis-*, *re-*
- by adding or changing the suffix, e.g. *-ate*, *-fy*, *-ise/ize*, *-y*, *-en*
- by adding another word as prefix, e.g. *back-*, *down-*, *out-*, *over-*, *up-*
- by adding or changing both prefix and suffix
- by making internal changes

Word formation **3** Read the strategy on page 167, then do the task.

> EXPERT STRATEGIES page 167

For questions 1–8, read the text below. Use the word given in CAPITALS at the end of some of the lines to form a word that fits in the gap in the same line. There is an example at the beginning (0).

Built-in obsolescence

Built-in obsolescence is a classic feature of **(0)** _consumerism_ . Products are designed	**CONSUMER**
to have a limited lifespan, and manufacturers are always developing new products,	
which will supersede those currently available. This is, therefore, a business strategy	
that aims to maintain demand for products by **(1)** ensuring that people feel a need to	**SURE**
buy a replacement for what they already have, **(2)** respectfully of its state of repair.	**RESPECT**
	irrespective
This practice is particularly **(3)** unprevail in the electronics industry, where there is	**PREVAIL**
prevalent	
seemingly constant **(4)** updating and remodelling of gadgets. What's more, the time	**DATE**
span between the launch of a product and the launch of its **(5)** successor, or the	**SUCCEED**
version with the latest 'must-have' feature, is often **(6)** remarkably short. Similarly, car	**REMARK**
manufacturers encourage us to view their products as indicators of our social status,	
making us more likely to feel we should go for an **(7)** upgrade.	**GRADE**
But is built-in obsolescence such a bad thing? One marketing guru views it as a	
natural **(8)** extension of the free-market economy, fuelled by technological advance –	**EXTEND**
maybe he has a point.	

6/8

Discussion **4** Discuss the following questions.

1 Do you agree with the final opinion mentioned in the text? Why/ Why not?
2 What other examples of built-in obsolescence have you come across or can you think of?
3 It has been said that we live in a consumer society. How could you best summarise that concept in one sentence?

Writing 2 (Paper 2 Part 1: Essay)

Lead-in **1** Have a mini class debate about the following statement.

'We believe that fashion is a multi-million dollar industry that serves no useful function in society. It should be banned.'

- One team should think of at least three ideas in support of the statement and the other team should think of at least three arguments against the statement.
- Whichever team argues the most convincingly and gets the most class votes wins!

Understand the task **2** Read the task below. Identify the two main points each text refers to.

Read the two texts below. Write an essay summarising and evaluating the key points from both texts. Use your own words throughout as far as possible, and include your own ideas in your answers.

Write your answer in **240–280** words.

1 **Ever-changing fashion**

The problem with fashion is that it never stands still for very long – it's always changing. Cars, clothes, interior décor: if we wanted to keep up with it we'd have to be changing everything every few years! However, in a sense it makes life interesting and ensures that we never get bored! It's also fascinating to see how fashions change over the years and even how fashions come back again, if you wait long enough. Unfortunately, though, when they do come back they're never exactly the same, so it's no use trying to hang onto your clothes for thirty years.

2 **Fashionable items: a historical viewpoint**

Fashion is only interesting from the point of view of what is not in fashion! That is to say, good and fine things mostly appreciate in value the longer they are around. Vintage cars, old paintings by well-known artists, rare books, antique furniture: these are just some of the examples of the way the interest value of items often increases with the years. Think, too, of how many museums and art galleries would not have any proper function if objects and works of art had not been preserved. In this way, changing fashions supply us with a means of experiencing a past world that somehow lives on.

Analysing a model answer

3 Read the first part of a model answer to the task below.

1 What essay plan is the student following?
2 Do you agree with the opinions stated?
3 Underline the phrases where the student:
  • summarises in their own words.
  • expresses an opinion.

> The writer of the first text refers to the fact that many aspects of our lives are related to what is popular and in fashion at a particular time and how quickly this can change. However, the text also mentions that this very fact brings variety into our lives and means that we don't have to see the same things all the time. The writer makes the point, though, that when certain fashions reappear, there is always a subtle difference the second time round.
>
> I agree with the viewpoint that fashion relieves boredom to a certain extent, although the fact that fashions in clothing change so rapidly can mean that people have to go to quite a lot of expense in order to keep up with them. It's true that fashions reoccur but I think it's unlikely that we will ever wear what they used to wear in the 18th century, for example!

Language and content: referring to the writer

4a You will need to mention what each writer says as part of the summarising procedure. Here are some examples:

argues for/against (+ noun or *-ing*)
claims (*that …* or *to* + inf)
supports (*the idea that* or *of* + *-ing*)
outlines the importance of (+ noun or *-ing*)
makes particular mention of/mentions/states (+ noun or *-ing*)
refers to/advocates/suggests (+ noun or *-ing*)
makes the point (*that …*)

You can also use the phrases on page 126 (Writing 1).

b Write three sentences about the opinions expressed in Exercise 2, text 2, using some of the phrases in Exercise 4a.

Write your essay

> EXPERT STRATEGIES page 169

5 Do the task in Exercise 2, substituting the text below for text 1 in the task.

| Designer vs. High Street fashion

The world of designer fashion – or *haute couture*, as it's called – often seems to be a million miles away from our day-to-day reality, although it sometimes gets filtered down to us lesser mortals through the more easily accessible High Street fashion outlets. Still, would life be any more interesting if it didn't exist? That's possibly much the same as saying that art or classical music shouldn't exist. Who are we to judge? In the meantime, we continue to roll our eyes in amazement at some of the fantastic creations that appear on our catwalks and wonder whether anyone actually ever wears them!

Check your essay

> EXPERT WRITING page 191

6 Edit your essay, using the checklist on page 191.

Review

1 Match the features with their meanings.

1 skylight	5 furnishings
2 porch	6 beam
3 parquet	7 alcove
4 loft	

a a type of flooring made of small flat blocks of wood

b the furniture, plus curtains, etc. in a room

c an entrance covered by a roof outside the front door

d a window in the roof of a building

e a room or space under the roof of a building

f a place in the wall of a room that is built further back than the rest of the wall

g a long heavy piece of wood used in buildings

2 Complete the text with the discourse markers below.

so	similarly	of course	just as	in particular
in other words	in a word	as I see it		

The issue of beauty in art has always been a thorny problem and one that has culminated in numerous heated discussions. **(1)** _____ , the role of art and architecture should be to add something of beauty – not ugliness – to our world. **(2)** _____ , the role of art and architecture should be to enhance our lives, perhaps even taking them to a different aesthetic level. **(3)** _____ we all like to see things of beauty in the world around us, **(4)** _____ surely we should want to see that beauty reflected in our art forms. **(5)** _____ , it might be argued that music has much the same role in our lives – it should be a thing of harmony that reflects, as people have said in the past, the harmony of the cosmos. **(6)** _____ , this view is not shared by everyone, **(7)** _____ those artists who display ugly, everyday objects in the name of Modern Art or those musicians whose music is full of clashes and discordant sounds! **(8)** _____ , beauty remains in the eye of the beholder and what we personally believe to be beautiful is rarely the result of rational deliberation.

3 Choose the correct words to complete the sentences.

1 Take a _____ look at that portrait, Alice – don't the eyes seem to follow you around the room?
   A near   B short   C strong   D good

2 He made a _____ decision to buy the painting even though it was a bit pricey.
   A brief   B poor   C snap   D fast

3 That private art gallery has benefitted _____ the interest of wealthy patrons.
   A with   B about   C from   D by

4 It's no _____ hoping you'll get round the museum quickly – there's just too much to see!
   A use   B point   C hope   D prospect

5 They are going to _____ finding an interior designer for their new house.
   A look after   B give up   C take up   D look into

6 I'm afraid he has no _____ of finding a buyer for that collection of cracked old records!
   A potential   B chance   C objection   D difficulty

4 Complete the text with the words below.

trouble	tendency	need	mood	likely	lengths
keen	how	bound	advisable		

Imagine that you and your family are either moving to a new house or have decided to redecorate your present one. You are in no **(1)** _____ to fork out a lot of money on this but you are **(2)** _____ to change the colour scheme and generally upgrade the look. Never fear! Here are a few quick and easy tips as to how you can maintain your sanity during this period of transformation!

- Firstly, there is no **(3)** _____ to go to great **(4)** _____ to choose wallpaper or think up elaborate patterns for the walls. Simply choose one main colour then paint the house in different shades of that colour. The effect will be both restful and chic.
- A few pots of paint don't cost the earth and if you know **(5)** _____ to wield a brush or a paint roller, you're **(6)** _____ to find the whole process relatively easy.
- If you have a **(7)** _____ to be messy, it's **(8)** _____ to cover all the furniture with plastic sheeting before you start! Of course, some splashes are **(9)** _____ to happen but try and wipe these off with a soft cloth before they dry.
- Once the painting is done, take the **(10)** _____ to change a few details of the decor as well: for example, the light switches, the door handles, the lamp shades. You'd be surprised how much difference that makes. Happy painting!

Overview

9A
➤ **Reading and Use of English:** Multiple choice (Part 5); Word formation (Part 3)
➤ **Listening:** Multiple matching (Part 4)
➤ **Language development:** Sentence adverbials; Gradable and ungradable adjectives
➤ **Writing:** Essay (Part 2); Developing your points

9B
➤ **Listening:** Multiple choice (Part 3)
➤ **Speaking:** Individual long turn (Part 3): Food and nutrition
➤ **Reading and Use of English:** Multiple-choice cloze (Part 1)
➤ **Language development:** Adjectives + prepositions; Prepositional phrases; Mixed prepositions
➤ **Writing:** Essay (Part 2); Effective use of discourse markers

Lead-in

1   What kind of skills and personal attributes are necessary for the sports depicted [shown] in the photographs? Use the words below to help you.

determination   dedication   stamina   mental and physical agility   passion

2   In pairs, discuss the quotations below. Which one(s) do you agree with? Which ones would you try to use as a motto for life in general?

'Only those who risk going too far can possibly find out how far one can go.'
(T. S. Eliot, poet)

'One man can be a crucial ingredient on a team, but one man cannot make a team.'
Kareem Abdul-Jabbar, former basketball player

'If all the year were playing holidays; To sport would be as tedious as to work.'
King Henry IV (William Shakespeare, playwright)

Reading (Paper 1 Part 5)

Before you read

1a What is the correct definition of 'sportsmanship'?

1. (1) behaviour that is fair, honest and polite in a game or sports competition
2. the act of showing remarkable determination in a sport
3. the act of being a strong member in a team

b Discuss the importance of sportsmanship in sport.

Skimming

2 Quickly read the text and decide which of the following statements summarises it best.

1. The impact of Wimbledon's longest-lasting match on tennis as a world sport was insignificant.
2. Following their epic tennis match at Wimbledon, John Isner and Nicolas Mahut struggled to deal with the attention they received from the media.
3. Isner and Mahut will go down in history for their tennis match but they have mixed feelings about its impact on their tennis careers.

Multiple choice

> EXPERT STRATEGIES page 168

3 You are going to read an extract from a magazine article. For questions 1–6, choose the answer (A, B, C or D) which you think fits best according to the text.

Task analysis

4 Justify your choice of answers to a partner by referring to the passage. Do you need to change any of them?

5 Check the meaning of these key words from the text.

> **EXPERT WORD CHECK**
>
> incongruous   stalemate   gangly   fidget   baggy   languid   partisan
> epic   stagger   jostle

Discussion

6a How do you think international sporting events can influence understanding between nations?

b Why do some people take up endurance sports like marathon running, the triathlon and pentathlon?

The match that would never end

In 2010, the Wimbledon tennis tournament saw the most extraordinary game of tennis in its 125-year history

If you go to the Wimbledon tennis museum, next to the famous courts where the international tournament is played each year, you can see clips and images of all the major champions. The display that attracts most attention, however, features two players who never won a title there. In 2010, Nicolas Mahut and John Isner played the most extraordinary match in the tournament's history. I was lucky enough to be there. Yet curiously, it's not an image that I recall from the match, but a sound. At seemingly incongruous moments, the spectators collectively emitted a nervous giggle, something higher and finer than laughter. It was the noise of people watching a tightrope walk, not a tennis match. And it told you one thing: they were on the edge of their seats, enthralled by the idea that a result could sit on a knife edge for so long.

It's usually impossible for professional tennis matches to go on for eleven hours. The rules at major tournaments provide for tie-breakers, designed to end the stalemate if no player wins by a clear margin after a given number of games. Wimbledon is one of only three major tournaments to play men's singles with no tie-breaker. Although in theory, matches could go on forever, most finish within a predictable time frame. Few people expected a classic on that warm Tuesday evening. The gangly Isner was fancied to beat the low-ranked Mahut in routine fashion. When the players walked onto court to light applause, Mahut fidgeted with the necklace underneath his Lacoste shirt. Isner, dressed in baggy whites and backwards cap, looked disarmingly languid. There was no hint of the epic struggle to come. When play was suspended for bad light, the score was level, with no clear victor emerging.

The following day, the match continued in the same vein, with neither player able to break the deadlock. Some spectators began to split into partisan camps, whilst others started to get anxious for the players, especially Isner, who appeared shattered. He could still hit the ball cleanly but between points he staggered around, often with a towel hanging out of his mouth. Mahut meanwhile, skipped out of his chair at the restarts and sprinted for every ball. That contrast in body language is what stays with me as an abiding image. 'I could see he was very tired,' remembers Mahut. 'I was tired too, of course, but I wanted him to think I was unstoppable. It was a second fight, a psychological fight.'

Meanwhile, news of the extraordinary match had trickled around the championship. Spectators began to jostle for room in the standing area above the official seating. In the wider world, too, the pair had caught the public imagination – the drama had hypnotised them and the pair had officially entered the record books. During the latter stages of Wednesday's play, Isner couldn't believe how Mahut managed to keep going. The answer was adrenalin. Mahut remembers sitting down at the changeover and 'feeling the electricity from the crowd'. By Thursday morning, the seemingly endless tennis match had gone viral – the eyes of the world were upon them.

How did it feel to play tennis like that? 'It was the biggest moment of my life,' says Mahut, gravely. 'It was magical.' He still finds the moment of defeat difficult to discuss. 'In my mind, it was the only tennis match I have ever played where I knew I couldn't lose,' he says. 'So, when I did … ' Certainly, in the immediate aftermath, he suffered a breakdown, weeping inconsolably in the locker room. Finding it hard to stand or breathe, he kept asking the same question: 'Did I lose the match, or did he win it?'

A week later, Mahut sent Isner an email, telling him he showed 'incredible fair play' throughout, and 'real class' by celebrating his victory in a humble manner. He also thanked Isner, because the match had taught him that 'everything that had been written about my physical and mental boundaries was wrong'. These lessons, however, were slow to register, with Mahut experiencing injuries and depression before recovering his form as a player. The match inspires, rather than haunts him: 'I can see now that this isn't going into the history books as a loss or a win, but because we both achieved something unbelievable.' Oddly, Isner now finds the match more painful to discuss than Mahut. 'I'm trying to get over it, in my head,' he says. 'I want to be remembered for more than that one match.'

---

1 Why does the writer mention a sound made by spectators?

   A It revealed the effect the match was having on them.
   B It seemed to represent a spontaneous group response.
   C It reflected their frustration with the scoring system.
   D It marked a turning point in the match for the players.

2 The writer describes the scene at the start of the match in order to

   A emphasise the fact that the two players were virtually unknown.
   B underline how unprepared the spectators were for what followed.
   C provide readers with an insight to the atmosphere at tournaments.
   D suggest why the players were unable to finish the match that day.

3 On the second day of play, the writer recalls feeling

   A struck by the contrast in the two players' behaviour.
   B touched by the anxiety the crowd showed towards Isner.
   C concerned about the signs of exhaustion from both players.
   D impressed that the spectators supported both Mahut and Isner.

4 The writer suggests that, by the end of the second day

   A the crowd was distracting the players.
   B interest in the tennis itself had waned.
   C a milestone in tennis history had been reached.
   D the players' commitment was beginning to flag.

5 According to the writer, after the match Mahut felt

   A totally exhausted.   C extremely relieved.
   B utterly devastated.   D incredibly inspired.

6 In the final paragraph, the writer reveals his surprise that

   A a feeling of empathy has developed between the two players.
   B Mahut now regards the match as a wholly positive experience.
   C it took both players so long to get over the effects of the match.
   D Isner has difficulty coming to terms with the impact of the match.

137

Vocabulary

Adjective + adverb collocations

1 Choose the adverb which best completes the collocation in the following sentences.

perceptibly   bitterly   perfectly   remarkably   deeply
painfully

1 Rachel was _bitterly_ disappointed when she lost the match against Carrie.
2 Construction of the new football stadium has been _painfully_ slow, due to adverse weather conditions.
3 Ellen MacArthur is _remarkabl_ talented, having achieved a great deal both in the sailing world and through her charity work with sick children.
4 The crowd showed _perceptibly_ more interest when Kenya's marathon runner Geoffrey Mutai walked onto the race track.
5 Alice was _deeply_ moved by her opponent's show of respect towards her.
6 Petra assured her coach she was _perfectly_ capable of finishing the race, despite her broken arm.

Words of endurance

2a Complete the text with the words below. Use each word only once.

ordeal   challenge   isolation   resourceful
remarkable   endurance   overcome   perseverance

Endurance ✗

Epic tales of (1) _isolation_ at sea abound, but Steven Callahan's story of survival is in a league of its own. In 1981, this (2) _remarkable_ sailor drifted in a life raft across the Atlantic Ocean but unlike other adventurers who have undertaken solo transatlantic voyages, his was unplanned. The sudden sinking of his yacht forced him to abandon ship into an inflatable life raft. With nobody aware that he was missing, he then had to endure a seventy-six day (3) _ordeal_ in this tiny leaking raft, fully aware that his food and water supplies were mournfully inadequate. Showing (4) _remarkable_ fortitude, he confronted the (5) _challenge_ of obtaining food and water with both ingenuity and a great deal of (6) _endurance_. He struggled at times to (7) _overcome_ feelings of (8) _perseverance_ and despair but the fact that he survived to tell the tale is a testament to this man's courage and determination.

b _Endurance_ and _perseverance_ are not only applicable to sports – describe a situation in which you or someone you know displayed some of the qualities listed below.

resourcefulness   stamina   drive   persistence
willpower   perseverance

Expressions with *keep*

3a Which of the following expressions with *keep* mean 'to persevere or persist' in doing something?

keep it up   keep it back   keep going   keep trying
keep him in   keep at it   keep to   keep out of

b Match the most suitable responses of encouragement to the statements. Some may fit more than one statement. Decide which one is best in each case.

1 Coach said I ran faster today. (A) (C)
2 I've run 64 of the 70-mile race. (C) (D)
3 I haven't finished my training programme but I'm exhausted. (D) (A)
4 I didn't make it onto the team this week. (B)

a Keep at it.
b Keep trying.
c Keep it up.
d Keep going.

Phrasal verbs with *get*

4a Choose the correct particle(s) to complete the phrasal verbs in the following sentences.

1 John Isner had difficulty getting *on with / over* his win against Nicolas Mahut.
2 We need to get *down / up* to some serious training if we're going to win the championship.
3 Jodie is doing extremely well, and has got *on / through* to the semi-finals.
4 Raoul is trying to get *ahead / along* in Formula 1 racing, but he needs to join a stronger team if he wants to win.
5 Enrique hates after-match parties, and is trying to get *over / out of* going tonight.
6 Isner and Mahut ended up getting *about / along* and have remained firm friends since their epic match.
7 Not having a car, Keira gets *ahead / about* mainly on horseback, using public transport only to go into the city.
8 Yelena is trying to get *round / in* with the basketball coach at college, as she wants to be chosen for the team.
9 The athlete got away *with / from* using performance enhancing drugs for several years but was finally caught just weeks before the Olympic Games.
10 John studied physical education but then got *down to / into* sports therapy.

b Make your own sentences with the phrasal verbs from Exercise 4a that did not fit.

Idioms with *get* and *keep*

5 Match the first half of the sentence in column A with its ending in column B.

A

1 There's a lot of truth in the saying *When the going gets tough, the tough*
2 Training hasn't being going well, and
3 Laura was easily defeated by her opponent, and she
4 The match starts in 20 minutes, so you'd better
5 I firmly believe in proverbs such as *An apple a day*
6 Yarek found ice hockey hard at first but he's starting to
7 Damian really wants to win this match, so
8 Ellen has got a new personal trainer, so I

B

a *keeps the doctor away.*
b get the hang of it.
c *get going.*
d wonder how she's getting on.
e found it hard to keep a stiff upper lip after the match.
f keep your fingers crossed.
g it's getting her down.
h get a move on.

Word formation: use of the prefixes *over* and *under*

6a Match the words below with the prefixes *over* and *under*. Some may go with both.

come	estimate	mine	cover	take	shadow
head	hand	cut	dog	awed	board	go
crowded	developed	wrought	power	pin	

b Explain the use of the words in *italics* in the following sentences.

1 When I watch a tennis match, I often favour the *underdog*, as I enjoy seeing people win against the odds.
2 The spectators' show of support towards Ken's opponent began to *undermine* his confidence.
3 *Overawed* by the fact that he was playing for such a famous team, Christian's first match for Real Madrid was not a good one.
4 Alex *underestimated* the difficulty of the climb, and found he was unable to make it to the summit.
5 The Olympic Games were *overshadowed* by the discovery that some athletes had been taking illegal steroids.
6 Realising his companion was unable to move with a broken ankle, Carl *undertook* the task of going for help.
7 Devastated at losing the race by a millisecond, the *overwrought* athlete shouted abuse at his trainer.
8 Ellen MacArthur *overcame* many hardships when participating in the Vendée Globe single-handed round-the-world yacht race.

Use of English 1 (Paper 1 Part 3)

Word formation

> **EXPERT STRATEGIES** page 167

1 For questions 1–8, read the text below. Use the word given in CAPITALS at the end of some of the lines to form a word that fits in the gap in the same line. There is an example at the beginning (0).

Edison Peña

Edison Peña is living proof that sport can be a **(0)** _powerful_ tool. The Chilean miner was trapped two-thousand feet underground with thirty-two others for sixty-nine days. Most people would find this appalling situation **(1)** UNBEARING (ADJ) UNBEARABLE and Edison almost lost his battle against **(2)** DESPONSIBI (N) DESPONDENCY. Amazingly, what helped him to overcome such feelings was jogging through the **(3)** EXTENDED (ADJ) EXTENSIVE system of underground tunnels. He believes he managed to survive his ordeal by concentrating on the **(4)** MAINTAIN (N) MAINTENANCE ANCE of a strict fitness routine. Running around six miles a day, his **(5)** PERSISTON (N) PERSISTENCE paid off, and he emerged from the ordeal in relatively good shape. **POWER**

BEAR

DESPOND

EXTEND

MAINTAIN

PERSIST

Competitor
Competetor

Following the miners' dramatic rescue, Peña was invited to attend the New York Marathon, not as a **(6)** COMPETITOR (N) but as an honoured spectator, the organisers having been impressed by his story. They **(7)** UNDERESTIMATED (ADJ) him, however, because he asked to compete. Disarmingly **(8)** CHARMED (ADJ) CHARMING, Peña captivated the New York crowds. Not only did he run the race, but he finished it in less than the six hours he had set himself. **COMPETE**

ESTIMATE

CHARM

Discussion

2 Why do some people run for the sake of running?

Writing

3 Sport and sporting personalities have often been a source of inspiration to people of all ages. Write a short article outlining one example of this. Use words and phrases from this section to help you express your ideas.

Listening 1 (Paper 3 Part 4)

Before you listen

1 Sporting accidents occur frequently. What are some of the risks involved in the following sports?

sailing   show jumping   karate   basketball   skiing   sky diving

2 Describe a situation in which you took a risk. Use the words below to express how you felt:

a at the time.   **b** after the incident.

exhilarated   shattered   petrified   excited   overwhelmed   relieved
ashamed

Multiple matching

> EXPERT STRATEGIES page 171

3 T2.10 Read the strategy on page 171, then do the task.

You will hear five short extracts in which footballers are talking about injuries.

Task One
For questions **1–5**, choose from the list (**A–H**) what caused each speaker's injury.

Task Two
For questions **6–10**, choose from the list (**A–H**) the long-term impact of the injury on each speaker.

You will hear the recording twice. While you listen, you must complete both tasks.

A a kick to the head	
B a momentary loss of concentration	1
C a badly timed attempt to prevent a goal	2
D hesitation before diving for the ball	
E a poorly-aimed tackle	3
F two blows in the same game	4
G a teammate's misjudgement	5
H misinterpreting an opponent's intentions	

A anxiety at the start of each match	
B limitations in performance	6
C fear of causing injury to others	7
D abandoning the sport	
E reluctance to engage with the ball	8
F slow return to full fitness	9
G acceptance of the risks involved	
H reduced speed on the field	10

Discussion

4 Discuss the following question.

What attracts people to team sports?

• the challenge   • being part of a team   • keeping in shape

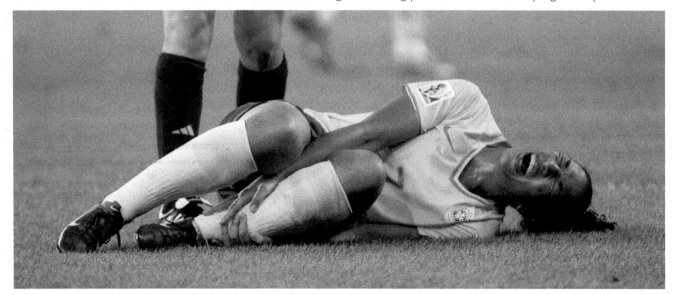

Language development 1

Sentence adverbials; modifying and intensifying gradable and ungradable adjectives

> EXPERT GRAMMAR page 187

Sentence adverbials

1a The penultimate sentence of the text in Exercise 4 begins with *Incredible though it may sound*. What is the effect of using this phrase?

b Complete the following responses with the words and phrases below.

Surprisingly   Incredible though (x2)   Believe it
Difficult as

---

1 'So, were you surprised when Helena won the race?' '_____ or not, I'd been expecting it.'
2 'It's odd that Jamie hasn't contacted us since he left for Liverpool, isn't it?' '_____ it may sound, I'm not worried at all, as I've heard he's training hard.'
3 'I thought you'd given up riding after your accident.' '_____ it is to believe, I couldn't wait to get back in the saddle.'
4 'Where's Sonya these days?' '_____ enough, she's head of the physical training department at the college down the road from here.'
5 'I thought you'd be playing basketball professionally by now.' '_____ it may seem, I've given up playing altogether.'

Common adverb + adjective collocations

2 Circle the adjective that does NOT collocate with each of the following adverbs.

   1 bitterly   *cold / disappointed / opposed / exhausted*
   2 deeply   *ashamed / angry / moved / unhappy / attached / upset*
   3 entirely   *beneficial / unexpected / shattered / true / different / satisfactory*
   4 heavily   *guarded / loaded / armed / polluted / trained*
   5 highly   *likely / qualified / captivated / trained / critical*
   6 painfully   *slow / aware / bored / obvious / shy*
   7 perfectly   *capable / confident / balanced / normal / safe / serious*
   8 totally   *convinced / excited / harmless / inadequate / unbelievable*
   9 utterly   *devastated / crazy / shattered / useless / beneficial / impossible*
   10 widely   *available / known / publicised / used / read / opposed / understood*

3 In sentences 1–6, circle the adverb (A–D) which CANNOT be used.

   1 Jake's performance in the match today was _____ awful!
     A absolutely   B completely   C perfectly
     D thoroughly
   2 Stoke City's 3-0 win against Liverpool was _____ unexpected.
     A deeply   B totally   C utterly   D entirely
   3 I think it's _____ unlikely that Heather will win the race in Gateshead tomorrow.
     A highly   B utterly   C extremely   D fairly
   4 Don't worry! Kirsty will be _____ safe swimming in the lake with her new coach.
     A deeply   B perfectly   C completely   D totally
   5 I'm not _____ sure that amateurs can enter this competition.
     A entirely   B absolutely   C thoroughly
     D completely
   6 Ivan was _____ ashamed of his rude behaviour towards the umpire in the cricket match yesterday.
     A deeply   B painfully   C totally   D thoroughly

4 Complete the text below with the adverbs below. Use each adverb only once.

---
deceptively   quite   absolutely   stupidly
reassuringly   rather   thoroughly   slightly
somewhat   pretty   decidedly   totally

Leaving Dover

The wind was already rising in a **(1)** _____ alarming manner, and the outlook for the next few days was **(2)** _____ bleak. Jeff looked at me and said, 'It's going to get **(3)** _____ rough out there. Are you sure you still want to come?' The inner harbour in Dover was **(4)** _____ peaceful at the time, and, **(5)** _____ convinced that I could handle anything, I replied there was no way I was going to miss it. I had no idea how **(6)** _____ naive I was being.

We motored out, and my eyes eagerly sought the outer harbour entrance to the sea and the elements beyond. It took me a few moments to realise that the reason I couldn't find it was that the sea had swollen to the same height as the thick outer sea wall, making it look like one solid mass.

(7) _____ shocked by this, I couldn't believe it when Jeff told me to take the wheel while he put up the mainsail. The boat was already swaying considerably, and I wondered how I was going to control it. Jeff, **(8)** _____ matter-of-fact, explained that partially raising the sail would help steady the boat. I had no choice but to grit my teeth and hang on. Jeff staggered around on deck, struggling with the sail, and at times I was **(9)** _____ terrified that he was going to fall overboard, but he finally managed to hoist the sail. I was **(10)** _____ relieved to find that the boat did indeed become steadier and **(11)** _____ easier to handle. Incredible though it may sound, given the appalling weather, once we were in the open sea, the voyage was actually **(12)** _____ enjoyable. Mind you, I wouldn't want to repeat the experience!

Writing 1 (Paper 2 Part 2: Essay)

Developing points to express your opinion in an essay

1 Read the question below and underline the key points. Then answer the questions.

> Your English teacher has asked you to write an essay evaluating the following quotation:
>
> *'Sport can teach us some valuable lessons for life. Through sport many of us first learn that fear can be overcome; that there is pride in working as part of a team, and that it is important to work together to achieve your goals.'*
>
> Write your essay, giving examples to support your views.

    1 Who is the essay for?
    2 What do you have to write about?
    3 Do you agree with the points made in the statement?

Model answer

> EXPERT STRATEGIES page 169

2a Work in pairs. Place these sentences in order to form a paragraph.

____ A Admittedly, we may have been kicking a ball around the garden with Dad at the weekend since we were toddlers, but it is at school that we tend to learn to play in groups.

____ B Furthermore, we will come to recognise the abilities of opponents, and also learn about the danger that lies in underestimating them.

____ C Through practice, however, we can learn that to do so will ultimately increase the chances of getting the desired result.

____ D Many of us first come into contact with team sport at school, and one of the most valuable lessons we gain from this is that of respect, both for our teammates and perhaps more importantly for our opponents.

____ E For instance, passing the ball to a team mate who is in a better position than us is not always easy for those of us who want to score a goal on our own.

____ F Sports such as football, basketball and volleyball teach us to share and offer each other support.

b What is the main point of the paragraph in Exercise 2a? What examples are given?

3 Write a final sentence for the paragraph in Exercise 2a to reinforce the point being made. Begin with the following words:

In this way, _____ .

4 Look at the following counter-argument to the point made in Exercise 2a. Underline the point being made, the example given to support it and the reinforcement of the point.

> Nevertheless, we should remember that not all of us are good at sport. There are many for whom the physical education lesson at school conjures up nothing but memories of shame and humiliation, simply because they did not fit into the 'team', were never chosen to be on anybody's 'side', and ended up feeling like outcasts. For them, the lessons learned from sport were often cruel ones, for you are more likely to be admired by your peers in school for your skills in sport than any academic achievement you may make.

5a Place the full paragraphs from Exercises 2, 3 and 4 in a suitable order to form the main body of an essay in answer to the question in Exercise 1.

b Write a suitable introduction and conclusion to complete the essay.

Listening 2 (Paper 3 Part 3)

Before you listen **1** Discuss the meaning of the following terms. How do these issues affect our daily lives?

- genetically-modified (GM) food
- organic farming
- pesticide and herbicide use in farming
- additives and preservatives in food
- nanotechnology

Multiple choice **2** 🎧 T2.11 Read the strategy on page 171, then do the task.

➤ EXPERT STRATEGIES page 171

You will hear two nutritionists, Fay Wells and George Fisher, discussing methods of food production. For questions 1–5, choose the answer (A, B, C or D) which fits best according to what you hear.

1 Looking at reports on the subject of GM foods, Fay feels

A pleased to read that the problem of food shortages is being addressed.
B surprised that the fears of the public are not allayed by them.
C frustrated by contradictory conclusions.
D critical of the scientists' methodology.

2 What does George suggest about organic foods?

A Consumers remain surprisingly poorly informed about them.
B People need to check out the claims made about them.
C They need to be made more attractive to meat-eaters.
D They may become more widely affordable in future.

3 What is George's opinion of 'vertical farming'?

A It could provide a realistic alternative to existing methods.
B It's a highly impractical scheme dreamt up by architects.
C It's unlikely to go much beyond the experimental stage.
D It has the potential to reduce consumption of energy.

4 George and Fay agree that the use of nanotechnology in food production will

A reduce the need for dietary supplements.
B simplify the process of food-labelling.
C complicate things for the consumer.
D introduce potential health risks.

5 In Fay's view, returning to self-sufficiency is only an option for people who

A have no need to get a return on their investment.
B are willing to accept a high level of regulation.
C reject the values of a consumer society.
D already have sufficient set-up funds.

Discussion **3** Check the meaning of these key words and phrases from the audioscript.

> **EXPERT WORD CHECK**
>
> kick off   hype   residue   be clued up (about)   afoot   prohibitive
> far-fetched   barrage   red tape   toe the line

Speaking (Paper 4 Part 3)

Vocabulary: food and nutrition

1 How do the terms in the word *cloud* relate to your daily diet? Are you careful about what you eat?

balanced diet
additives
preservatives
carbohydrates
protein
vegan
dairy
energy
nutrition
vegetarian
fibre
iron
olive oil
raw salads
fluids
fats
trans fats
pasta

2 *Food for thought*: How much do you know about what you eat? Do the quiz and find out.

1 In what foods do you find Omega 3 fatty acids?
a oily fish   **b** eggs

2 Lentils are part of which food family?
a vegetables   **b** pulses

3 Apart from sunlight, what is the next best source of Vitamin D?
a cheese   **b** salmon

4 What are calcium and iron?
a minerals   **b** vitamins

5 Which is an example of a complex carbohydrate?
a fruit   **b** wholemeal bread

6 What is a good source of protein apart from meat, fish and dairy products?
a nuts   **b** pasta

7 Which type of meal is best to eat before participating in sport?
a high-protein   **b** high-carbohydrate

8 What type of foods are convenience foods?
a low-fat   **b** pre-prepared

9 What types of food contain more iron?
a dairy products   **b** dried fruits

10 Which is worse for your health?
a margarine made out of hydrogenated oils   **b** butter

Useful language: discourse markers

3a 🎧 T2.12 Listen to a conversation between two native speakers of English about a change in lifestyle. As you listen, note down your answers to these questions.

1 Why does Maria say she doesn't buy vegetables 'out of season'? What does she imply by that?
2 What did the athletics coach suggest that Maria should do first?
3 Note down three changes that Maria made to her diet.
4 What does Maria say she's careful about in the supermarket?

b 🎧 T2.12 Now listen again and tick the discourse markers you hear in the conversation.

1 after all ☐	5 in any case ☐	9 in the same way ☐	
2 at any rate ☐	6 in fact ☐	10 on top of that ☐	
3 basically ☐	7 in particular ☐	11 to begin with ☐	
4 for one thing ☐	8 in the first place ☐	12 well actually ☐	

c Complete or connect the following sentences with the discourse markers you didn't tick in Exercise 3b.

1 The best way to keep healthy is to eat a variety of different foods, _____ , foods that you can cook from scratch. _____ , if they have been processed, then they are bound to have lost a lot of their goodness.

2 It's no wonder that people feel unhealthy if they eat all the wrong foods. _____ , it's hardly surprising that they feel sluggish if their way of life is completely sedentary. _____ , lots of people say they're too busy to take up a sport on a regular basis. My advice would be to start with a little exercise and build up – that's better than nothing, _____ !

4a Maria uses a couple of food idioms when talking to Emma: *in a nutshell* and *have a lot on my plate*. What do you think they mean?

b Here are some more useful food idioms. Substitute the underlined parts of the sentences with the correct form of the idioms below.

food for thought   pie in the sky   go bananas/nuts   hot potato
a piece of cake   walk on eggshells

1 Tim gets irritated very quickly – I always feel as if I <u>have to be very careful what I say to him</u> all the time.
2 My trainer <u>was furious</u> when I told him I was going off to the Bahamas on holiday for ten days!
3 Jane's scheme for setting up a restaurant is <u>very unlikely to ever happen</u> – she's got no money, for a start!
4 I wouldn't say that walking ten kilometres was <u>easy</u> but I managed to do it and felt very proud of myself!
5 That talk we went to about new farming technologies certainly gave us <u>something to reflect on</u>.
6 At the meeting, everyone avoided discussing the plans to build a road right through private farmland – it was a bit of a <u>difficult issue</u>.

Part 3 Individual long turn

➤ EXPERT STRATEGIES page 171

5a Work in pairs. Student A should respond to the question on Task card 1 on page 205 and talk for about two minutes. ⏱ There are some ideas on the card for you to use if you like. Student B should respond briefly to their question. Try to use some of the discourse markers from Exercise 3.

b Student B should respond to the question on Task card 2 on page 205 and talk for about two minutes. ⏱ There are some ideas on the card for you to use if you like. Student A should respond briefly to their question.

Developing the discussion

6 Discuss the following questions about nutrition in general.

1 Some people say that eating healthily is unaffordable for the average family. Do you agree?
2 In the modern world, what problems do we have to deal with regarding the purchase and preparation of food?
3 What is your opinion of fast food? Is it all unhealthy?

Language development 2

Adjectives + prepositions; prepositional phrases; mixed prepositions

> EXPERT GRAMMAR page 187

Adjectives + prepositions

1a Complete the sentences with the prepositions below. You will need to use some prepositions more than once and there are some extra prepositions you don't need.

against	at	for	in	of	on	to	with

1 People whose diet is **deficient** _____ vitamins are more **vulnerable** _____ illness.
2 I found it **difficult** _____ understand why he was so indifferent _____ what he ate.
3 Working in a cake shop was **fraught** _____ danger: I was **liable** _____ pick up a jam doughnut at the drop of a hat!
4 When Lucy was training for the marathon, she went out running every day, **irrespective** _____ the weather.
5 Unfortunately, insects and weeds that are sprayed with pesticides or herbicides eventually become **resistant** _____ the chemicals, and mutate into different forms.
6 Many people who develop diabetes become **dependent** _____ insulin injections to keep their blood sugar level down.

b Work in pairs. Think of some other situations where you could use the phrases in Exercise 1a.

Prepositional phrases

2a Complete the sentences with the words below. Then underline the completed prepositional phrases (preposition + noun) you have found.

belief	coincidence	collaboration	extent	fail
fault	impression	jeopardy	mistake	reach
response	verge			

1 There were loads of applicants in _____ to the advertisement for a personal trainer on a cruise ship!
2 The new TV chef is working in _____ with various ecological groups.
3 We were under the _____ that she was a vegetarian but we saw her having a steak the other day!
4 I'm starting my new exercise regime on Monday, without _____ !
5 I'm afraid his place in the team is in _____ after his poor performance in Australia.
6 The children were on the _____ of fainting with hunger by the time we arrived at the hotel.

7 Body-building seems to have taken over Ben's life, to a great _____ .
8 Chrissie cut into the avocado pear by _____ , thinking it was a real pear!

b Make sentences with the remaining words, using a prepositional phrase. Check the list in Expert grammar on page 188 if you are unsure.

Mixed prepositions

3a Complete the text with the missing prepositions.

Brain foods for increased intelligence

>> Your brain, which takes up at least 20 percent of your daily calorie intake, also requires a balanced and varied diet to feed your neutrons! So what foods are good **(1)** _____ your brain? Firstly, the Omega 3 fatty acids are crucial **(2)** _____ the production and maintenance **(3)** _____ brain cells and also play a part **(4)** _____ neuron activity. Weakening brain function and memory trouble can often be traced back **(5)** _____ a deficiency **(6)** _____ Omega 3. Oily fish, as we know, are one of the best sources **(7)** _____ Omega 3.

>> The brain depends **(8)** _____ glucose for its capacity **(9)** _____ memorise but beware of indulging **(10)** _____ sugary foods and confectionery. Foods like pulses, on the other hand, are rich **(11)** _____ complex sugars which don't lead **(12)** _____ sudden surges and drops **(13)** _____ your blood sugar level. Green leafy vegetables – spinach, for example – also play an active role **(14)** _____ the development of memory.

>> Shellfish provide us **(15)** _____ certain minerals that help in the fight **(16)** _____ anxiety and mental stress. Similar foods are wholemeal bread or wheatgerm. Other 'happy' foods we can benefit **(17)** _____ include bananas, berries and cocoa!

>> Avocados contribute **(18)** _____ keeping the brain young, and liver (or beef) can bring about a substantial improvement **(19)** _____ cognitive function.

>> Remember that intellectual athletes need to train their brain through study, doing puzzles, and so on. Adequate sleep, too, is essential **(20)** _____ the brain's regeneration: don't burn the candle at both ends!

b Do you think you might follow some of the nutritional advice in Exercise 3a to help you prepare for and take your examinations? Which parts of the advice might you find most helpful?

Use of English 2 (Paper 1 Part 1)

Lead-in	**1a**	When we talk of a 'balanced diet', is there only one kind of diet that suits all types of lifestyle?
	b	What kind of foods are suitable for athletes?
Reading for gist	**2**	Quickly read through the text below about the Tarahumara. What is unusual about their lifestyle?
Multiple-choice cloze	**3**	Read the strategy on page 167, then do the task.

➤ EXPERT STRATEGIES page 167

For questions 1–8, read the text below and decide which answer (A, B, C or D) best fits each gap. There is an example at the beginning (0).

The Tarahumara diet

Running **(0)** _A_ naturally to a Tarahumara. These fascinating people live in a remote region of northwest Mexico, an area totally **(1)** _C_ to normal means of transport. Even horses have difficulty **(2)** _A_ parts of the unforgiving rocky terrain. As a result, the Tarahumara **(3)** _B_ to running as a way of getting around, sometimes covering distances of up to eighty miles a day. How do they do it?

Studies suggest that alongside the physical conditioning, **(4)** _D_ by their lifestyle, diet plays an important role. The Tarahumara diet **(5)** _D_ largely of complex carbohydrates, and is almost meat-free. They generally rely on cooperative agriculture to feed the community as a whole. Pinole, a powder made of toasted corn, is the staple food, along with squash, beans and chilli. Fish and all wild plants growing nearby also **(6)** _A_ prominently in their diet. Indeed, the fact that the Tarahumara experience a low incidence of blood pressure and heart problems **(7)** _B_ weight to the argument that their diet is perfectly in **(8)** _C_ with their particular lifestyle.

	0	A comes	B works	C seems	D gains
	1	A inhospitable	B unapproachable	C inaccessible	D unattainable
	2	A negotiating	B overcoming	C embarking	D undertaking
	3	A opt	B resort	C rely	D employ
	4	A ordered	B elicited	C requested	D induced
	5	A contains	B consumes	C composes	D consists
	6	A feature	B appear	C occur	D reveal
	7	A provides	B lends	C gains	D delivers
	8	A adjustment	B compatibility	C harmony	D consensus

Task analysis	**4**	Compare your answers with a partner, then check the following. 1 Did you consider the context before making your choice of word? 2 Did you check the grammatical structures that follow each option?
Discussion	**5**	Discuss the following question. Would the Tarahumara diet suit your lifestyle? Why/Why not?

Writing 2 (Paper 2 Part 2: Essay)

Lead-in 1 How do you think future developments in food production might affect our diet? Consider the following aspects.

· GM crops   · organic farming   · processed foods

Understand the task 2 Read the exam writing task below, then answer the following question.

What should the two main paragraphs of your answer focus on?

> Following a discussion on the sources and methods of food production, your English tutor has asked you to write an essay on the benefits and drawbacks of being a vegetarian today. You should give examples to support your views.
>
> Write your essay in **280–320** words.

3a Read the model answer to the task in Exercise 2, then complete it with the words and phrases below.

Few can deny that   However   Assuming, that is   This is now
The question is   Providing   The problem with this   Generally speaking
In contrast   For one thing

b Underline the main arguments it makes.

c Highlight the example which follows each point, and the reinforcing statement which consolidates the points the writer makes.

An increasing number of people are making a conscious decision to stop eating meat. Their reasons for doing so vary. **(1)** _____ , with the present methods of commercial food production involving such things as pesticides and herbicides, and the controversy surrounding the introduction of genetically-modified crops, are they really able to maintain a healthy diet?

(2) _____ vegetarianism is potentially beneficial for your health. **(3)** _____ , by not eating red meat, you avoid the risk of some of the negative effects it can have, particularly since most livestock is packed with antibiotics and chemical hormones. **(4)** _____ you ensure a daily intake of foods like pulses and nuts, which provide nutrients present in meat, it is possible to have both a balanced and healthy diet. **(5)** _____ fairly easy to achieve because most large supermarkets stock a huge variety of food products, covering all kinds of dietary needs.

(6) _____ , the recent rise in the number of genetically modified foods on the world market has caused concern among some people over whether what we are buying is really that good for us. Some experts argue that altering the genetic makeup of plants has adverse effects on the nutrients they contain, and fear that this in turn will have a negative impact on our bodies.

(7) _____ , others claim that GM foods are perfectly safe, and are preferable to eating normal foods that have been sprayed with all kinds of pesticide. Studies conducted so far have proved inconclusive in this respect, and so it remains a hotly debated issue.

(8) _____ , with the long-term effects of chemicals and modifications largely unknown, it would seem wise to favour organic produce when shopping. **(9)** _____ , of course, is that it tends to be more expensive, and not everyone can afford to be choosey. So, the best solution might be to grow your own fruit and vegetables. **(10)** _____ , you can find non-modified seeds!

Plan your essay

4 Read the exam task below, then answer the question from Exercise 2.

> Your teacher has asked you to write an essay outlining how age, work and exercise affect a person's dietary needs.
>
> You should give reasons for your choice, and present examples to support your views.
>
> Write your essay in **280–320** words.

5a Work in pairs. Brainstorm some ideas about what factors influence the kind of diet that is suitable for a person.

• age • work • exercise

b Make a list of the way in which these factors affect the kind of food a person should eat. Think of an example to illustrate each point.

> 1) age: effects young person - food for growth; old person - healthy heart Example: young person - proteins/carbohydrates; old person - less fatty food
>
> 2) work: effects _____ Example: _____
>
> 3) exercise: effects _____ Example: _____

c Write a suitable introductory paragraph mentioning the points you intend to include.

Language and content

6a Use the ideas you brainstormed in Exercise 5 to complete the following statements.

1 There seems to be a general consensus of opinion over the fact that a person's dietary needs vary according to their age. For instance, it is widely understood that a young child needs _____ , whereas an adult _____ .

2 The reason for this _____ .

3 Admittedly, a lot depends on _____ .

4 However, in comparison with adults, children need a lot more
_____ .

5 Another point worth noting is _____ . This can be seen in
_____ . Clearly, this would suggest that _____ is true.

b Make other statements with points from Exercise 5, using some of the words and phrases below. Using your answers from Exercise 5a, build some of them into your two or three main paragraphs.

Many people believe   In general   A number of people tend to think that
Nevertheless   In this respect   In comparison with   On the other hand

Write your essay

➤ EXPERT STRATEGIES page 169

7 Write an essay in answer to the question in Exercise 4. Remember to write between **280–320** words.

Check your essay

➤ EXPERT WRITING page 191

8 Edit your essay, using the checklist on page 191.

Review

1 Circle the correct words to complete the sentences.

1 Henry was *shattered / petrified* after the marathon, and took a while to recover.
2 David was rather *overwhelmed / overwrought* after all the criticism he'd received during the training session, and really snapped at me.
3 Laura proved herself to be quite *resourceful / reckless* by managing to find her way down the mountain despite the thick fog.
4 I know you like doing parkour, but jumping from the roof of one building to the next was extremely *foolhardy / remarkable*!
5 Initially, I had trouble getting *ahead / the hang* of the rules of cricket but now I really enjoy playing.
6 Stan's *persistence / endurance* in entering competitions paid off when he won a gold medal.
7 During tennis matches, I tend to favour the *daredevil / underdog*, as I enjoy watching players beat a stronger opponent.
8 In the championship, Ivan faces the *challenge / ordeal* of improving on last year's poor performance.

2 Complete the sentences with a suitable adverb.

bitterly   heavily   deeply   entirely   highly   painfully
perfectly   totally   utterly   widely

1 Diana was _____ convinced she would win the championship.
2 Snowboarding and skateboarding require _____ different skills.
3 *You Are What You Eat* is a popular book on nutrition that is _____ read by dieticians and health professionals.
4 Jake was _____ disappointed at not being selected for the Olympic team.
5 Sally is a _____ trained karate instructor.
6 After the accident, Kate's recovery was _____ slow and frustrating.
7 Ian's diet is _____ balanced to suit his rigorous training programme.
8 The team coach was _____ moved when the players presented him with a leaving present.
9 Throughout the competition, the athletes were _____ guarded in case of trouble from over-enthusiastic supporters.
10 The tennis champion was _____ shattered at being knocked out in the quarter finals.

3 Complete the sentences by forming a suitable word from the words in CAPITALS.

1 Anna UNDERWENT surgery after she tore a ligament during training. **GO**
2 The success of the tournament was ~~shadowed~~ *overshadowed* by a dispute between two rivals. **SHADOW**
3 I think the way you got that job was ~~robbhanded~~ *UNDERHAND*. You should have been more honest about it. **HAND**
4 Sarah UNDERTOOK the task of organising the welcoming ceremony for the visiting teams. **TAKE**
5 Some of the athletes were UNAWARED and a little intimidated by the size of the new Olympic stadium. **AWE**
6 The organisers of the competition OVERESTIM *ATED* the popularity of the sport, and were unable to sell half the tickets. **ESTIMATE**
7 In many sports, spectators will often support the brave *UNDERDOG* dogger, the unknown player who challenges a champion. **DOG**
8 The basketball hall was OVERCROWDED with spectators and the atmosphere was stiflingly hot. **CROWD**

4 Complete the text with the words below.

packed   effects   mindful   crucial   lapse   demands
committed   prone

Nutrition is (1) _____ to an athlete's performance, and the optimal diet varies from sport to sport. Endurance sports such as triathlon, running, swimming and cycling place great (2) _____ on the body, especially during training. Athletes are (3) _____ to injury and fatigue due to overtraining, and this can have adverse (4) _____ on their long-term health. While most are (5) _____ to following a strict diet (6) _____ with optimal nutrients during peak training periods, some (7) _____ into bad habits during the rest of the year, exposing themselves to health problems. Some nutritional experts, (8) _____ of the dangers, now focus on creating long-term nutritional plans for athletes, including foods suitable for recovery periods as well as those geared towards rigorous training.

10A
- ➤ **Reading and Use of English:** Multiple matching (Part 7); Open cloze (Part 2)
- ➤ **Listening:** Sentence completion (Part 2)
- ➤ **Language development:** Reporting verbs; Ways of rephrasing and summarising; Impersonal report structures
- ➤ **Writing:** Discursive essay; Note-taking and working from notes (Part 1)

10B
- ➤ **Listening:** Multiple matching (Part 4)
- ➤ **Speaking:** Individual long turn (Parts 1, 2 & 3): Thinking and learning
- ➤ **Reading and Use of English:** Word formation (Part 3)
- ➤ **Language development:** General verb phrases; Phrases with *come*, *go*, *make* and *take*; Nouns from phrasal verbs
- ➤ **Writing:** Discursive essay (Part 1); Using impersonal statements; Agreeing and disagreeing with ideas

In the interview they told me the job would involve some paperwork.

Lead-in

1 Discuss the following questions. Here are some common areas of work.

• Business and Law   • Education   • Healthcare   • Information Technology   • Media

1 Can you think of any more to add to the list?
2 Which areas do you find most interesting? Why?
3 What specific jobs can you think of within each field?
4 What qualifications do you need for your chosen field?

2 How do you see the job you are either doing now or hope to be doing in the future – will it be a job for life, do you think? What might be some possible effects of the increasing use of technology in the workplace?

3 What are the elements of a job that create 'job satisfaction'? Discuss, make a list and compare ideas.

4a Here are some common abbreviations from the worlds of business and education. Discuss what you think they might mean and to which area they belong.

• BA   • CEO   • CMO   • HE   • HR   • IB   • MBA   • MD   • MEd   • MSc   • PhD

b What other useful abbreviations do you know in English?

Reading (Paper 1 Part 7)

Before you read

1 People often make mistakes in their personal or professional lives. What is the best way to deal with any mistakes you make, and why? Why don't people always react like that?

Skimming: understanding gist

2 Quickly read through the text on page 153. Each section (A–D) is written by a successful businessperson. What do you think each person learns from their experiences? Choose which of the following points could relate to each text.

- Don't let yourself get so carried away by enthusiasm that you fail to put in place a careful planning strategy.
- It's best to do things properly if you're going to do them at all.
- In business, you must be on your guard and always have a plan B to fall back on.
- Stay with what you know best and remedy any mistakes you make as soon as possible.

Multiple matching

➤ EXPERT STRATEGIES page 168

3 Read the strategies on page 168, then do the task.

Answer questions 1–10 by referring to the article about the sort of problems businesspeople have to overcome. For each question, choose from the best answer from sections A–D. Some of the choices may be required more than once.

Which businessperson mentions

initial success being the source of later problems?	1 _____
not paying attention to wise advice?	2 _____
underestimating the effect of cultural differences?	3 _____
being unable to raise sufficient levels of investment?	4 _____
not responding to an instinctive feeling about a proposal?	5 _____
failing to realise that integrity could not be assumed?	6 _____
overreacting to an unrepresentative trend in sales?	7 _____
not tackling fundamental problems soon enough?	8 _____
approaching the staff of rival companies as a form of recruitment?	9 _____
suffering a feeling of personal inadequacy at one stage?	10 _____

Discussion

4a The sayings below could be applied to one or more of the situations in the texts. Which do you agree with most, and why?

- Every cloud has a silver lining.
- If at first you don't succeed, try, try again.
- Nothing ventured, nothing gained.
- You have to learn to walk before you can run.

b How far do you agree with the idea that people can learn from their mistakes? Does this also apply to language learning?

5 Check the meaning of these key words and phrases from the text.

> **EXPERT WORD CHECK**
>
> canny   restraint   venture capitalist   naivety   burgeon   backlog
> detract (from)   untenable   flounder   headhunt

When things don't go right in business

Some personal experiences

A Michaela James: Food industry

I emerged from business school raring to go. My area of expertise was supplying the catering industry with ingredients for use in fast-food outlets. I'd thought of a new idea for how to organise the distribution network and thought I could make a go of it. I immediately set up a company, despite my canny parents urging restraint and patience. I sunk all my savings into the company, took out loans, ran up an overdraft but was still underfunded. So I explained my idea to an expert, a venture capitalist, and asked him if he could help me attract backers. Little did I know that he'd go straight to one of the big players in the industry and sell my idea to them behind my back. In my naivety, and desire to set the ball rolling, I'd omitted to get him to sign a confidentiality agreement – an omission which I paid dearly for in subsequent months, and years. My idea was certainly a money-spinner but sadly not for me. I lost out there but chalked it up to experience. Before long, I'd been taken on by a rival company and found my niche. Luckily, my injured pride soon recovered!

B Sam Liddle: Lifestyle management business

Our particular problem was not lack of expansion but rather over-expansion, in the sense that it all happened too fast without our having done the necessary groundwork. In our business, we commit to respond to our clients' requests – whether it's for concert tickets, a hotel booking, a golfing holiday – within a very short timescale. However, when the number of requests suddenly burgeoned into over 10,000 a month, we recruited staff in the heat of the moment, simply to clear the backlog. I guess we thought that level of business would be sustained, but it turned out to be no more than a blip. After that, we faced the prospect of radical cost-cutting, reduction in staffing levels and motivational talks for our reduced workforce. It paid off in the end but I was certainly out of my comfort zone for a while. I thought I'd messed up totally – and that's putting it mildly!

C Liz Andrews: Online translation company

Our business successfully provides translation services for business or individuals. Some years ago, a multi-millionaire with more money than sense, persuaded us to take on a major project for him. He wanted us to translate his 'philosophy of life' into fifty-seven languages so that he could then create a dedicated website for this purpose. He also requested that we help him with the content. Since his financial input was going to be considerable and he seemed trustworthy, we felt we could hardly refuse, although our gut feeling told us otherwise. Although we recruited additional staff specifically for the project, it still detracted from our core values and the focus on improving our services for the general public. Eventually, we simply couldn't produce the material fast enough and the situation became untenable, so we agreed to call it a day. As a company, the upside is that we got and retained two excellent managers, but the fact remains that the whole situation dragged on for an inexcusable length of time before we faced up to it.

D Josh Black: Email security business

A year after our business was established, I insisted on sending a small team over to the USA to start up an office there, assuming that a small-scale operation would be a good way of assessing the market potential for our product. Due to lack of funds and inadequate on-site backup however, the operation floundered. We were getting nowhere fast. Marketing a product in the USA is a different kettle of fish from the UK: the expectations are greater and the market is so huge in comparison. Really, a fully-functioning base was needed out there, so I suggested we set it up in New York as a fairly self-contained enterprise. That was the only way I could see it would work. So we duly went over there and headhunted some key people from a competitor – so far so good. That was the point at which, however, it came to light that our charges to users were quite a bit above the going market rate – and our hands were tied; we'd committed to the new setup. In the end, it all worked out for us and the USA became our biggest market with five million users by the time we sold the company.

Vocabulary

Phrasal verbs

1a Match the phrasal verbs from the texts on page 153 with their meanings in context. Then complete the sentences with the correct form of one of the phrasal verbs.

1 set up (text A)	7 mess up (text B)
2 take out (text A)	8 take on (text C)
3 run up (text A)	9 drag on (text C)
4 lose out (text A)	10 face up to (text C)
5 take sb on (text A)	11 start up (text D)
6 pay off (text B)	12 work out (text D)

a accept and not run away from a difficult fact or problem

b agree to do some work or be responsible for sth

c agree with or support sb/sth

d be successful, have a good result

e continue for too long

f use so much of sth or owe so much money that you owe a lot

g make a financial or legal arrangement

h found a business/company/organisation (2 verbs)

i make a mistake and do sth badly

j not get sth good or valuable because sb else gets it instead

k start to employ sb

Some **expert** advice

» If you're thinking of becoming self-employed and (1) _____ your own business, it's a good idea to build up some savings beforehand and not (2) _____ too many debts. You'll find that careful planning always (3) _____ in the end.

» It's always best to (4) _____ any problems you have and not let them (5) _____ . Inevitably, you'll find they get worse!

» In some deals, you might (6) _____ through wrong judgement on your part but learn from your mistakes. If you (7) _____ once or twice, it's not the end of the world.

» In whatever you do, don't settle for second best. If you find things aren't going so well, step up your efforts and you'll soon find that things will (8) _____ . Sometimes you'll need to take professional advice – in that case, go along with whatever you are told. Experts usually know best!

---

b What other phrasal verbs can you find in the sentences in Exercise 1a? Highlight them and discuss their meaning.

Collocations

2a Read what a professional translator has to say about her job. Match the words below with the words in bold in the text to make collocations.

background	internet	job	lifelong	open	print
realistic	research	sound	subject	target	team

Translation –
a changing profession

The **(1)** _____ **profile** of a translator is changing constantly. It is no longer defined solely by criteria such as source and **(2)** _____ **languages**, specialisation areas and freelance or payroll status. Translation skills and love of language are essential but so, too, are a(n) **(3)** _____ **attitude** to new technologies, **(4)** _____ **spirit**, and reliability.

Translators have direct **(5)** _____ **access** and are efficient at researching and finding information from online and **(6)** _____ **resources**. Upon entering the workforce, most graduates have a repertoire of translation techniques. However, few have an adequate concept of the complexity of many texts and the overall **(7)** _____ **knowledge** required to translate such material reliably while meeting **(8)** _____ **deadlines**. It pays to embrace any technology that can enhance efficiency and reduce repetitive processes.

A typical personal profile for a freelance or payroll translator would include qualifications as varied as excellent translation skills, **(9)** _____ **knowledge** of office software and good (internet) **(10)** _____ **skills**.

(11) _____ **learning** has special relevance in our profession. Not only do we need to keep abreast of changes and evolving terminology in the **(12)** _____ **matter** we translate, we also need further training if we wish to keep up-to-date with trends or simply broaden our perspective of ourselves and the world we live in.

b Look back at the text in Exercise 2a and find the words that collocate with these verbs. Can you think of any other words that collocate with the same verbs?

meet   embrace   enhance   broaden

c Talk about a career that interests you, using some of the ideas and collocations from Exercise 2a. In what way do you think that career might be affected by recent technological innovations?

Proverbs/Idioms

3a Discuss the meaning of these sayings within the context of success or failure.

1 It's no use crying over spilt milk.
2 Where there's a will, there's a way.
3 Whoever laughs last, laughs longest.
4 Strike while the iron's hot.
5 Practice makes perfect.
6 Don't count your chickens before they hatch.
7 Bite off more than you can chew.
8 Actions speak louder than words.

b How far do you agree with the sayings? Are there similar sayings in your own language? Which do you think could be applied to people or situations you know well?

Word formation: *in-* or *un-*?

4a Here are some verbs from which you can create adjectives and adverbs with *in-* or *un-*. Create a short dialogue with two or three.

conceive   decide   describe   foresee   inform
recognise   rely   vary

b Discuss the question below. Use some of the vocabulary and ideas you have learnt in this section.

What qualities do you think employers look for in job applicants and which characteristics would they not want to see?

Use of English 1 (Paper 1 Part 2)

Open cloze

1a Think of two or three contexts in which you could use the word *network*. What does a network facilitate?

b Now do the task below.

For questions 1–8, read the text below and think of the word which best fits each gap. Use only one word in each gap. There is an example at the beginning (0).

➤ EXPERT STRATEGIES page 167

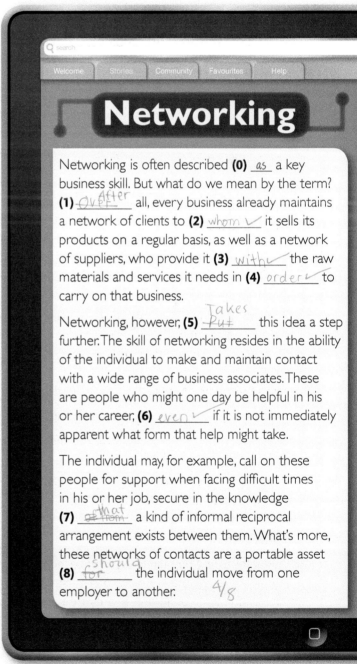

Networking

Networking is often described **(0)** _as_ a key business skill. But what do we mean by the term? **(1)** _Over/After_ all, every business already maintains a network of clients to **(2)** _whom_ ✓ it sells its products on a regular basis, as well as a network of suppliers, who provide it **(3)** _with_ ✓ the raw materials and services it needs in **(4)** _order_ ✓ to carry on that business.

Networking, however, **(5)** _Put/Takes_ this idea a step further. The skill of networking resides in the ability of the individual to make and maintain contact with a wide range of business associates. These are people who might one day be helpful in his or her career, **(6)** _even_ ✓ if it is not immediately apparent what form that help might take.

The individual may, for example, call on these people for support when facing difficult times in his or her job, secure in the knowledge **(7)** _that/from_ a kind of informal reciprocal arrangement exists between them. What's more, these networks of contacts are a portable asset **(8)** _for/should_ the individual move from one employer to another. 4/8

Discussion

2 Discuss different ways that people can network with other professionals in their field.

Listening 1 (Paper 3 Part 2)

thatched cottage at Blaise hamlet, near Bristol, UK

terracotta roofs made out of clay tiles in Carcassonne, SE France

Before you listen

1a Look at the buildings in the photographs. Do you see roofs like this anywhere near where you live? Discuss what you know about the different processes involved in making these roofs.

b Making thatched roofs out of straw is a traditional skill that has been around for hundreds of years. Discuss what the following traditional skills involve.

- weaving
- stained glass
- glass-blowing
- stone/wood-carving
- basketry
- topiary
- dry-stone walling
- carpentry

2 Have you seen these crafts being put into practice in your country or elsewhere? Do you know of any other traditional skills that are in use in your country?

Sentence completion

➤ **EXPERT STRATEGIES** page 170

3 🎧 T2.13 Read the strategy on page 170, then do the task.

You will hear a man called Kevin Arden, who works as a thatcher, talking about his job. For questions 1–9, complete the sentences with a word or short phrase.

Kevin Arden: thatcher

The subject which Kevin studied at university was ⬚ **1** .

Kevin explains that thatchers create a roof using ⬚ **2** which are made of straw.

Kevin says that ⬚ **3** is the key personal quality needed for building a career as a thatcher.

Kevin mentions the use of ⬚ **4** to explain why thatchers need to be physically fit.

Kevin points to recent ⬚ **5** as the cause of rising demand for his thatching skills.

People are surprised to hear that Kevin doesn't use ⬚ **6** when he's planning a thatched roof.

Kevin uses the term ⬚ **7** to indicate the impact thatching has on the natural environment.

Kevin gives the example of preparing ⬚ **8** as a less enjoyable aspect of running his own business.

Kevin always has what he calls a ⬚ **9** to fall back on when adverse weather conditions upset his schedule.

Discussion

4 Discuss the following questions.

1 Thatching is an example of what is called a 'labour-intensive' industry, that is one that depends more on people than machinery to deliver the product. What other labour-intensive industries can you think of?

2 What do you think the future of labour-intensive industries is? Will they ever die out completely, in your opinion? Why/Why not?

Language development 1

Reporting verbs; ways of rephrasing and summarising; impersonal report structures

> **EXPERT GRAMMAR** page 189

Using reporting verbs: rephrasing and summarising

1 🎧 T2.14 We can often rephrase what people tell us by using reporting verbs. Listen to a dialogue between two friends which is in three parts. After each part, rephrase the points you heard using the correct form of the verbs below. Then listen again to check what you have written.

promise   insist   object   prefer   congratulate   regret

Part 1

1 The day before, Mel's boss

_____ .

2 However, Mel

_____ .

Part 2

3 Jack's boss

_____ .

4 Jack would

_____ .

Part 3

5 Mel said that Jack

_____ .

6 Mel _____ .

Using phrasal verbs as reporting verbs

2a Complete the sentences with the correct form of the phrasal verbs below.

call for   come in for   come up with   drive at   fill in
get through to   put down   reel off   spell out   touch on

1 If we go for a coffee, I'll _____ (you) on everything that happened at work today.
2 I feel like I'm banging my head against a brick wall! Why can't I _____ him!
3 We only _____ the theme of profits and losses in the tutorial today: we'll be going into greater detail tomorrow.
4 When I asked him what he wanted for his birthday, Tim _____ a list of books he'd seen for sale on eBay.
5 Entrepreneurs such as Stelios Haji-Ioannou, Richard Branson and Alan Sugar are well known for _____ some very bright ideas!
6 It's really not the done thing to _____ (a colleague) in front of their workmates.

b Look at the list of phrasal verbs in this category in Expert grammar on page 190. Choose three which were not used in Exercise 2a and think of an example sentence to use them.

More ways of rephrasing and summarising; impersonal report structures

3a Discuss the exact meaning of the verbs below, then complete the sentences with the correct form of the verbs.

allege   confess   confirm   consider   deny
doubt   state

1 The CEO openly _____ to embezzling the company funds.
2 It was officially _____ yesterday that Yvonne is to be named Businesswoman of the Year. We all knew that it was a foregone conclusion!
3 I seriously _____ whether Darren will make a good teacher, but you never know.
4 James strongly _____ having designs on the manager's position in the company.
5 His company is _____ to be one of the top 100 in the country.
6 Ruth and Paul _____ categorically that they would have nothing to do with the new venture.
7 I'm afraid the business _____ to be in serious financial trouble but no one knows how far the rumours are true.

b Another way of summarising what people say is by the use of nouns. Complete the sentences with nouns formed from the verbs below.

allege   approve   criticise   demand   recollect
require

1 Bill was quick to deny all the _____ of fraud made against him.
2 It was impossible to meet all the workers' _____ for equal pay.
3 Toby had no _____ of what he'd done with the file.
4 The rest of the team were quick to show their _____ of her innovative idea.
5 The _____ levelled at him was totally unjustified as he was really hard-working.
6 What exactly are the _____ of the job?

Discussion

4 Do you know the names of any other successful entrepreneurs, apart from the ones mentioned in Exercise 2a? What makes a good entrepreneur?

→ Write down an schedule with some basic guidelines that leads. (Even for a small business)

→ Stands out, fill a gap. = success.

→ Professional advice. NOT GESSWORK.

→ Think big = Keep an eye on the competitors and move a step according to their failures.

→ Determination to overcome difficult...

→ Take the constructive criticism in.

→ Avoid the negative pessimism.

1 Small is good

Not everyone wants to be in big business and create a huge international company but even if you just want to start up a small business, you still have to do it properly and follow certain basic guidelines. A good starting-point is to find an area in the market where there is a gap: do something a bit different from everyone else and you'll have a chance of success. Then you'll need to do your homework about how to run a business and make sure to get professional advice. Guesswork in this area is not helpful and is more likely to be a recipe for disaster.

2 Bigger is better

Successful entrepreneurs don't even see 'small' as an option: they think 'big' and they will do whatever it takes to achieve that goal. They have an overwhelming inner drive to succeed which means keeping an eagle eye on any potential competitors and expanding their own businesses accordingly. What can sometimes be seen as arrogance from the outside is simply a refusal to admit defeat, combined with a steely determination to overcome any obstacles in their path. These entrepreneurs have achieved success not only by accepting constructive criticism and putting it to good use but also by ignoring anything they judge to be negative pessimism.

My notes on the first text:

If you set up a small business, you should:
- *research carefully what you want to do*
- *face up to any difficulties*
- *always aim higher*
- *realise it's not going to be easy*
- *imitate the success of big businesses*

My opinion
- *Don't really agree with some of the ideas*
- *If so many small businesses fail, then isn't it best to do something else?*
- *Most successful big businesses have small beginnings so don't quite see logic of advice*
- *Would acceptance of this advice mean not really trying to improve?*
- *However, good idea to learn about running a business and not run away from mistakes*

b Which reporting verbs do you think Lily could use to summarise the writer's arguments in the first text? Look at the list on page 189 in Expert grammar to refresh your memory!

c Match Lily's notes on her opinion to sentences 1–5 from her essay. Complete the gaps in the sentences with an appropriate word.

1 Does the author intend _____ discourage people _____ having goals in life, I wonder?
2 I admit that it's impossible _____ succeed without having an understanding _____ how businesses work and being strong enough to face up _____ your mistakes.
3 I confess _____ having doubts _____ the validity of some of the ideas mentioned here.
4 It could be argued _____ everyone has to start from somewhere and I object _____ the idea that everyone does not have the same potential _____ success.
5 The thought _____ only a minority of small businesses succeed puts me off wanting to set one _____ myself.

d Do you agree with her opinions? Make a few notes about what you think of the text.

2 Read text 2. Make notes to summarise the ideas expressed and give your opinion. Compare your ideas with the rest of the class.

3 Now do the task in Exercise 1a.

> EXPERT STRATEGIES page 169
> EXPERT WRITING page 191

Listening 2 (Paper 3 Part 4)

Before you listen 1 Online distance learning is gradually gaining in popularity. What reasons can you think of that might attract people to this method of studying? What might be the disadvantages?

Multiple matching 2 🎧 T2.15 Read the strategy on page 171, then do the task.

➤ EXPERT STRATEGIES page 171

You will hear five short extracts in which people are talking about distance-learning courses they have done.

Task One
For questions **1–5**, choose from the list (**A–H**) each speaker's reason for doing a distance-learning course.

Task Two
For questions **6–10**, choose from the list (**A–H**) the unexpected benefit of doing the course which each speaker mentions.

You will hear the recording twice. While you listen, you must complete both tasks.

Task One		Task Two	
A a need to develop language skills	1	A gaining promotion	6
B a long-held ambition to study		B greater self-discipline	
C a desire to feel fully occupied	2	C academic recognition	7
D family pressure	3	D increased respect from peers	8
E health issues		E discovering hidden talents	
F a wish for improved job security	4	F developing personal relationships	9
G an overseas posting	5	G changing career path	10
H a lack of theoretical background		H realising previous mistakes	

Discussion 3 What might tempt you to do an online course of study? Or is it out of the question for you? Give your reasons.

4 Check the meaning of these key words and phrases from the audioscript.

> **EXPERT WORD CHECK**
>
> knock (sb) down with a feather   fall into place   (be) at a loose end   hooked
> bowled over   flabbergasted   grasp   muck about   gobsmacked   hanker

Speaking (Paper 4 Parts 1, 2 & 3)

Vocabulary:
thinking and learning

1a Learning may once again have reached a critical point in time, as new paradigms, or generally accepted sets of ideas and practices, are being proposed. Read the short text and choose the correct words.

Sir Ken Robinson in his Royal Society of Arts lecture entitled 'Changing Education Paradigms', proposed changing the (1) *traditional / ancient* methods of educating children. He (2) *repeated / quoted* studies which have found that children's ability to use (3) *sideways / lateral* thinking skills, or to think 'outside the box' as they say, (4) *reduces / diminishes* with the number of years they go to school!

Salman Kahn of Kahn Academy has (5) *collated / collected* a couple of thousand videos on an internet site where students of all ages go and learn for free and which schools are starting to use as a (6) *foundation / source* of teaching material. His philosophy is that the one-on-one (7) *education / tuition* that students get from his videos enables them both to move at their own (8) *pace / stride* and to learn more effectively than they do in the classroom situation.

YouTube Edu (YouTube Education) is home to thousands of free instructional videos (9) *initiating / originating* from universities, including subjects such as science, maths, business, engineering, humanities, history, social sciences, medicine, law, arts, education and languages; the online TED (Technology, Entertainment and Design) series of conferences and lectures inform us about every subject under the sun. The list is (10) *endless / interminable*. The question remains: where is learning going and where do we go from here?

b Where do **you** think learning is going?

Part 1

> EXPERT STRATEGIES page 171

2 In pairs, discuss the following questions, then report back to the class.
- What aspect of learning do you find most rewarding?
- What is your preferred method of learning?
- Can you see yourself becoming an educator? Why/Why not?

Part 2 Collaborative task: TV documentary – the future of education

3a In pairs, look at photographs 2 and 3. Talk together about how useful you think these learning situations are. ⏱ You have about one minute for this.

b Now look at all the photographs. Imagine that a television documentary is being produced about the future of education. These photographs show some of the issues that will be discussed. Talk together about the different issues relating to the future of education that these photographs show. Then suggest one other issue related to the topic that might be included in the documentary. ⏱ You have about three minutes for this.

Part 3 Individual long turn: learning

4a Work in pairs. Student A should respond to the question on Task card 1 and talk for about two minutes. ⏱ There are some ideas on the card for you to use if you like. Student B should respond briefly to their question.

> **Task card 1**
>
> Do you learn more by making mistakes or by doing everything perfectly?
> - in life
> - in education
> - at work

Question for Student B:
- How do you feel about making mistakes?

Follow-up question for Student A:
- What do you think?

b Student B should respond to the question on Task card 2 and talk for about two minutes. ⏱ There are some ideas on the card for you to use if you like. Student A should respond briefly to their question.

> **Task card 2**
>
> Should education prepare you for a job or for life?
> - academic qualifications
> - general knowledge
> - personal development

Question for Student A:
- What, in your view, have you gained most from your education?

Follow-up question for Student B:
- Do you agree?

Developing the discussion

5 Discuss the following questions about learning in general.
1 Does learning stop once you finish your formal education, that is after you leave school or university?
2 Does a subject have to interest you in order for you to learn about it effectively?
3 Can you learn from other people or only from books or digital material? Why/Why not?

Language development 2

General verb phrases; phrases with *come, go, make* and *take*; nouns from phrasal verbs

> EXPERT GRAMMAR page 190

General verb phrases

1a Choose the words below to complete the verb phrases in **bold** in the sentences.

aback	comparison	concern	disposal	exempt
justification	making	practice	question	short

1 Fortunately, the charity my brother set up **is _____ from** tax.
2 My tutor informed me that taking an extra year to finish my degree **is out of the _____** .
3 **There's no _____** between the course here and the one at other universities.
4 In the exam, I'm going to **put into _____** everything I've learnt this year!
5 'Your future is in your hands,' the speaker said. **'It's all of your own _____** what you end up doing in life.'
6 Sue**'s not _____ of** creativity, but she's lacking in organisational skills.
7 **There's no _____** for not turning up to class – you were all given the timetable two weeks ago!
8 The professor apologised for not **being at our _____** this term but he was teaching abroad!
9 I must admit I **was taken _____** by the high standard of English required.
10 To be honest, **it's no _____ of mine** if they want to waste their time doing nothing.

b In pairs, make up and act out a dialogue between a tutor at college and his/her student. There is a problematic situation which the tutor is trying to resolve. In your dialogue, use as many phrases from Exercise 1a as you can.

Phrases with *come, go, make* and *take*

2 Study the groups of phrases on page 190, then read the beginning of the following short story. Underline the phrases you find. In pairs or groups, write the remainder of the short story, including at least four more of the phrases.

BRASSERIE

Philip was a very keen student of French. His university tutor thought he had a good chance of going for a doctorate after he graduated. As the summer holiday approached before his final year at university, he came to a decision. He would take the opportunity to go backpacking around France and practise his French. It went without saying that he'd have to take some textbooks with him but he was pretty fit so he should manage OK. While Philip was in France, he picked up a strange bug which meant he had to stay in bed for a day – and study – but he then made a swift recovery and hitched a lift with a lorry that was going to the Dordogne area. The lorry dropped him at the foot of a little hill, and as Philip came to an exhausted halt outside a little brasserie, who should he see but …

Nouns from phrasal verbs

3 A number of compound nouns are formed from phrasal verbs. Combine the words below with the particle given and complete the sentences. (The particle may come either at the beginning or at the end of the word.)

break	come	draw	feed	goings	look	put
take (x2)	turn					

1 If your _____ (out) are more than your _____ (in), then you're in trouble!
2 After the _____ (up) in the company's finances, they put in a _____ (over) bid for a rival firm.
3 Unfortunately, there was a _____ (down) in communication amongst the members of the team.
4 You should be on the _____ (out) for any new work opportunities since many companies have reduced their _____ (in) of new graduates.
5 I wonder why the factory's _____ (out) has decreased in recent months? Perhaps we need to investigate some of the workers' complaints.
6 The only _____ (back) of her research project was that the _____ (back) for her questionnaire was going to come from multiple sources. Very time-consuming to collate!

Use of English 2 (Paper 1 Part 3)

Lead-in **1** How good are you at time management? Do you ever feel that there aren't enough hours in the day? Discuss the time management skills required by:

- a student at school or college
- a professional at work
- a professional who works from home
- a professional with a family

Developing skills: forming nouns ending in -ance/-ence, -ency, -ity, -ship

2 These words all form nouns using the suffixes -ance/-ence, -ency, -ity and -ship.

1 Classify them into the correct group, writing the noun form.
2 Then find their other forms: verb, adjective, adverb, opposite (where applicable).

able	allow	apprentice	confide	efficient	entrepreneur	exist
experience	fluent	hard	literate	maintain	patient	prior
proficient	relevant	secure	signify	visible		

- -ance/-ence: _____
- -ency: _____
- -ity: _____
- -ship: _____

Word formation

➤ EXPERT STRATEGIES page 167

3 Read the strategy on page 167, then do the task.

For questions 1–8, read the text below. Use the word given in CAPITALS at the end of some of the lines to form a word that fits in the gap in the same line. There is an example at the beginning (0).

The Swiss Cheese Approach

For anyone who works from home, time **(0)** _management_ can be a real problem. Poor planning is often to blame, like not knowing how to **(1)** p_____ tasks effectively. Similarly, an **(2)** _____ to say no can lead people to take on more work than they can **(3)** _____ deal with. But there are solutions.

MANAGE

PRIORITY PRIORITISE ✓
INABILITY
ABLE ABILITY UNABILITY
REALISTIC
REALISTICALLY ✓

One useful tip is something called the Swiss Cheese Approach. A large complex project can seem daunting, so it can be hard to make a start on it. Yet even a few minutes a day devoted to such a project could make quite an **(4)** _____ difference. By 'eating away' at it, the task can be moved forward in ways that make it seem more **(5)** _____.

APPRECIABLE APPRECIATABLE
APPRECIATE APPRECIATE
APPRECIABLE APPRECIABLY
ACCESS ACCESSFUL accessible

One aspect of this can be the keeping of a daily record of work, which can provide valuable **(6)** _____ into whether time is being used **(7)** _____ or not. A clear policy on **(8)** _____ can also be useful. Just because someone works from home, it doesn't mean they have to be available to friends 24/7.

SIGHT INSIGHTS ✓
PRODUCT PRODUCTIVELY
INTERRUPT INTERRUPTIONS

5/8

Task analysis **4** How many changes did you have to make to the base words? Did you get them all?

Discussion **5** Discuss the following statements.

1 'Worrying about things can waste time, and 80 percent of the things we worry about never actually happen!'
2 'The way to get things done is to focus the mind on what the priority is at any given moment. Everything else can wait till later.'

Writing 2 (Paper 2 Part 1: Essay)

Lead-in   **1**   Discuss the advantages and disadvantages of a university education. What are the alternatives?

Understand the task   **2**   Read the task below. Summarise in one sentence the main ideas expressed in each of the texts. What do you think about the topics?

Read the two texts. Write an essay summarising and evaluating the key points from both texts. Use your own words throughout as far as possible, and include your own ideas in your answers.
Write your answer in **240–280** words.

1 The future of higher education

It's true to say that higher education remains the goal for a large number of young people, since nothing much can beat the satisfaction of acquiring a university degree. Even as we speak, however, fundamental changes to the system are in progress and it's anybody's guess what university study will be like in twenty years' time. For one thing, relative ease of international travel means that in the future, more students may not choose to go to university in their home country. Then there's the increase in online teaching, although the general consensus is that this will never wholly substitute face-to-face teaching.

2 An alternative to higher education

Apprenticeships offer young people vocational training rather than academic study as such, and studies have shown that this type of training has a more positive effect on their happiness level than university study! Indeed, there are many advantages to doing an apprenticeship, whether it's from the age of 16, 17 or 18 – or even later on in life. The possibilities are varied, ranging from veterinary nursing to boat-building to creating sets for the theatre. Granted, the final salary isn't always huge but at least you get an income during the apprenticeship and a reasonable guarantee of a job after finishing.

Plan your task   **3**   Make notes summarising the two texts, as you did on page 158. Then decide where you want to include your evaluation of the ideas.

Relative ease of International travel and the enhance in online teaching have begun to show a change in the higher education methodology hitherto.

**Language and content
Using impersonal statements**

4 These are a useful way of making general statements in a more formal way.

It is often claimed/suggested …
It is widely/generally understood/believed/accepted …
Many/Certain people claim/assume …   It has been pointed out that …
It is common knowledge that …   It seems as though …

Use impersonal statements to comment on some of the ideas in the texts in Exercise 2.

Using text adverbials

5 Text adverbials can be very useful to introduce or link your points. Choose an adverb or adverbial phrase from the list below to complete the sentences. Sometimes, more than one is possible.

apparently   chiefly   evidently   in some respects   mainly   on the contrary
presumably   theoretically   to a certain extent   up to a point

1 _____ more students are choosing to study technology and engineering than arts subjects these days.
2 _____ a university education should give you a broader perspective on life, although sometimes you wouldn't think it!
3 _____ , studying abroad would be interesting but in other ways it would be more challenging.
4 I agree with his views _____ but there are some areas where we differ.

Expressing grades of agreement

6 Choose an appropriate way of agreeing or disagreeing with the following statements.

Agreement
Without a doubt, …   Undoubtedly, …   I'm (absolutely) convinced …
I totally agree …   I'm very much in favour of …

Partial agreement
I tend to feel that …   Most of the writer's arguments are plausible although …
I'm fairly certain that …   I'm inclined to agree with …

Disagreement
I'm not (entirely) convinced that …   It's doubtful that …

Strong disagreement
I seriously doubt whether …   It's highly unlikely that …
I'm strongly against/opposed to …

1 Education is a waste of time. It's better to get out into the world and learn through experience.
2 You can learn more about life through books and learning than you can through simply living.
3 Practical skills are as important as gaining a good education – where would we be without them?
4 Manual and intellectual skills should be paid equally.
5 Football stars deserve to be paid huge salaries.
6 The average number of career changes during our lifetime is five to seven, so why specialise?

Write your essay
➤ EXPERT STRATEGIES page 169

7 Do the task in Exercise 2, using the strategies on page 169 and some of the phrases on this page to help you.

Check your essay
➤ EXPERT WRITING page 191

8 Edit your essay, using the checklist on page 191.

Review

1 Complete the sentences with the correct form of the words in brackets.

1 I am at a loss to understand why Damian is _____ (vary) late for class!

2 I must admit, in the photo of her twenty years ago, she's quite _____ (recognise).

3 Jenny was lucky to have the _____ (secure) of a steady job.

4 Setting an example of successful _____ (entrepreneur) can give a positive example to young people.

5 I don't think you can say that any of our students are _____ (sufficient) prepared for their exams – they're all excellent!

6 The talk we heard about Italian Renaissance art was _____ (forget) – particularly since it took place in a building overlooking the Grand Canal in Venice!

7 The food in that restaurant was _____ (describe) bad – that's definitely one to cross off the list.

8 Can anyone tell me what the _____ (signify) of the Latin language was in the development of modern English?

2 Complete the second sentence so that it has a similar meaning to the first sentence. Use between three and eight words.

1 Paul didn't want us to leave the party so early.
(objected)
Paul _objected on leaving_ to our leaving the party so early.

2 After the meeting, the employees voiced their thoughts about the way the management was behaving.
(commented)
After the meeting, the employees _commented about_ on the management's behaviour.

3 Some big businesses have been criticised for their lack of sustainability programmes. (in criticism) for
(come)
Some big businesses _have come_ critise because of their lack of sustainability programmes.

4 Would you like me to bring you up-to-date with the latest developments?
(fill)
me fill you in on
Would you like _to be filled with_ the latest developments?

5 They suggested that I should summarise what we had decided.
(sum) was suggested tha I sum up
has to be summed up by me
It _summed up_ what we had decided.

6 The office workers persuaded their boss to let them have an extra half-day holiday.
(talked)
their boss into giving
The office workers _talked to their boss to_ them an extra half-day holiday.

3 Complete the text with the words below.

access   board   comparison   granted   justification
question   saying   short   surprise   worse

It's funny how we all tend to take education for **(1)** _____ these days but only a couple of hundred years ago, a good education was out of the **(2)** _____ for the majority of the population. Education was the prerogative of the select few and it was only in the last century that schooling became widely available for all children up to the age of 16 or 18. The trouble is, familiarity breeds contempt, as the saying goes, so it comes as no **(3)** _____ that a large number of schools come under attack nowadays, both from students and from parents. Some of the comments you might hear are: 'Education is going from bad to **(4)** _____ !' or 'Our schools are so **(5)** _____ of funds they can't create any more sporting facilities!' However, it's very easy to forget that, generally speaking, most children nowadays have **(6)** _____ to a pretty good all-round education. It goes without **(7)** _____ that there's no **(8)** _____ between the facilities generally available nowadays in schools and colleges and what was around last century. Not only that, but so much knowledge is on hand at the click of a mouse. So, one might say, there is absolutely no **(9)** _____ for ignorance or narrow-mindedness in today's world. Well, that's a thought to take on **(10)** _____ , isn't it?

4 Choose the correct words to complete the sentences.

1 My opinion is that you shouldn't ____ producing anything that is less than your best.
   A take on   B settle for   C start up

2 I try not to ____ other people's opinions unless I totally agree with them.
   A go along with   B face up to   C drag on

3 We're lucky in that our tutor sets us realistic ____ for our assignments.
   A profiles   B resources   C deadlines

4 What is the subject ____ of tomorrow's lecture?
   A matter   B topic   C lesson

5 The company has been warned that their ____ must increase otherwise it will be closed down.
   A outgoings   B outlook   C output

6 This year's ____ of graduate students is of a very high calibre.
   A income   B intake   C takeover

Exam reference

Paper 1: Reading and Use of English 1 hour 30 minutes

There are seven parts to this paper:
• Part 1: four-option multiple-choice cloze – one short text with eight questions
• Part 2: open cloze – one short text with eight questions
• Part 3: word formation – one short text with eight questions
• Part 4: key word transformations – six separate items
• Part 5: Four-option multiple choice – one long text with six questions
• Part 6: gapped text – one long text with seven questions
• Part 7: multiple matching – one long text or several short texts with ten questions

There are 53 questions overall. For Parts 1–3, each correct answer gets one mark, for Part 4 each correct answer gets up to two marks, for Parts 5 and 6, each correct answer gets two marks and for Part 7, each correct answer gets one mark. Total number of marks = 72.

The texts come from a wide range of sources, including magazine and newspaper articles, non-fiction, academic publications and literature.

EXPERT TASK STRATEGY (ALL TASKS)

• Watch the time carefully. Allow yourself 5–10 minutes for tasks 1–4 and 15–20 minutes for tasks 5–7. Once you have finished each task, move on straightaway to the next one. Make sure you answer all the questions and if you have time at the end, quickly check through your answers.
• For all the text-based tasks, read the heading and skim the text quickly to understand the general meaning. Read the rubric carefully before starting the task.

Part 1: multiple-choice cloze

This is a four-option multiple-choice task with eight gaps, based on a text of between 150–170 words. The focus is on vocabulary, which may also be tested within the framework of collocations (e.g. *freedom of the press*), fixed phrases (e.g. *off the beaten track*), idioms (e.g. *a twelve-year stint*), complementation (the structures that follow different types of verbs), phrasal verbs (e.g. *stand up to*) or semantic precision (choosing the correct word for the context).

EXPERT TASK STRATEGY

• Some options have similar meanings but are used in different contexts or collocate with different words. Consider the exact meaning and use of each option carefully before deciding which word fits the context.
• Look carefully at the words that come before and after the tested item. The correct word might be followed by a particular preposition or particle.

• Once you have made your choice, read through the completed sentence together with the word you have chosen. If it is wrong, it may not 'sound' right to you.

Part 2: open cloze

This is a task with eight gaps, based on a text of between 150–170 words. The focus is mainly on an understanding of grammar but there may also be some testing of vocabulary. The missing words may include prepositions (e.g. *in, on, against*), verb forms (e.g. *being*), pronouns (e.g. *they, this*), conjunctions (e.g. *as, because, when*), etc. and may often form part of a set phrase, a lexical chunk or a phrasal verb.

EXPERT TASK STRATEGY

• Read through the whole text quickly to get the general idea, before you start trying to find the missing words.
• After reading the text, complete the gaps, looking carefully at the context of the sentence and the paragraph to help you.
• Do not use contractions.
• Once you have completed the gaps, read the text through again carefully and check that your answers accurately reflect the overall meaning of the text.

Part 3: word formation

This is a task with eight gaps, based on a text of between 150–170 words. The focus is on vocabulary and the formation of words from a stem, making use of affixation (prefixes and suffixes), internal changes and compound words. There may also be a grammatical element (plurality, verb tenses, participles, etc.) to the changes that need to be made. Some of the words you have to form may be part of fixed expressions or collocations.

EXPERT TASK STRATEGY

• In order to find the correct word, remember to read each sentence in the context of the paragraph and the text as a whole.
• Use your knowledge of grammar to understand what part of speech the missing word is (noun, verb, adjective, adverb) and think through the range of possible affixes, including particles and negative prefixes or suffixes.
• Look carefully at the way the sentence is constructed to decide whether the missing word should be positive or negative. Look for evidence of antithesis (two opposing ideas).
• When the stem presents several possible derivatives, look at the context carefully to check that you have the derivative with the correct meaning.
• Remember that more than one change to the stem word can often be required.

Part 4: key word transformations

This is a task with six sentences which have to be rewritten using a given key word. The focus is on grammar, vocabulary and collocation, e.g. verb phrases, prepositional phrases, and so on. You must use between three and eight words, including the key word. Contracted words are counted as two words. You must not change the key word.

EXPERT TASK STRATEGY

• Read both sentences carefully to understand the meaning of what is missing in the second sentence.
• The key word will normally form part of a fixed phrase or grammatical structure. Use the phrase correctly to fit in the gap, together with any other words or phrases that might be necessary.
• Read the completed sentence through again to make sure that it accurately reflects the meaning of the original sentence.
• All elements of the first sentence must be included in the second sentence, although they will be expressed in different language.

Part 5: multiple choice

This is a text of about 700–750 words followed by six four-option multiple-choice questions. The focus of this task includes an understanding of the writer's opinion and purpose for writing through attitude, tone and implication, together with an ability to grasp the significance of detail and text organisation features.

EXPERT TASK STRATEGY

• Whenever you answer questions on a text, it is important to keep the overall context and the writer's intention in mind.
• Read the multiple-choice questions before you read the text. This will give a focus to your reading and ultimately save you time.
• Read the question stem carefully, plus all the options. Then read the relevant section of the text to find the answer.
• All of the options will seem possible answers to the question but only one will match the information in the text or the view of the writer. Check that the option you choose does both.

Part 6: gapped text

This is a text of about 800–1,100 words from which six paragraphs have been removed and put in jumbled order. There is one extra paragraph that does not belong to the text. The focus of this task is on an understanding of the text as a whole, with regard to the flow of the argument it presents (coherence), the way it all logically fits together (cohesion) and its overall meaning. It is also necessary to examine the detail of the text structure (through the use of reference words, e.g. *it, there, afterwards*) to identify which paragraphs should go where.

EXPERT TASK STRATEGY

• Read through the base text first, then the missing paragraphs.
• Paragraphs in a text are linked in various ways. Look at how the main text develops, and try to assess the purpose of the gapped paragraph. For example, it may develop a line of argument, give an example to illustrate a point, introduce a new person or point, or refer to something in the past.
• Make sure you check the paragraphs immediately before and after the gapped paragraph to ensure there is cohesion. Look out for textual clues such as time references, the use of direct or reported speech, referencing through the use of pronouns, parallel phrases, etc. that should help you to identify the missing paragraphs.
• Notice the development of the writer's narrative or description and consider whether the opinions being expressed are the writer's or someone else's.
• When you have finished the task, remember to check that the whole passage makes sense.

Part 7: multiple matching

This is a text of 650–700 words, or several short texts, preceded by ten questions which you need to match to sections of the text. The task tests the ability to identify specific information in the text or texts together with an understanding of attitude and opinion.

EXPERT TASK STRATEGY

• Read each question first, then find the sections of the text or texts that seem to match each question. You may find two or three possible sections.
• Read these sections carefully. Examine the detail in order to find the one which matches the question exactly.
• You may find it helpful to underline key words in the sentences as you read through them.
• If the task involves finding points that have been mentioned by the writer, then these need to be clearly stated, not simply implied.

Paper 2: Writing (1 hour 30 minutes)

There are two parts to this paper:
• Part 1 is a compulsory essay.
• Part 2 consists of a choice between five questions. The task types may include an essay, a review, an article, a letter and a report.

The instructions clearly specify the type of writing, the target reader and the purpose for writing, and each question carries equal marks. Candidates should read the instructions carefully, as an answer must include all the relevant information in order to receive a good mark.

> EXPERT WRITING Page 191

Part 1

Part 1 is based on input material consisting of two texts of approximately 100 words each. The texts are on the same topic and each one has two clear main points. The texts may present opposing or complementary views and may be extracts from newspapers, books, magazines, online source material or could be based on quotations made by speakers during a discussion. The question instructions are standard, and candidates are required to write an essay summarising and evaluating the key points in the texts. You must use your own words as far as possible and include your own ideas in your answer. You must write 240–280 words.

> EXPERT WRITING Page 192

EXPERT TASK STRATEGY

• Before you start writing your essay, analyse the writer's main ideas in both texts and make notes on the key points that are mentioned. Use your own words as far as possible. Then make a few notes about your opinion of the ideas in the texts.
• Use the notes you have made as a basis for your essay.
• Careful planning is essential for this task during the note-making stage. Do not forget to use appropriate linking phrases to ensure your essay has a logical flow.
• Your aim in your essay is to create a new piece of original writing, with a new target reader and purpose, which draws on the views and information in the two texts.
• Make sure your answer:
  contains a clear and concise summary of the key points of the two texts
  analyses and evaluates the main ideas or opinions expressed in the texts
  includes possible counter-arguments and points the writer has failed to consider when presenting his/her view (It is important that you address these in your answer, even if you in fact agree with what the writer says)
  includes your own views and opinions on the topics of the texts.
  is organised into clear paragraphs.

Part 2

In Part 2, you have to choose one of five tasks. The task types include an essay, article, report, letter or review. Questions 2–4 provide candidates with a clear topic, purpose and target reader for their answer. All tasks are formal or semi-formal, and the target reader may be the editor of a newspaper or magazine, the director of an international company or a school or college principal. Question 5 contains a choice between two tasks based on the set reading texts. You should not attempt this question if you have not read the texts or seen the corresponding film. Your answer will be marked on its ability to answer the question, appropriate style and register, as well as use of language. You must write 280–320 words.

> EXPERT WRITING Page 194

EXPERT TASK STRATEGY

For all task types, you should:
• consider the target reader carefully, and ensure you use the appropriate register
• organise your answer in a way that is appropriate to the task type
• display a suitable range of vocabulary and grammar, using a variety of sentence structure and more complex language
• use discourse markers effectively
• endeavour to capture the reader's interest.

Article – This should be written in a suitable style for publication in an English-language newspaper, magazine or newsletter. You will need to convey information through your article, and your answer may need to include examples of descriptive, narrative, evaluative or anecdotal language.
• Organise your article in a way that it will have maximum impact on the reader, particularly if it is semi-formal.
• Plan your article carefully. Include an introduction that will make the reader want to read further and a suitable conclusion. The conclusion can also include a rhetorical question to the reader.

Report – Make sure you organise your answer carefully into paragraphs with sub-headings, which address all the points specified in the question.
• A report will include mostly factual information but you will also be able to bring in some of your own ideas and experience.
• Give your reason for the report in the introduction and include a summary of what you have said, plus a recommendation in the conclusion.

Review – When analysing the question, consider the kind of language you need to use in your answer. This may be narrative, descriptive, explanatory or evaluative.
• Think of sub-topics and core vocabulary connected with the subject of the review.
• Think of appropriate adjectives/adverbs to express praise or criticism.

- Plan your review and decide how to order your points. Give your review a title.
- A good review is an interesting and informative review. Remember that, based on what you say, your readers will either go and see that film, read that book, go to that restaurant or not!

Letter – This will be a response to a situation specified in the question and may contain a narrative element, requiring you to describe a personal experience or it may be largely factual. Some other possible genres might be letters of complaint or advice.

- Make sure you use a range of appropriate language.
- Include appropriate opening and closing phrases for letter-writing.
- Ensure that your language is at the correct level of formality to suit the context.

Essay – Make sure your main paragraphs make a main point, give examples to support the point, then reinforce that point.

- Clarity and a logical presentation and organisation of ideas are essential for essay-writing.
- Spend 5–10 minutes planning the outline of your essay before you start writing. In this way, your essay will flow much better.

Set text – Questions may be any of the task types mentioned previously and will specify which aspects of the text you should focus on, e.g. character development or significance of events.

- You should not attempt this task if you have not read the prescribed text.
- Make sure you restrict your answer to the aspects outlined in the question.
- You should also make detailed reference to appropriate sections of the text to support your arguments.

Paper 3: Listening
(approximately 40 minutes)

There are four parts to this paper:
- Part 1: three-option multiple choice – three short extracts with two questions each
- Part 2: sentence completion – a monologue with nine questions
- Part 3: four-option multiple choice – discussion involving interacting speakers, with five questions
- Part 4: multiple matching – five themed monologues with ten questions

Each correct answer gets one mark.

Part 1: multiple-choice questions

For this part, you will hear three short, unrelated extracts from monologues or exchanges between interacting speakers. Each extract has two three-option multiple-choice questions. You may need to identify the speaker's feeling, attitude, opinion and purpose; agreement between speakers, gist or detail.

EXPERT TASK STRATEGY

- Read the context sentence and then the questions before you listen. Think about the type of text you will be listening to and the specific information (opinion, detail, etc.) you will be listening for.
- Consider the speaker's attitude to what they are talking about: how they feel, what their opinion is.
- Listen also for expressions of agreement or disagreement between interacting speakers.
- Remember that what you hear will not be using the same words as are in the questions.

Part 2: sentence completion

In this part, you will hear a monologue which may be part of a talk, lecture, speech or radio broadcast. You will have to complete nine gapped sentences which summarise the main points in the audioscript. You must identify specific information and stated opinion that you hear.

EXPERT TASK STRATEGY

- The sentences you are given summarise the information from the audioscript text, but use different words and expressions. The sentences give an outline of what you can expect to hear.
- Before you listen, read through the gapped sentences carefully, to identify the kind of information you are looking for. Try to predict the missing word or words.
- The words you have to write are the exact words you will hear on the audioscript, although they may come in a different order. The target words are concrete pieces of information, and so are usually nouns or noun phrases.

- The first time you listen, try to understand where the relevant information appears for each question. Listen out for discourse markers and topic shifts in the audioscript that relate to the sentences. Then focus on the target language the second time you hear the script.
- You will hear other answers that could logically fit the gap but that are not the correct answer. Check the sentence carefully to see which answer is correct.
- Once you have completed the task, read through the completed sentences to make sure they make sense.

Part 3: multiple choice

This part is an interview or discussion between two or more speakers. There are five four-option multiple-choice questions, and the focus is on identifying gist, detail, attitude, opinion and inference.

EXPERT TASK STRATEGY

As for Part 1 but in this part you should also listen for:
- attitudes and opinions which are stated indirectly by the speakers
- cues in the audioscript that should signal the next question
- discourse markers that indicate a change in topic, speaker's attitude, or agreement or disagreement with another speaker's view
- words and phrases in the audioscript that have a similar meaning to the options. Be careful, as some options contain words from the script but the meaning of the whole sentence is different.

Part 4: multiple matching

This part contains five short monologues on a related theme. You must complete two tasks containing five questions each. Each task requires you to choose from a list of eight options. The focus is on interpreting gist, main points, attitude and the context. You will hear the rubric on the audioscript but not the options.

EXPERT TASK STRATEGY

- Before you listen, read both the task rubric and options carefully, to understand what the task focus is and what information you need to listen for.
- The first time you listen, complete task one, and the second time you listen, complete task two.
- You will hear similar ideas expressed by some of the speakers. However, only one of the options will accurately match the ideas expressed by each speaker. Look back at the task rubric as you listen to remind yourselves of what type of information you are listening for.

Paper 4: Speaking (16 minutes)

There are three parts to this paper:
- Part 1: social interaction – a conversation between the interlocutor (the examiner who participates in the interaction with the candidates) and each candidate on general topics relating to the candidate. (2 minutes)
- Part 2: collaborative task – a two-way decision-making task between the candidates, based on visual and written prompts. (4 minutes)
- Part 3: individual long turn – each candidate has to speak for about two minutes in response to a task card which has a question and some prompts on it. The other candidate has to respond, and then the interlocutor leads a discussion about the topics covered in each individual long turn. (10 minutes)

Candidates are assessed on their ability to:
- use a wide range of grammar and vocabulary appropriately
- maintain a coherent dialogue or monologue
- take part effectively in interpersonal interaction
- use correct pronunciation and intonation.

EXPERT TASK STRATEGY

Part 1
- Do not forget to expand your answers by giving additional information or a reason for your answer. Express your ideas in an interesting and lively way.
- You should try to use different language from your partner when answering questions about yourself, to demonstrate your knowledge of a range of vocabulary.

Part 2
- Interaction is vital in this part of the Speaking paper. Aim to achieve a balance with your partner, by actively encouraging each other to speak in the following ways:
  1 When you make a point, finish by asking for their agreement or opinion.
  2 Respond to what they say by commenting on it, then adding another point.
- Aim to give your opinion clearly and succinctly. Your goal is to express yourself within the time limit, conclude your turn and move on by including your partner.

Part 3
- To help you expand your views, use the following techniques to help you.
  1 Introduce the topic by talking about it in general terms before saying how it affects you personally.
  2 Support your views with examples from personal knowledge or experience; if not your own, then someone close to you.
- Listen carefully to what your partner says and consider your own opinion, as the examiner will ask you a follow-up question. Do not repeat your partner's exact words and phrases but it is a good idea to refer to things he/she mentions to support your response.
- Use discourse markers to structure your talk and also to give yourself time to think.
- Remember that the points on the task cards are simply a guideline and you do not have to mention them all. You can also introduce points of your own, if you wish.

Expert grammar

1

Present and past tense review
(page 13)

A Continuous forms

We use present and past continuous forms when we are:
1 talking about temporary events.
   *The film **is showing** at the local cinema tonight.* (present continuous)
   *We **were filming** in the studio last week.* (past continuous)
2 talking about repeated actions.
   *Mobile phones **were ringing** all through the concert.* (past continuous)
3 talking about ongoing events.
   *We **are rehearsing** a play.* (present continuous)
   *I**'ve been drawing** since I was a child.* (present perfect continuous)
   *I**'ve been meaning** to invite you to come to our new show.* (present perfect continuous)
4 setting the background to narrative events.
   *I **was listening** to the concert when a mobile phone rang.* (past continuous)
   *People **had been queuing** outside the theatre for hours in order to get tickets.* (past perfect continuous)
5 focusing on the action or situation.
   *James **was always doodling** at school.* (past continuous, characteristic behaviour)
   *I**'ve been sitting** at my computer all day, and I'm very stiff now.* (present perfect, leading to present result)

B State verbs

Some verbs describe states and are not normally used in a continuous form. State verbs often:
1 describe emotions or mental states or processes.
   adore, appreciate (= value), approve of, believe, care, consider (= hold an opinion), detest, dislike, doubt, expect (= think), fear, feel (= have an opinion), find (= realise), forget, gather (= understand), hate, imagine, know, like, loathe, love, need, mind, perceive, prefer, realise, recall, recognise, recollect, regret, remember, require, see (= understand), see through sb (= understand hidden motives), suppose, suspect, think (= have an opinion), trust (= believe, have confidence in), understand, value, want, wish
   Exceptions: *enjoy, long for*
2 refer to the senses.
   feel, hear, see, smell, sound, taste. Also: *notice, observe*
3 refer to communication.
   agree, apologise, deny, disagree, mean, promise
4 refer to exterior appearance.
   appear, look (= seem), seem
5 refer to possession.
   belong to, have, owe, own, possess

6 Other state verbs include:
   be, concern, consist of, contain, cost, depend on, deserve, exist, fit, hold (= contain), impress, include, involve, keep (= continue), lack (BUT is lacking in), matter, resemble, signify, suit, surprise, weigh

Note
We can use state verbs in the continuous when they describe an action
*I**'m thinking** about/**considering** taking ballet lessons.*
*He**'s always promising** to introduce me to Johnny Depp.*
*I**'m seeing** the director tomorrow.*
*We**'re having** a great time, doing this show.*

C Perfect forms

We use perfect forms:
1 when we are talking about events or states that happened or obtained before a point in time.
   *So far, all the audiences **have enjoyed** the show.* (present perfect for time up to now)
   *James Quigley **has made** money from advertising work that funds his own films.* (present perfect for a past event or action that is relevant now)
   *Several mobile phones rang after Sir Peter **had asked** people to switch them off.* (past perfect for something that happened before another event in the past)
2 after reporting verbs.
   *I think it**'s been** scientifically **proven**.*
3 with superlatives or *ever/never*.
   *I**'ve never seen** a musical like 'Mamma Mia'!*
   *Hannibal Lecter was the worst villain Anthony Hopkins **had ever played**.*
   ***Have** you **ever met** Sir Peter Maxwell Davies?*
4 with certain phrases.
   *This is the first time I**'ve been** to the opera!*
5 for reporting new information.
   *A Chinese adaptation of 'Mamma Mia' **has just opened** in Beijing.*

D Tense forms often confused

1 Present perfect and past simple

1 We use the **present perfect** to show present relevance. We often use it for announcing news or things that have recently changed.
   *Jane **has just started** her drama course.*
2 We use the **past simple** for finished action and often refer to a specific time in the past.
   *She **met** the director yesterday.*
3 We use the **present perfect** for talking about experiences, and unfinished time periods.
   *Animators **have learned** to exploit technology.*
4 We use the **present perfect** with *ever/never* for general experiences.
   *The director **has never achieved** his goal of creating reality.*

5 We use the **past simple** for talking about finished actions/events in the past.
*James **made** a short film called 'Happy Cow' while he was at art college.*

2 Past continuous and past simple

1 We use the **past continuous** for talking about background states or incomplete events in the past.
*James **was studying** art.*

2 We use the **past simple** for talking about completed actions, and events that interrupt another action in the past.
*James was studying art when he **made** a film.*

3 Present perfect simple and present perfect continuous

We use the **present perfect simple** for completed actions, with present result.
*Chinese folk dances **have replaced** some Western choreography in the new adaptation of 'Mamma Mia'.*

4 Past perfect simple and past perfect continuous

1 We use the **past perfect simple** to show that one event finished before something else happened.
*By the time we arrived, the film **had already finished**.*

2 We use the **past perfect continuous** to talk about a longer period up to a specified time in the past.
*Sara **had been dancing** for a long time before she joined the Royal Ballet.*

E Time words

1 We use the **present/past perfect simple** with *still/yet* to refer to a period of time up to the moment of speaking.
*We **still haven't heard** from her.*
*Six days had passed and we **still hadn't heard** from her.*
*Sally **hasn't appeared** in a film **yet**.*
BUT also note the construction: *Sally **has yet to appear** in a film.*

2 We use the **present perfect simple** or **present perfect continuous** with *recently/lately/before*, etc. to mean 'at some time up to now'.
*I **haven't seen** Alice **lately**, have you?*

Note
Recently can also be used with the **past simple** + an affirmative verb.
*I **saw** Toby **recently** and he was asking after you.*

3 We use the **present perfect continuous** to focus on the length time of an uncompleted action.
*They **have been working** on the translation **for** five years.*

4 We use the **present/past perfect continuous** for repeated actions.
*She **has been dancing** the lead role in 'Swan Lake' **for six weeks**.*
*I'**d been ringing** Anne Hathaway's agent **all morning** but with no luck.*

Notes
1 We use *for* with a period of time (e.g. *for five months*) and *since* with a point in time (e.g. *since last November*).
2 The use of the **past perfect** in these sentences is unusual because it refers to a time later than the action of the main verb.
*Jo's agent sold the book before she'**d finished** writing it.*
*The critics decided they hated the show before they'**d seen** it.*
3 When we want to emphasise an action, we use *do/did* + infinitive (mainly spoken with stress on the auxiliary verb).
*James **did do** some work for children's books – I remember now!*

Future tense review (page 18)

A *will* and *going to*

1 We use *will* to make predictions, spontaneous decisions and offers.
*I think set design **will** change a lot in the next twenty years.* (prediction)
*'We need a director for our film.' 'OK, I'**ll** do it!'* (spontaneous decision, offer)

2 We use *going to* for predictions based on evidence and for plans.
*The show has had good reviews. It'**s going to** be a success.* (prediction based on evidence)
*I'**m going to** be a dancer.* (plan)

B Present simple and present continuous

1 We use the **present simple** for timetables and programmes.
*The show **starts** at 7.15.*

2 We use the **present continuous** for arrangements and planned events.
*We'**re starting** rehearsals on Saturday, and we'**re opening** the show in September.*

C *will* and future continuous

1 We use *will* for predictions.
*You **won't** be able to get a job unless you're highly computer literate.*

2 We use the **future continuous** for events that will be in progress in the future.
*We'**ll be working** at the Edinburgh Festival this summer.*

D Future perfect

We use the **future perfect** for an action that will be completed before a certain time in the future.
*Set design **will have changed** a lot by 2020, and designers will need to be computer literate.*

E Present simple or present perfect?

We use the **present simple** or **present perfect**, not *will*, for future time after time conjunctions (*after, as soon as, when*, etc.).
*Let me know **as soon as** you **decide/have decided**.*
*The hard work really starts **when/after** you **graduate/have graduated**.*

*We won't know whether Benny and Bjorn like the adaptation of 'Mamma Mia' **until** they**'ve seen** the show. **After** he**'s given** his presentation, James will answer the children's questions about becoming an animator.*

F Expressions with future meaning

1. To talk about fixed, planned events, we use:
   be to + infinitive.
   *'Mamma Mia' **is to be** the first Western musical to be translated into Chinese.*

2. To talk about events that will happen very soon, we use:
   be about to + infinitive
   *The world **is about to find out** whether the Chinese 'Mamma Mia' will be a success.*
   on the point/verge of + -ing/noun.
   *Some veteran musicians are **on the verge of retiring**.*

3. To talk about probability, we use:
   be likely/unlikely to + infinitive.
   *A rock music concert **is likely to attract** people of different ages.*
   expect (sb/sth) to + infinitive
   *Joe's **expecting** his agent **to call** him any day now.*
   stand to + infinitive.
   *If he gets the film part, he **stands to make** a lot of money.*

4. To talk about things we feel certain about, we use:
   bound to + infinitive.
   *Gemma's accident **is bound to set** us back.*

5. To talk about planned events or actions that didn't happen, we use:
   just about to + infinitive
   *Thanks for ringing, I was **just about to call** you.*
   was/were going to + infinitive
   *They **were going to have** wonderful special effects but the computer broke down.*
   supposed to/due to + infinitive.
   *We were **supposed/due to meet** the director tomorrow but he's cancelled the meeting.*

2

Passive forms (page 29)

A Use

We use **the passive** when:
1. the agent is unknown.
   *More food **will be imported**.*
2. the agent is obvious or not important.
   *The Kayapo's territories **will be flooded**.*
   *Some tribes in the Amazon **have been contacted**.*
3. we do not want to say who the agent is (non-accusatory).
   *New hydroelectric dams **are planned** across Brazil and Peru.*
   *Something **should have been done**.*
   *Forests **are being cut down**.*

We use **the passive + by + agent** when:
we want to focus on the agent.
*The crops **are pollinated by insects**.*

We use **the passive** when we want to be formal and impersonal:
1. in academic and scientific works
2. for giving rules, orders and instructions, often on notices
   *Dogs must **be kept** under control.*
3. for talking about events and achievements
   *The lion cubs **have been reintroduced** into the wild.*
4. for describing processes
   *First, the cubs **are trained** to hunt and kill …*

Notes
1. We cannot use intransitive verbs in the passive, because there is no object to become the subject.
   *The elephant **died**. (not ~~The elephant was died.~~)*
   *We **arrived** at the river at dawn. (not ~~The river was arrived at dawn.~~)*
2. We cannot always use the indirect object of a transitive verb as a subject for a passive sentence.
   ***They explained** the route to us. (not ~~We were explained the route.~~)*
   Alex likes eggs, so a neighbour suggested he keep chickens. (not ~~Alex was suggested to keep chickens.~~)
3. Some verbs describing states cannot be used in the passive.
   *The tribes **lack immunity** to western diseases. (not ~~Immunity to western diseases is lacked …~~)*

B Form

1 Passive infinitives

1. We form passive infinitives using **be + past participle**.

Tense	Active	Passive
simple	to write	to be written
perfect	to have written	to have been written
continuous	to be writing	to be being written (rarely used)
perfect continuous	to have been writing	to have been being written (rarely used)

2. We often use passive infinitives in set expressions.
   *There's nothing **to be done**.*
   *It's nowhere **to be found**.*
   *It's only **to be expected**.*

2 Modal passives

We form the passive of modal verbs using **modal verb + be + past participle** in the present, and **modal verb + have + been** in the past.

	Active	Passive
Present	We mustn't destroy the forest.	The forest must not be destroyed.
Past	Tourists shouldn't have approached the animals.	The animals should not have been approached.

3 Passive -ing forms and infinitives

1. Some verbs and expressions can be followed by the **passive infinitive**.
   Active: *People **have to sort** rubbish into different containers.*
   Passive: *Rubbish **has to be sorted** into different containers.*

2 Other verbs and expressions (e.g. adjectives + prepositions) can be followed by the passive -ing form.
Active: *They were **terrified of people taking their children** into slavery.*
Passive: *They were **terrified of their children being taken** into slavery.*

3 Both forms can also come at the beginning of a sentence.
***To be asked** to give a talk on the environment was quite a surprise.*
***Being made** to leave their homes and move to the city wasn't easy for the tribe.*
***Having been kept** in cages all their lives, the chickens didn't know what to do when they were finally released.*

Notes

1 Some verbs (*make, hear, see, help*) are followed by an object + infinitive without *to* in the active but require a *to* infinitive in the passive.
Active: *They **saw** the orang-utans **use** leaves as gloves.*
Passive: *Orang-utans **were seen to use** leaves as gloves.*

2 *Let* cannot be used in the passive when it is followed by a verb phrase. We have to use *allow*.
*They let us take photos. (not ~~We were let to take photos.~~) We **were allowed** to take photos.*

3 Some verbs are followed by an *-ing* form.
Active: *Loggers **keep destroying** the forests.*
Passive: *The forests **keep being destroyed** (by loggers).*

4 *need + -ing*
When we say something *needs doing*, this can have a passive meaning.
*Endangered species **need protecting** = Endangered species **need to be protected**.*

C Impersonal passive structures

1 We use impersonal passive structures after reporting verbs (e.g. *say, know, ask, suggest, explain*).

2 We form impersonal passives in three main ways.
   - subject + passive verb + *to* infinitive
   *Orang-utans **are known to use** leaves as gloves.*
   - *It* + passive verb + *that* clause
   *It **is acknowledged that** logging damages the environment.*
   - *There* + passive verb + *to be*
   *There **are thought to be** over 180 uncontacted tribes in the Amazon region.*

Note

We can also make passive structures with impersonal pronouns.
***Something should have been done** about the oil spill.*
***Nothing was done** to save the animals.*

D *have/get* + object + past participle

We use *have/get* + object + past participle to:
1 talk about something which someone else does for us.
*We **had our photos taken** before we left.*
2 describe an accident or unexpected event, often unpleasant.
*They **had their land stolen**.*

Language in use: collocational phrases (page 34)

A Verb phrases

Some verbs are part of fixed phrases that often include a noun or adjective and a prepositional phrase. Here are some examples that often appear in *CPE* exams. Add to the list any others that you find.

1 General verb phrases

be in charge (of)
be thanks to
bring (sb) up-to-date
bring (sth) to an end
buy (sth) on a whim
buy in bulk
capture the attention of (sb)/capture (sb's) attention
meet (our) goals
meet the needs/demands/requirements/conditions, etc. (of)
place importance/value/emphasis (on sth)
place/take an order/advertisement (for sth)
put (sb) at (their) ease
put plans into action
show (no) signs of
show/make a profit
take (an) interest (in)
take place

2 Phrases with *have*

have access to
have an/a major/no impact on
have dealings/relations with
have no decision
have no inclination to
have serious/far-reaching/disastrous consequences
have strong/no views on

B Prepositional phrases

1 Phrases with *by*

by accident   by chance   by choice

2 Phrases with *in*

in all likelihood	*in sb's wake*
in captivity	*in the end*
in living memory	*in the west*
in my view	*in the wild*
in peace	*in tune with*

3 Phrases with *on*

on Earth   on occasion

4 Phrases with *out*

out of breath   out of the way

5 Phrases with *with*

with ease	*with reference/regard to*
with enthusiasm	*with the advent/arrival of*
with pleasure	

3

Conditionals tense review (page 45)

A Overview

1 We use the **zero conditional** to talk about real events and things that are always true.
  - *If/When* + present simple + present simple
  If/When you *know* you can do something, you *feel confident.*
  - *If/When* + past simple + past simple
  When Pearsall *reviewed* the book, he *showed* it was nonsense.

2 We use the **first conditional** to talk about possible or likely events/situations in the future.
  - *If/When* + present + modal verb/present continuous/*going to*/imperative
  If you *practise*, you*'ll improve.*
  If you *don't try*, you*'re not going to* succeed.
  When you*'re ready*, we *can* start.

3 We use the **second conditional** to talk about unlikely or unreal situations in the present or future, and for giving advice.
  - *If* + past + *would/could/might* + infinitive
  If you *read* this book, you *might understand* the problem. (advice)
  If they *didn't want* to be happy and successful, people *wouldn't* buy these books. (unlikely situation)

4 We use the **third conditional** to talk about unreal/impossible situations or events in the past.
  - *If* + past perfect + *would/could/might* + *have* + past participle
  If Emma *hadn't found* good advice on the website, she *might have become* ill. (= She did find advice, and she didn't become ill.)
  If you *had worked* harder, you *might have succeeded.* (criticism)

B Mixed conditionals

We can also use mixed conditionals to talk about unreal situations.
- Unreal past + unreal present
  If she*'d stayed* in that job, she*'d be* the director by now.
- Unreal present + unreal past
  James wouldn't be an actor if he *hadn't read* the book.

C Alternatives to *if*

We can use other conjunctions to replace *if.*
- *unless* (= *if ... not* or *only if ...*)
  Unless he apologises, I won't speak to him again. (= If he doesn't apologise ...)
- *provided/providing (that), on condition that, so/as long as* (= *only if*)
  I'll lend you the book, provided that you promise to give it back to me.

but for
  Emma would have left her job, **but for** the advice she found online. (= if she hadn't found advice online)
- *whether ... or not*
  Whether you agree with Paul McKenna **or not**, you'll enjoy reading his book.
- *suppose/supposing/what if/imagine ...* (imaginary situations)
  Supposing you **take** the course, what job would you get afterwards? (present simple, suggests that the condition may be fulfilled)
  What if you **took** the course, how would it help you? (past, suggests that the condition is unlikely to be fulfilled)
  Imagine you **hadn't read** the article, Emma, what would you have done? (past perfect for unreal past)
- *assuming that* (= *in the possible situation that ...*)
  Assuming that the company paid for you, would you take the course?
- *in case* (= *as a precaution*)
  Write the telephone number down, **in case** you forget it.
- *otherwise* (= *if not ...*)
  Speak confidently, **otherwise** they won't believe you.
- *without*
  Without their help, Emma couldn't have overcome her problems.
  You shouldn't take these pills **without** consulting your doctor.
- *Given (that)* (= *Since/Because*)
  Given that you're not feeling well, it would be better to go to bed.

D Omission of *if*

In formal English we can invert the subject and the auxiliary verb, and omit *if.*
Should you find yourself with such difficult problems ... (an unlikely situation = *If you found ...*)
Were it not for that book, I wouldn't have had the courage to tell my parents I wanted to be an actor. (unlikely or unreal situation)
Had his wife not been the therapist, Rick would have gone to laughter classes. (unreal past)
When we omit *if*, we do not contract negatives.
Had she not stood up to him, he'd still be bullying her.

E Other phrases with *if*

Even if you're self-confident, you can enjoy reading this book.
If I **were** to recommend a laughter club, would you go to one?
If you **should/happen to** come across a laughter club, give it a try.
If talking helps, you can call a friend. (If + present participle)
If taken too seriously, self-help books can be depressing. (If + past participle)
If in doubt, consult a specialist. (= If you're in doubt .../If you're not sure ...)
If necessary, you can take a pill to help you calm down. (= If you need to ...)
It would be a pity **if** you couldn't express your emotions. (preparatory it)
Do you feel negative all the time? **If so**, a laughter club could help you. (= If you do feel negative ...)

Do you have the potential to be a concert pianist? **If not,** *give yourself a break and do something else.* (= *If you don't have the potential ...*)
If it **weren't/hadn't been** *for her friends' help, Emma wouldn't have recovered.* (= *If she hadn't had her friends' help ...*)

Introductory and emphatic *it* and *there* (page 50)

A Introductory *it* and *there*

1   In sentences that say something exists, we can use **there** as an introductory subject and put the real subject after the verb. We often use this structure with subjects that have indefinite or no article or indefinite determiners (*some, any, no*) or indefinite pronouns (*something, nobody,* etc.).
There's a feature on relaxation techniques in the magazine this month. (This is more natural than *A feature on relaxation techniques is in the magazine this month.*)
There are some good suggestions about how to relax.

2   When the subject is an infinitive expression, we avoid putting this at the beginning of a sentence by using introductory *it*.
It's easy to relax when you listen to music. (This is more natural than *To relax when you listen to music is easy.*)

3   We often use *it* + *be* + **name** to say who is talking (when the person can't be seen).
Hello, it's Jenny here.

4   We can also use introductory *it* as an object.
Ariana and Jarek found **it** *difficult to choose the photos for the article.*

B Emphasis with *it* + *be*

1   We can use **introductory** *it* + *be* for emphasis, often contrasting or contradicting a previous statement.
Ariana suggested gardening as a good way to relax. (no emphasis)
It was Ariana who suggested gardening as a good way to relax. (emphasising the subject)
It was gardening that Ariana suggested as a good way to relax. (emphasising the object)
It was as a good way to relax that Ariana suggested gardening. (emphasising the prepositional phrase)

2   We can also use this structure to emphasise a condition.
If it weren't for gardening, I'd never be able to relax.
If it hadn't been for laughter therapy, I couldn't have continued giving lectures.

Some common phrases with emphatic *it*

We often use expressions with *it* to express anger and frustration.
That does **it**!
I've had **it**!
I can't stand **it**!
I won't stand for **it** *(any longer).*
Also note these phrases:
It's a matter of making the decision to do it.
It's a question of finding the right solution.
It's a pity you were out when I called.
It makes no difference, whatever I say, she keeps on talking.
This is it.

C Inversion

The following expressions can be placed first in a sentence for emphasis. The subject and verb are then inverted. We use *do/does/did* if there is no auxiliary.

- *little, never, rarely, scarcely*
  Never have I seen so many people.
  Little did we know that he had followed us.
- *no sooner ... than, barely/hardly ... when*
  No sooner had he got the job **than** *he asked for a pay rise.*
  Hardly had I got through the door **when** *the phone rang.*
- *at no time, under no circumstances, on no account, no way* (informal)
  Under no circumstances should you let anyone in.
- *not since, not for, not a (person/thing), not only ... (but also)*
  Not since the 90s has he written such a superb novel.
  Not a soul did we see on our journey.
  *Not only do they want a pay increase, they (**also**) want reduced hours.*
- *only + time expression or prepositional phrase*
  Only now/after all these years has the crime been solved.
  Only when I got to the airport did I realise that I had forgotten my passport.

4

Modals 1: obligation, necessity, advice and criticism (page 61)

A Obligation, prohibition, necessity and lack of necessity

1   We use *must/mustn't* when:
   - we decide for ourselves that something is necessary, obligatory or prohibited.
     I **must** *answer my emails.*
     You **mustn't** *interrupt me while I'm working.*
   - we express strong opinions.
     We **must** *meet more often.*
   - we give instructions, especially in writing.
     Mobile phones **must** *be switched off for take-off and landing.*
     You **mustn't** *talk loudly in the library.*

2   We use *have to, need to* for an obligation imposed by someone else.
   You **have to** *say where you got the information from.*
   You **need to** *write a report.*

3   We use *must, have to, need to* to express general necessity.
   We **must** *try to talk to each other more.*
   We **have to** *reduce our dependence on technology.*
   We **need to** *take control of our lives.*

4   We can also use these other expressions of obligation and necessity.
   - *be required to* + infinitive
     You're **required to say** *where you got the information from.*
   - *be to* + infinitive
     The next task **will be to** *find out how people use their phones.*

- *had better* + infinitive
  *You'd **better finish** your homework before you start playing computer games.*
- *feel/be obliged* + *to* infinitive
  *I **feel obliged to answer** my emails straightaway.*
  *We're **obliged to attend** all the lectures.*
- *It's (your) duty/responsibility* + *to* infinitive
  *It's the moderators' **duty/responsibility to** ensure that nobody is bullied online.*
- *ought to*
  *You **ought to** apologise for being so late.*
- *the onus* ~~is on sb to do~~
  *The **onus** is on you to keep the information secure.*
- *be up to (you) to*
  *It's **up to you to** make sure the information is accurate.*

5 We use **not have to**, **need not**, **not need to** when there is a lack of necessity.
  *Safaricom users **don't need to** have a bank account.* (= not necessary)

Notes

1 There is a difference in meaning between *not need to* and *needn't have* + past participle.
  *The customers **didn't need to** have a bank account.* (= We don't know whether they had bank accounts or not.)
  *He **needn't have** brought his laptop.* (= He brought his laptop but it wasn't necessary.)

2 We also use *need* as an ordinary (not modal) verb, followed by a *to* infinitive or a noun phrase.
  *They **need to reduce** the time they spend online.*
  *I **need a new phone**.*

3 We can also use these other expressions for lack of necessity.
  - *be under no obligation to*
    *The café is **under no obligation to** provide free WiFi.*
    *You **are under no obligation to** give them your email address.*
  - *there is no need to*
    *There's **no need to** go to the library, all the information is online.*

B Advice and criticism

1 We use **must** for strong advice and recommendations.
  *You **must** keep your PIN secret.*

2 We use **should/ought to** when the advice is less strong.
  *You **should** charge up your phone before you go out.*
  *You **ought to** be careful what you put on the website.*

3 We use **could**, **would** and **might** to make suggestions and recommendations.
  *You **could** try looking it up on Wikipedia.*
  *I **would** market the games in a different way.*
  *It **might** be a good idea to make the games more exciting.*

4 We use **might have**, **would** and **should(n't) have** to criticise people.
  *You **might have** told me you'd borrowed my phone.*
  *I warned her to leave him alone but she **would** keep texting.*
  *You **shouldn't have** read my email.*

Note

We avoid using *ought to* in questions and negative statements.
*You ~~didn't ought to~~ **shouldn't** borrow my phone without asking.*
*Do you think you ~~ought to~~ **should** have posted that photo on your website?*

C Special uses of *should*

1 We often use **should** + subjunctive in *that* clauses after verbs used to make requests (e.g. *ask, request*) and suggestions (e.g. *suggest, recommend, propose*) or to give orders (e.g. *insist, demand, require*) or warnings (e.g. *warn*).
  *Jemima **asked/recommended/insisted that** the family **should spend** the weekend offline.*

2 We can also use *should* in *that* clauses after adjectives expressing importance (*important, essential, vital, necessary*) or reactions (*sorry, surprised/surprising, interesting, horrified, worried/worrying*).
  *It's **important/essential that** we **should** relate to the people we're with at the moment.*
  *It's **worrying that** Artley **should** feel obliged to obey these machines.*

3 In formal English we can omit *should* after *that* clauses.
  *Powers **recommends that** families **spend** time together.*
  *It's **vital that** we **balance** work and home life.*

4 We can also use *should* in clauses of purpose, to give a reason.
  *The company has a response team in place **so that** negative comments **shouldn't** go unanswered.*
  *People put photos on social networking sites **in order that** their friends **should** see them.*

5 We can also use *should* with some verbs (e.g. *hope, imagine, say, think*) to express uncertainty.
  *I **should hope** there's nothing embarrassing on your website.*
  *I **should imagine** that an employer would use social networking sites to find out about candidates.*

Modals 2: ability, possibility, probability and deduction (page 66)

A Ability

1 We use **can/can't** for general ability in the present and future.
  *You **can** charge up your mobile phone when you get home.*
  *You **can't** access the internet from here, there's no signal.*

2 We use **could** for general ability in the past.
  *People in rural areas **could** communicate with mobile phones.*

3 We use **was able to** for ability in a specific situation in the past.
  *They **were able to** enjoy the weekend together without being interrupted by mobile phone calls.*

4 We use **wasn't/weren't able to** or **couldn't** for negative ability in the past.
  *Will **couldn't** resist checking his emails and text messages.*
  *They **weren't able to** use their phones at the farm.*

Note

We can also use **be able to** for ability in the present and future.
*Readers **are able to** post comments immediately after an article.*
*Everyone **will be able to** see your photos on the website.*

B Possibility and probability

1 We use *can*, *could*, *may* for things that are possible and sometimes happen.
Damaging comments can destroy your company's reputation.
Jemima couldn't take a photo because she didn't have her phone.

2 We use *could*, *may*, *might* for possibility in the present or future.
Thousands of people could see an embarrassing photo on the internet.
People may post criticisms on a blog or in a forum.
You might find it difficult to delete the comments.

3 We use *could* for something that did happen from time to time.
The comments on his blog could sometimes be unpleasant. (= On some occasions, the comments were unpleasant.)

4 We use *could* + *have* for a theoretical possibility in the past.
They could have found the information on the internet.
(= It's possible but we don't know if they did or not.)

5 We use *can*, *could*, *may*, *might* + *have* + past participle for specific past possibilities.
Shakespeare could have used a writing table.
We think Shakespeare might have used a writing table because he shows Hamlet using one.
Desktop publishing may have led to a decline in quality.

6 We use *could/might* (+ *have* + past participle) to express criticism or annoyance.
You might have switched off the computer when you had finished using it.

7 We use *may/might* (*well*) to acknowledge something is true before introducing a contrast.
It may well be in the newspaper, but it isn't true.

8 We use *should/shouldn't* for probability.
We should be able to find the answer in the dictionary.
It shouldn't take long to work it out.

C Deduction

1 We use *must* to make deductions in the present.
There must be something wrong with my computer. It keeps crashing.

2 We use *must* + *have* + past participle to make deductions about the past.
Working together must have given them an advantage.

3 We use *can't/couldn't* for deduction in negative sentences.
It can't be true. I don't believe it.
It couldn't have been an interesting article, there were no comments.

5

Language in use: words with a similar meaning; confusable words; homophones
(page 77)

A Words with a similar meaning

It is important to choose the correct word for the meaning you want to express.

- *associate/compare*
  We associate the library with studying. (= When we think of the library, we think of studying.)
  We compare the library with other places to study: *The library is quieter than my room at home.*

- *contain/enclose/entail*
  The box contains (= holds inside) *books.*
  The dictionary contains (= includes) *hundreds of new words.*
  This product may contain (= have as part of it) *nuts.*
  The school is enclosed (= surrounded) *by a high brick wall.*
  A card is enclosed (= also in the envelope) *with this letter.*
  Trading with the outside world entails communication.
  (= Communication is a necessary part or result of trading.)

- *difference/discrepancy*
  There is a difference between the books we display and the books we read for pleasure. (= They aren't the same books.)
  There's a discrepancy between the books he says he reads and the books he actually reads. (= They should be the same books but they aren't.)

- *differentiate/discern/separate*
  It's important to differentiate (= recognise the difference) *between fact and fiction.*
  From looking at the books on the shelf, we discerned (= noticed) *that he was a keen cook.*
  You can't separate (= divide) *the language from the culture.*

- *match/similarity*
  There's a match (= suitability, close connection) *between your books and your personality.*
  There is no similarity (= likeness) *between the book and the film.*

- *opportunity/possibility/potential*
  Clive Thomas's work with Enduring Voices gave him the opportunity (= chance) *to study endangered languages.*
  Clive is optimistic about the possibility (= it may happen) *of saving endangered languages.*
  Clive sees the potential (= quality that makes it possible) *for minority languages to survive.*

- *rare/scarce*
  Old books in perfect condition are valuable because they are so rare (= uncommon).
  We must make the most of scarce (= few or little available) *resources.*

- *refrain/refuse/reject*
  We refrained from laughing (= We wanted to laugh, but we didn't.) *at her attempts to appear sophisticated by quoting poetry.*
  The restaurant reviewer refused (= said 'no' to) *the offer of a free meal.*

*The teacher **rejected** (= refused to accept, believe in or agree with) the boy's excuse that the dog had eaten his homework.*

B Confusable words

Some words sound very similar and have similar spellings, and related meanings but it is important to use the correct word.

accept/except: *Please **accept** this gift. / I can resist everything **except** temptation.*

affect/effect: *Your decision will **affect** everybody. / Her words had the desired **effect**, and we all agreed.*

disinterested/uninterested: *The judges must be **disinterested** (= impartial, not personally affected by the outcome) but we don't want them to be **uninterested** in (= bored by) the competition.*

emigration/immigration: ***Emigration** to Australia increased in the second half of the 20th century. / The **immigration** officials looked closely at everyone's passports as they entered the country.*

exhausted/exhaustive: *We looked everywhere, we made an **exhaustive** search. / We walked all day, so we were **exhausted**.*

historic/historical: *There are several associations that look after and maintain **historic** houses. / James was very good at remembering **historical** facts.*

industrial/industrious: *There are lots of factories in **industrial** cities. / Joe is an **industrious** boy, he works hard.*

loath/loathe: *The boys are **loath** (= don't want) to join the book group because they **loathe** (= hate) chic-lit.*

personal (= belonging to you)/**personnel** (= staff of an organisation)

suites (= a set of, e.g. rooms, furniture, music) / **suits** (= sets of clothes that match, men who wear suits at work, one of the four types of cards in a set of playing cards)

C Homophones

It is important to know the difference between these words that sound the same but have different spellings.

air = the gas we breathe / **heir** = someone who will inherit
aloud = audibly / **allowed** = permitted
assent = approval, agreement / **ascent** = upward climb
bite = with your teeth / **byte** = piece of electronic data
buoy = a floating object / **boy** = a young male person
complimentary = free, or saying you admire someone or something / **complementary** = go well together
counsellor = advisor / **councillor** = member of the council
ensure = make certain / **insure** = protect against something
fazed = confused / **phased** = done in stages
feet = part of the body / **feat** = achievement
foul = dirty, unpleasant / **fowl** = birds
gorillas = type of ape / **guerrillas** = unofficial military group
historic = an important place or event in history / **historical** = related to the past
leant = in a sloping position / **lent** = let someone borrow
lessen = diminish, grow smaller / **lesson** = period of instruction
nose = part of the face / **knows** = has knowledge of

pause = stop for a short time / **paws** = the feet of some animals / **pores** = small holes in the skin / **pours** = makes a liquid flow
peak = the highest point / **peek** = a quick look / **peke** = short for Pekinese dog / **pique** = feeling of being annoyed
prey = victim of a predator / **pray** = speak to God
principal = main, most important / **principle** = moral rule or belief
reek = smell very bad / **wreak** = cause damage
reins = used to guide a horse / **rains** = wet weather
scent = perfume / **sent** = past of *send*
sees = with your eyes / **seize** = grab hold of / **seas** = the oceans
serial = a story in several parts, one after the other / **cereal** = a plant grown for grain, e.g. wheat, barley, etc.; breakfast cereal
sight = something you see / **site** = a place / **cite** = mention
sort = type / **sought** = past of *seek*
sauce = liquid served with food / **source** = place where something starts or comes from
stationary = not moving / **stationery** = writing equipment, pens, paper, etc.
steak = piece of meat / **stake** = a stick used as a support
sun = bright object in the sky / **son** = sb's male child
toe = part of the foot / **tow** = pull along
wine = drink / **whine** = complain

More emphatic structures; nominal relative clauses; noun collocations (page 82)

A More emphatic structures (cleft sentences)

When we want to emphasise a point, we can split a sentence into two clauses. This is called a cleft or divided sentence. The emphasis is on the information that follows the first verb. Cleft sentences are common in both speech and writing. In writing they show an emphasis that cannot be signalled by intonation.

1 We form cleft sentences with a *wh-* clause (with a verb) + correct form of *be* + emphasised information.

2 We use this structure to emphasise the subject, object or complement of a sentence.
   Your book collection creates a good impression. (neutral)
   *What creates a good impression is **your book collection**.* (emphasis on subject)
   *Your book collection is what creates **a good impression**.* (emphasis on object)

3 The clauses can be reversed.
   ***A good impression** is what your book collection creates.*

4 We use this structure to emphasise the action of a sentence. We usually use the auxiliary verb *do*.
   ***What your book collection does**, is create a good impression.*

5 We use cleft sentences with an introductory phrase to focus on a thing, person, place, time or reason. The *wh-* clause acts like a relative clause.
   ***The thing that** creates a good impression is your book collection.*
   ***The person who** wrote the best-selling detective stories was Agatha Christie.*

*The place **where** I like to read is on the beach.*
*The time **when** I'm most relaxed is when I'm lying on the beach with a book.*
*The reason (**why**) I enjoy detective novels is that they're exciting.*
*All **I'd ever wanted** was to become a novelist.*
*All **I know is**, I prefer real books to e-books.*

B Nominal relative clauses

1 In nominal relative clauses, the relative pronoun acts like a noun + a relative pronoun together.
*I needed a bookcase and IKEA had exactly **what** I was looking for.* (= exactly the thing which I was looking for)

2 We do not use another pronoun or relative pronoun with a nominal relative pronoun.
*A cheap stylish bookcase was ~~the thing~~ **what** I was looking for.*

3 **What** is the most common nominal relative pronoun but we can also use:
  • **whatever/whoever/whichever/wherever**
    *I read **whatever** is available.*
    *Romantic stories are all the same, **whoever** the author is.*
    *Take **whichever** book you like, I don't mind.*
    *I read all the time, **wherever** I am.*
  • **when**
    *Do you remember **when** you first saw a Shakespeare play?*
  • **where**
    *Is this **where** they put the classic novels?*
  • **who**
    *Do you know **who** you're going to meet at the party?*
  • **how**
    *It's interesting to see **how** people display their books.*
  • **why**
    *Can you explain **why** you like e-readers?*

4 Nominal relative pronouns **what**, **when**, **where**, **who** and **how** can be followed by a *to* infinitive.
*We couldn't work out **how to assemble** the bookcase.*
*I didn't know **where to find** the books I wanted.*
*I was so confused, I didn't know **what to do**.*
*I don't know **who to give** this book to.*
*Amy is so irritating. She doesn't know **when to stop** talking.*

5 Nominal relative pronoun **what** can be followed by a noun.
***What enjoyment** we had came from books.* (What = 'all the enjoyment' but it suggests that there wasn't much enjoyment.)

6 We can use **which** to refer to a whole clause, not just the preceding noun.
*He went to see a speech and language therapist, **which** was a major breakthrough.*

Language in use: noun collocations + *of*
(page 82)

We often use **of** to link two nouns. Here are some common noun + of + noun collocations. Add any more that you find to the list.

a kind/type/sort of + person/thing
balance of power
break of day
centre of attention/gravity
choice of career/books
cost of living
course of action/treatment
crack of dawn/thunder
language of love
life of leisure/crime/poverty/luxury
matter of principle/course/life or death/opinion/time
point of departure/order/principle/reference/view
point of no return
price of success/fame/gold/food
sign of trouble/the times/success
standard of living
time of year/day/the month/your life/life
train of thought

6

Present and past subjunctive and unreal past (page 93)

A Present subjunctive

We use the **present subjunctive** (the infinitive without *to*) in a few fixed phrases and in formal and impersonal language.

1 Present subjunctive in fixed phrases
Far be it from me … (= I shouldn't criticise, but I'm going to.)
Be that as it may … (In spite of what you have just mentioned, however …)
Suffice it to say … (That's enough to explain …)
So be it. (= I accept the outcome, although I don't like it.) *I want to travel by train, and if it takes longer, **so be it**.*
No matter what … (= whatever happens/should happen)
*I'm going to climb Mount Kilimanjaro, **no matter what**.* (= Nothing will stop me climbing Mount Kilimanjaro.)
Come what may (= whatever should happen to prevent it) *I'll get to the top of the mountain, **come what may**.*

2 Present subjunctive in formal and impersonal language
We use the **present subjunctive** after:
  • reporting verbs, e.g. *insist, suggest, recommend, propose, request, order*, etc.
  • adjectives and nouns, usually expressing the idea that something is urgent, important or desirable.
    *For Jan, **it's essential that she apply** for a visa before travelling to Russia.*
    *Rolf's **recommendation/advice** is that a traveller **(should) leave** his mobile phone behind.*

3 We can also use the present subjunctive after *if, whether* and *whatever*.
*If Paco **(should) find** himself in a familiar place, he tries to see it with new eyes.*
***Whether** he **revisit** a place or a person, he recognises an old friend.*
***Whatever** your situation **may be**, Benedict says you should enjoy travelling.*

B Past subjunctive and unreal past

1 We use the **past subjunctive** (*were*) in formal English. Its meaning is similar to unreal past.
*If he **were** really serious about visiting Greenland, he'd have gone last year.*

2 We use the **past subjunctive** or **unreal past** for impossible wishes, proposals, giving advice and polite requests.
*I **wish** I **were** able to come with you. (but I can't)*
*I'd **suggest** we travel together, but I'm afraid of flying.*
*If I **were** you, I'd go by train.*
*If you **were** able to meet me when I arrived, I'd be very grateful.*

C Hypothetical meanings

To talk about situations in the present, past or future which are imagined or unreal, we use *wish/if only, It's (high) time, would rather/sooner, would prefer, as if/though, suppose/supposing, what if* followed by past tenses.
*It's high time we **booked** our tickets.*
*I'd **rather/sooner have slept** in an igloo.*
*I **would prefer to have visited** Greenland.*
*The tour guide wasn't interested in our safety, it's **as if/though** he **weren't** responsible!*
*Suppose/Supposing we'd **fallen** in the ravine!*
*What if we **hadn't had** our mobile phones with us?*

1 *wish / if only*

1 We use *wish* and *if only* + **past** to talk about a present situation that we want to be different.
*I **wish** I **were** a more adventurous traveller.*
*If only I **knew** how to fly a helicopter.*

2 We use *wish* and *if only* to talk about something we want to change in the present or future, often to complain about someone or something.
*I **wish/If only** the airport **weren't** so crowded.*

Notes: differences between *wish* and *hope*

1 We use *hope* for something we believe is possible and likely.

2 We use *wish* for something we don't think will happen.
*I **hope** I'll see an iceberg when I visit Greenland next year.*
(= I think it's likely.)
*I **wish** you **would** come to Greenland with me. (= But I don't think you will.)*

3 We do not use *I wish + would* to refer to ourselves.
*I **wish** he **would** take his phone, so we could contact him.*
*I **wish** I **could** (not ~~would~~) contact him but he hasn't got his phone with him.*

4 We do not use *would* for something which we cannot change.
*I **wish/If only** Greenland **were** (not ~~would be~~) closer.*

5 We use *wish/if only* + **past perfect** to express regret about a past situation.
*I **wish** I'd **seen** the iceberg break up.*

Notes: differences between *wish* and *if only*

1 *If only* is usually more emphatic than *I wish*.

2 We can put a subject between *if* and *only* for emphasis.
If people only knew how beautiful Greenland is, more tourists would go there.

2 *It's time*

We use *It's time* to talk about something we think should be happening, but isn't.
It's time we realised the importance of the polar ice caps.

3 *would rather/sooner, would prefer*

We use these expressions to talk about preferences and what we would like to happen or not happen.
*I'd **rather/sooner** travel by train. (not ~~to travel~~)*
*I'd **prefer to travel** by train. (not ~~travel~~)*

4 *as if/as though*

1 We use *as if/as though* + **past tense** to indicate that a situation is unlikely.
*Strel makes it sound **as if/as though it was** (formal **were**) easy to swim along the Amazon. (= In fact, it's difficult to swim along the Amazon.)*
BUT *It sounds **as if you had** an exciting adventure.*
(= I think you had an exciting adventure.)

2 *As if/As though* + **present tense** indicates that something is likely.
*It looks **as if/as though** the road ahead **is** blocked.*
(= The road probably is blocked.)
*It looks **as if/as though** the ice **is melting**.*
(= The ice probably is melting.)
*It looks **as if/as though** the iceberg **has broken up**.*
(= The iceberg probably has broken up.)

5 *suppose/supposing, imagine, what if*

We use these expressions to talk about imaginary situations in the (unreal) past, present or future, and possible consequences.
Suppose the iceberg tipped over, what would happen to the fishing boats?
What if the iceberg had tipped over, could the fishing boats have escaped?
Imagine you'd been really hungry, you'd have had to eat seal meat.

Language in use: emphatic phrases with *whether, however, whatever, no matter what/how* (page 98)

We use these phrases to emphasise what we say.
Whether you like it or not, I'm going to join the expedition to the South Pole.
No matter how beautiful the animals may be, they are very dangerous, so stay in the car.
Whatever you do, make sure you tell us where you're going.
No matter what the time is, call me if you need help.
However long you stay in India, there'll always be more places to explore.

Note
After *whatever* and *however*, we can omit the verb.
*I'm going camping, **whatever** the weather (may be).*
*I'm determined to get to the top, **however** difficult the climb (is/may be).*

7

Relative clauses (page 109)

A Relative pronouns and adverbs

We can use a relative pronoun as the subject of a relative clause.
*Coffee shops were establishments **that** promoted discussion.* (= Coffee shops were establishments. The establishments promoted discussion.)
*Anyone **who** started a quarrel had to atone for it by buying a coffee for all present.* (= If a person started a quarrel, the person had to buy coffee for everyone.)
*People **whose** work is mental rather than physical find coffee stimulating.* (= Some people do mental work. These people find coffee stimulating.)

Notes
1 We do not use a subject pronoun (*he, she, it*, etc.) after a subject relative pronoun.
   Coffee shops were establishments that ~~they~~ promoted discussion.
2 We cannot omit a relative pronoun when it is the subject.
   ~~Anyone started a quarrel had to atone for it by buying a coffee for all present.~~
3 We can use a relative pronoun as the object of a relative clause.
   The people who you met in the coffee house were very interesting. (= You met people in the coffee house. They were very interesting.)
   *The coffee houses **that** people went to reflected their interests.* (= People went to coffee houses. The coffee houses reflected their interests.)
4 We do not use an object pronoun and a relative pronoun in the same clause.
   *The coffee houses **that** people went to ~~them~~ reflected their interests.*
5 We can omit the defining relative pronoun if it is an object.
   The coffee houses people went to reflected their interests.
6 We can use relative adverbs (*where, when, why*) as the subject or object of a relative clause.
   *The coffee house was the place **where** people heard the news.*
   *In the days **when** there were no regular postal services, people collected their mail from the coffee house.*
   *The friendly atmosphere is **why** everyone feels at home.*
7 We can use the relative pronoun *which* to refer to a whole sentence, not just the subject or object.
   *Going to the coffee house cost only a few pence, **which** was much cheaper than entertaining at home.*
8 We can also say *which (be) why/when/where/what*.
   *Cycling is a way to avoid traffic jams **which is why** I started going to work by bike.*
   *Everyone in my department joined the Cycle Challenge, **which was when** we started cycling again.*

B Defining relative clauses

We use defining relative clauses to identify or classify a noun/pronoun. Defining relative clauses are necessary to the sentence. We do not use commas.
*Coffee houses were popular with people **who** did mental work.*

C Non-defining relative clauses

We use non-defining relative clauses to add extra information. They are not necessary to the sense of the sentence. We use commas to separate the extra information from the rest of the sentence. Non-defining relative clauses are more common in written than spoken English.
*Robert Hooke, **who** was a scientist and polymath, visited dozens of coffee houses.*

Notes
1 In non-defining relative clauses we do not omit the relative pronoun.
2 We do not use *that* in non-defining relative clauses.

D Words used with relative pronouns

1 Prepositions and prepositional phrases

We can put a preposition in two positions: before the relative pronoun, or at the end of the clause.
*Coffee houses were places **in which** people of all classes felt comfortable.*
*Coffee houses were places **which** people of all classes felt comfortable **in**.*

Note
After the preposition we use *which* (not ~~that~~) for things and *whom* (not ~~who~~) for people.
*Coffee houses were places **which/that** everyone felt comfortable **in**.*
*Coffee houses were places **in which** everyone felt comfortable.* (more formal)
*Office workers were people **who** coffee was useful **for**.*
*Office workers were people **for whom** coffee was useful.*

2 Expressions of quantity

We can use expressions of quantity (e.g. *all, both, neither, some, many*) + *of* before the relative pronoun in non-defining clauses.
*Volunteers, **many of** whom were students, created a neighbourhood centre.*

3 Indefinite pronouns

We can use indefinite pronouns (e.g. *someone, nothing, everything, anybody*, etc.) before a relative pronoun in defining clauses, with *who* (not *whom*) and *that* (not *which*).
***Everyone who** comes to teach at the school is made welcome.*
*You can do **anything that** you want to do here – swimming, pottery, painting, sports.*

E Reduced relative clauses with participles and *to* infinitives

1 In reduced relative clauses we can use *-ing* forms after nouns and pronouns.
   *Homeowners **living** close to the main road are in favour of a bypass.* (*living* = who are living)
   • We can omit the *-ing* form when it is followed by a prepositional phrase of place.
     *A man **at a table by himself** was busily writing notes.*
   • With reduced relative clauses we can use stative verbs, not usually used in the continuous form.
     *Anyone **imagining/thinking** that life in rural Australia is dull will be surprised.* (*imagining/thinking* = who imagines/thinks)

2 In reduced relative clauses we can use past participles after nouns or pronouns.
*The authorities, **alarmed** at the potential for dissent, tried to outlaw the coffee houses. (alarmed = who were alarmed)*
***Anyone interested** in purchasing their olive oil. (Anyone interested = Anyone who is interested)*
- We can also use some adjectives in the same way.
*The **people responsible** for the Noan Olive Oil company are Margit and Richard Schweger. (people responsible = people who are responsible)*
*The coffee house is **a place welcoming** to all. (a place welcoming = a place that welcomes)*

3 We can use *to* infinitives to replace relative clauses containing modal verbs.
*London was the city **to go to** for the best coffee houses. (= where you should go)*
- We can also use *to* infinitives after expressions of quantity and indefinite pronouns.
*Surprisingly, there is **a lot to do** in rural Australia. (= a lot of things we can do)*
*In the coffee house there was always **somebody to talk to**. (= somebody who you could talk to)*
- We can also use *to* infinitives after phrases such as *the first, the next, the last, the only, the best,* etc.
*This was **the first** coffee house **to open** in London. (= that opened)*

F Reduced non-defining descriptive clauses

We can also add participle phrases or noun phrases to non-defining clauses when we want to give extra information.
*The coffee houses, **doubling as outlets for newsletters**, reflected the interests of their clientele.*
*The teachers, **determined to keep abreast of things**, established an online forum.*
*The shopkeepers, **concerned about losing trade**, opposed the bypass.*
*The volunteers, **mainly enthusiastic students**, run workshops on recycling.*

Clauses of time and reason, result, concession (page 114)

A Time and reason clauses

1 Time clauses

We use time clauses to say when things begin and end and whether one event happened earlier or later than, or at the same time as, another event. Time clauses are introduced by a conjunction (*when, while,* etc.) or an *-ing* form.

1 To say when events or situations began.
*We've reduced waste **since** we set up the repair centre.*
*I moved to rural Australia a year ago, and I've enjoyed it **ever since**.*
*I began to enjoy cycling **once** I got used to it.*
***Once** you've made the decision, you must stick to it.*
***Now that** the traffic signs are gone, everyone drives more slowly.*

2 To say that two things happened at the same time.
*Social differences were ignored **while/when** people were in the coffee house.*
*The customers exchanged news and ideas **while** they drank their coffee.*
*The popularity of coffee houses increased **as** the middle class expanded.*
*Scientists gathered in one coffee house, **meanwhile** philosophers exchanged ideas in another.*

3 To say that one thing happened after another.
*I took up cycling **after** a friend recommended it for medical reasons.*
*I hadn't been canoeing **before** I went to Australia.*

4 To say that one thing follows another very quickly.
***As soon as** we met, we became friends.*
***No sooner** had we met, than we became friends.*
***The moment** we met, we became friends.*
***On arrival**, we left our luggage at the hotel and went straight to the meeting.*

5 To say when things end.
*The meeting continued **until** six o'clock.*
***By the time** the meeting finished, it was dark.*

2 Reason clauses

We use clauses of reason to explain why things happen.
*I choose to be a non-driver for ethical reasons, and I cycle **because** it's so practical.*
*We like to repair things **since** it's so much more economical.*
*It's worth supporting the Noan Olive Oil company **seeing (that)** it's a fair trade enterprise.*
*The council **is planning on** removing all the traffic signs.*
*The council **is hoping to** make drivers slow down.*
*The Schwegers work closely with farmers **so that/in order that** the company respects the environment.*
*Take your phone **in case** you need to call me.*

B Result clauses

We use result clauses to show the consequences of actions or situations.
*The council organised a welcome party and **consequently** we all got to know each other very quickly.*
*The car broke down, **hence** we had a long walk!*
*Take a map, **otherwise** you could get lost.*
*The company is organised **in such a way that** it supports the farmers and educational charities.*
*The climate is **so harsh that** nothing can grow there.*
*We can't afford to buy new equipment and **that being the case** we try to repair anything that breaks down.*

C Concession clauses

We use concession clauses to introduce unexpected contrasts. Concession clauses introduce either the background information or information that conflicts with it. They can be the first or second clause in the sentence.
***Much as** I'd like to, I can't come to the party.*
***Difficult though** it is to organise volunteers, the club has a lot of members.*
*The school is very isolated; **nevertheless** there is a great professional network.*

I don't like sports; **even so** there is plenty to do in rural Australia.
Sceptics anticipate problems; **however**, there's no harm in giving the traffic proposal a try.
Ann is really good at her job. **Be that as it may**, her repeated lateness for work this month cannot be ignored.
Although we suffered some setbacks, we persevered and the centre is a success.
While homeowners were in favour, shopkeepers opposed the bypass.

Note

In spite of and despite are followed by a noun phrase or -ing form.
Despite/In spite of concerns about safety the council decided to remove the traffic signs.

8

-ing form (page 125)

A -ing form in clauses

We use the -ing form in clauses:

1 to show that two actions occurred at the same time, or that one happened immediately after the other.
Emerging from the Lincoln tunnel into midtown Manhattan, a yellow cab from JFK Airport takes you past an architectural masterpiece.
The escalators became central to the composition of the building, *falling* and *rising* diagonally.

2 to suggest a cause, reason or result. In these clauses, we can use stative verbs, not usually used in the continuous.
Believing that everyday objects should be useful or beautiful, Morris made the home a work of art.

3 to replace adverbial clauses of time or contrast. We introduce the participle clause with a conjunction.
After redecorating her own cottage, Sarah started a home-styling business.
Although working on a tight budget wasn't easy, Sarah enjoyed redecorating her cottage.

B Common words and expressions + -ing

Here are some of the common words and expressions commonly tested in CPE exams. Add to the list any other examples you find.
be a master/genius at: Sarah**'s a genius at renovating** houses on a small budget.
be to blame for: Rex **was to blame for ruining** Clare's picture.
for fear of
for the sake of: **for the sake of preserving** old buildings
for/with the purpose of: **for the purpose of adapting** the building for a new tenant.
in addition to
in spite of/despite
instead of: **Instead of employing** tradesmen, Sarah did the work herself.
be worth
be no good/use
the best way/the idea of (doing sth)
there's no hope of
there's no point in

there's no prospect of
through
with a view to
with the purpose of
without
Would you mind … ?
I don't mind …

C Adjectives + prepositions + -ing

accused of: The developers were **accused of wrecking** a historical building.
accustomed to: Wealthy developers are **accustomed to getting** their own way.
based on: Approval of the plans was **based on** the façade **remaining** intact.
better at: Architects are **no better at predicting** the future than the rest of us.

better off	opposed to
capable of	prone to
committed to	responsible for
excited/enthusiastic about	sorry for
guilty of	tired of
justified in	worried about
keen on	

D Verb phrases + -ing

be charged with (= made responsible for something)
be feted/honoured for: Architects are often **feted/honoured for designing** buildings whose form follows function.

be fined for	have difficulty in
be no likelihood of	have no intention of
be/get landed/stuck with	have no objection to
can't help	have no regrets about
can't stand	have no/little chance of
consider the possibility of	have/take responsibility for
feel like	keep (sb) waiting
hate the thought of	take advantage of
have a reason for	come/result from
have an/no excuse for	plan on

E Verb + preposition + -ing

Some verbs are followed by a preposition and then the -ing form of the verb.
believe in: Morris **believed in making** things by hand.
benefit from
come/result from
compliment sb on: They **complimented the architects on** their innovative design.
depend on: Sarah's renovation **depended on finding** cheap furniture.
dream of/about: Sarah **dreamt of/about restoring** her own house.
plan on
pride yourself on: Sarah **prided herself on keeping** to a budget.
specialise in: William Morris **specialised in creating** patterns from nature.
succeed in: The Arts and Crafts Movement **succeeded in changing** the relationship between art, society and labour.

F Phrasal verbs + *-ing*

burst out: Amy **burst out crying** when she saw the damage the storm caused to her house.
cut back/down on
cut out (also *be cut out for*)
end up
feel up to
get over
give up: Clare decided to **give up painting**.
go into (time/money/effort/hard work): A great deal of time, money and hard work **went into decorating** the house.
keep on: Sarah **will keep on renovating** houses.
look after (= be responsible for)
look into: The committee **looked into extending** Landmark status to interior features.
make up for (= compensate)
put off (= delay)
set about: Sarah **set about finding** cheap things on eBay.
take to
take up: Sarah decided to **take up renovating** houses as a full-time job.

Infinitive or *-ing* form? (page 130)

A *-ing* form, *to* + infinitive or infinitive without *to*?

We can use *-ing* forms, *to* infinitives and infinitives without *to* in a variety of ways.

1 As subject
   Adapting old buildings for new functions is difficult.
   To prevent the destruction of the elevated railway, the residents formed a protest group.
2 As object
   Sarah enjoys **finding interesting pieces of furniture**.
   Sarah's husband wanted **to help**.
3 Following *be*
   The purpose of the Landmark trust **is saving** beautiful buildings.
   Clare's intention **was to paint** a picture of her cat.
4 Following a noun or adjective
   There are **tenants waiting** for the building to be ready.
   The council took a long **time to decide** what to do about the banking house.
   It's **important to consider** the interior as well as the façade.
5 Adding a subject to a *to* infinitive clause
   We usually add *for* when a *to* infinitive clause has a subject.
   It's **essential for the architects to reduce** the budget.
6 Verb + object + *-ing* clause
   In formal language we use a possessive form as the object of an *-ing* clause.
   We **didn't like them changing** the use of the building. (= informal/spoken)
   The council **objected to their changing** the use of the building. (= formal)
7 Verb + continuous infinitive
   The figures **seem to be telling** us that people want to see the museum's permanent collection.

8 Verb + *in order to/so as to*
   Buildings must **evolve** and **adapt in order to stay** useful.
   The design **changed so as to retain** the façade.

B Verb phrases + *to* + infinitive

do your best/do what you can to: **Do your best/Do what you can to reduce** the costs.
feel the need to/there is no need to
go to great lengths to
have/be time to
have a tendency to
have no wish/desire to
know how to
make an attempt to
make an/every effort to
make up your mind to
take the trouble to (BUT *go to the trouble of*): It's worth **going to the trouble of painting** some details.

C Adjectives + *to* + infinitive

anxious
apt
bound
due
inclined: They are **inclined to ask** for the impossible.
liable: Inexperienced builders **are liable to make** mistakes.
prepared
ready
reluctant
(un)willing

D Other useful phrases + *to* + infinitive

be (un)likely: The website allows people to see things they **would be unlikely to get** to see in person.
be at a loss
be in no mood: You**'re in no mood to spend** a lot of money on redecorating.
be keen: They **were keen to improve** the decorations.
be under no obligation
don't want there to be
it was kind of you to let me come
nowhere to be seen
occur to (sb) to do something: It **didn't occur to me to ask** him to come back.
turn out

9

Language in use: sentence adverbials; modifying and intensifying gradable and ungradable adjectives (page 141)

A Sentence adverbials

We can use sentence adverbials to express the speaker's attitude to a statement. We often put these at the beginning of a sentence but we can also put them in the

middle. Here are some examples that are often tested in CPE exams. Add to the list any others that you find.
Believe it or not, …
Difficult as it is to believe …
Incredible as it may be/look/sound …
Surprisingly, … (also *Amazingly, … /Astonishingly, … / Fortunately, …/Incredibly, …/Unbelievably, …/Unfortunately, … ,* etc.)
To (somebody's) amazement, … (also *astonishment … / surprise … ,* etc.)

B Modifying gradable adjectives

We can grade most adjectives (e.g. *good, big, dangerous*) because they describe things that can have more or less of the quality.
1 We can intensify gradable adjectives (= make them stronger) by using *very, extremely, rather, pretty* (informal) *really, terribly, most* (formal).
2 We can modify gradable adjectives (= make them weaker) by using *a bit, fairly, quite* (= partially), *relatively, slightly, somewhat* (formal)

C Modifying ungradable adjectives

Adjectives that describe absolute qualities (e.g. *unique, fantastic, extraordinary, perfect*) cannot be graded.
1 We can intensify the extreme quality by using *really, totally, utterly, completely, quite* (= totally).
2 We can say that something approaches an absolute state by using *almost, practically, virtually, nearly.*

D Gradable and ungradable adjectives

Some adjectives may be gradable or ungradable, depending on the context.
*The place was **fairly** deserted.* (gradable = there weren't many people in the place)
*The place was **completely** deserted.* (ungradable = there were no people in the place)

E Common adverb + adjective collocations

We often use adverb–adjective collocations to modify or intensify the adjective. Here are some examples that often appear in CPE exams. Add to the list any others that you find.
absolutely *awful/convinced/excruciating/sure/terrified*
bitterly *cold/disappointed/opposed*
completely *awful/safe/sure*
deceptively *peaceful*
decidedly *bleak/rough*
deeply *ashamed/attached/moved/unhappy/upset*
entirely *beneficial/different/satisfactory/sure/true/unexpected*
heavily *armed/guarded/loaded/polluted*
highly *critical/likely/qualified/trained/unlikely*
painfully *aware/obvious/shy/slow*
perfectly *awful/balanced/capable/normal/safe/serious*
pretty *alarming/bleak/rough*
quite *bleak/enjoyable/relieved/rough/shocked*

rather *alarming/bleak/enjoyable/relieved/rough/shocked*
reassuringly *matter-of-fact*
slightly *alarming/easier/shocked*
somewhat *alarming/bleak/shocked*
stupidly *naive*
thoroughly *ashamed/convinced/relieved*
totally *ashamed/convinced/harmless/inadequate/safe/ unbelievable/unexpected*
utterly *crazy/devastated/impossible/shattered/unexpected/ useless*
widely *available/known/publicised/read/understood/used*

Language in use: adjectives + prepositions; prepositional phrases; mixed prepositions
(page 146)

These are common collocations and phrases that are often tested in CPE exams. Add to the list any other combinations that you find.

A Adjectives + prepositions

1 **+ by**
confused   impressed   surrounded

2 **+ for**
eligible   essential
*(im)possible: It's usually **impossible for** professional tennis matches to go on so long.*
normal   responsible

3 **+ in**
absorbed/engrossed   deficient   fluent   involved lacking   rich

4 **+ of**
devoid   independent   indicative   innocent irrespective   mindful   regardless   reminiscent   typical

5 **+ on**
based   centred   dependent   intent   tough

6 **+ to**
accessible	*integral*
allergic	*liable*
committed	*prone*
conducive	*resigned*
crucial	*resistant*
difficult/hard/painful	*sensitive*
immune	*slow*
impervious	*(un)able*
indifferent	*vulnerable*

7 **+ with**
blue (with cold)	*good (with children)*
breathless (with excitement)	*incompatible*
bursting (with health)	*obsessed*
concerned/concerned about	*packed*
fraught	

B Nouns + prepositions

1 + against
race: a **race against** time   fight/struggle

2 + for
capacity   justification

3 + in
deficiency   drop   improvement   surge

4 + of
hint: There was no **hint of** the epic struggle to come.
maintenance   production   source

5 + on
authority   information/information about

6 + to
capacity (+ verb): The brain depends on glucose for its **capacity to** memorise.

C Verbs + prepositions

1 + about
boast   decide   dream   protest   reminisce

2 + against
battle/fight/struggle   decide   discriminate   insure
protest   race
react: People might **react against** all these developments.

3 + at
glance   hint   marvel

4 + for
account   allow   apply (e.g. apply for a job)
blame (sb)   cater   count   opt
provide (for sb/sth): The rules **provide for** tie-breakers.
struggle   substitute

5 + from
abstain   ban   bar   benefit   derive   differ
distinguish/distinguish between   expel   distract
profit   stem

6 + in
confide   fail   implicate   indulge   involve   result
specialise

7 + into
divide/split something   poke your nose   pry

8 + of
consist   deprive   remind

9 + on
blame (sth on sb)   concentrate
congratulate (sb on sth)   comment   decide (= choose)
depend   elaborate   impose   lavish (sth)
pride oneself

10 + to
appeal   apply (oneself/sth)   attend   attribute
contribute   devote oneself   lead   react   refer
resort   subject (sb/sth)   tend   trace (back)

11 + with
acquaint   associate   coincide   collide   comply
confront   confuse   cram
deal: Are GM foods the best way of **dealing with** food shortages?
ingratiate oneself   provide
struggle: Jeff staggered around on deck, **struggling with** the sail.
tamper   trust

D Prepositional phrases

against the law
at fault
beyond a joke
beyond belief
beyond the shadow of a doubt
by coincidence
by mistake
far from the truth
for fear of
for the time being
in advance
in all likelihood
in collaboration with
in comparison with
in demand
in favour of
in jeopardy
in recognition of
in response to
in theory
on a knife edge
on a regular/long-term basis
on behalf of

on good terms (with)
on my mind
on purpose
on the edge of
on the safe side
on the verge of
out of breath
out of control
out of favour
out of hand
out of the ordinary
out of the question
to a great extent
under control
under the circumstances
under the impression
with good reason
with the exception of
within reach (of)
without delay
without exception
without fail

E Verb phrases + prepositions

acquire a taste for
be/have (no) room for
find a solution to
have a craving/thirst for
have a high level of
have a lot of influence on
have access to/access (v) sth
have an aptitude for

have an effect on
have complete disregard for
have success in
impose a ban on
make a comment on
play a part/role in
spring to mind
take responsibility for

10

Reporting verbs; ways of rephrasing and summarising; impersonal report structures
(page 157)

A Review of reported speech and reported questions

When we report what someone else said, we make changes to the verb tenses, pronouns and references to time and place, in order to be clear.

1 Tense changes

We change the tenses by 'backshifting' one step further back in the past.

*'I **feel** very proud of what I**'ve achieved**.'* (present simple, present perfect)

*Kevin **said** that he **felt** very proud of what he **had achieved**.* (past simple, past perfect)

We do not backshift:

- when the reporting verb is in the present.
  *Kevin **says** he feels proud of what he**'s achieved**.*
- when we use modal verbs.
  *'You **should** be proud of what you**'ve achieved**.'* – I told Kevin that he **should** be proud of what he**'s achieved**.
- with the past perfect.
  *'I **had done** a degree in engineering before I started thatching.'*
  *Kevin said that he **had done** a degree in engineering before he started thatching.*

We can choose whether to backshift or not if the present and future events are still true.

*'Thatch **keeps (will keep)** you warm in winter and cool in summer.'*

*Kevin said that thatch **keeps (will/would keep)** you warm in winter and cool in summer.*

Note

Shall changes to *should* when it is a suggestion.
*'**Shall** we start the meeting at 10 o'clock?' The chair asked if we **should** start the meeting at 10 o'clock.*

2 Changes of pronouns and adverbs

When we report what someone else said in a different time and place, we have to change the pronouns and adverbs to be clear.

*'The next meeting will be **here**, in **this** room, **tomorrow**, at two o'clock.'*

*The secretary said the next meeting would be **there**, in **that** room, **the following day**, at two o'clock.*

*'The deal was signed, on **this** very table, **last** year.'*

*The manager said the deal had been signed on **that** very table, the **previous** year/the year **before**.*

*'I hope sales **will improve next year**.'*

*The sales director (He/She) hoped that sales **would improve the following year**.*

3 Word order in reported questions

- When we report questions, we do not invert the subject and auxiliary verb as we do in direct questions. We use subject–verb as in statements.
  *'**Where are you** going?' He asked me **where I was** going.*
- With *what/who/which* questions + *be* + complement, we can put *be* before the complement.
  *'Who is your business partner?' She asked me **who my business partner was**./She asked me **who was my business partner**.*

B Using reporting verbs: rephrasing and summarising

We can report what people say by using reporting verbs. There are various patterns that we can use.

1 Verb + *that* clause (+ *should*)

add, admit, advise, agree, announce, answer, argue, ask, beg, claim, command, complain, confess, decide, demand, deny, expect, explain, hint, hope, insist, intend, mention, prefer, promise, propose, recall, recommend, regret, repeat, report, request, suggest, swear, threaten, warn

*Michaela's parents **suggested that** she **shouldn't** set up a company immediately.*

*He **requested that** we help him with the content.*

Notes

1 In more formal context we can omit *should*.
*The lawyer advised that she (should) **insist** on a secrecy agreement.*

2 In less formal contexts we use the normal progression of tenses for reported speech.
*Our advisor recommended that we **drew up** a business plan.*

2 Verb + *to* + infinitive

agree, ask, claim, decide, demand, expect, hope, intend, offer, prefer, promise, refuse, swear, threaten

*Michaela **hoped to get** some advice from a venture capitalist.*

*She **expected to be** successful.*

3 Verb + object + *to* + infinitive

advise, ask, beg, command, encourage, expect, forbid, intend, invite, order, persuade, prefer, recommend, remind, tell, urge, warn

*Michaela's parents **advised her to wait** a bit before she set up a company.*

*A millionaire **asked them to translate** his philosophy of life.*

4 Verb + *-ing* form

admit, deny, mention, prefer, propose, recommend, regret, report, request, suggest

*Sam **admitted launching** his product prematurely.*

*Liz **regretted taking** on a big project.*

5 Verb (+ object) + preposition (+ object/genitive) + *-ing*

accuse sb of, apologise to sb for, blame sb for, complain about, confess to, congratulate sb on, insist on, object to, warn sb about

*Michaela's parents **warned her about setting** up a company too soon.*

*Michaela **blamed herself for making** a mistake.*

Note

Some reporting verbs may be followed by a *wh-* clause.
*He told them **what he wanted**.*
*She explained **where she went wrong**.*

C Using phrasal verbs as reporting verbs

blurt out (= say sth without thinking), *call for* (= propose), *come back with* (= retaliate) (e.g. *a sharp response*), *come in for* (e.g. *heavy criticism*), *come out with* (e.g. *sth rude/contemptuous*), *come up with* (e.g. *a good idea*), *drive at* (= what sb is trying to say), *dwell on* (= think/talk too long about sth unpleasant) (e.g. *don't dwell on your problems*), *fill sb in on* (= update), *get through to* (= reach) (e.g. *I tried to phone but I couldn't get through to the company*), *put forward* (e.g. *a suggestion*), *put sb down* (e.g. *with sarcasm*), *put/get across* (e.g. *your message*), *read out* (e.g. *he read out the list of candidates*), *reel off* (= quickly recite a list) (e.g. *the sales manager reeled off the list of targets*) *sound off* (= express strong opinions about), *speak out against* (= protest about), *speak up* (= express your opinion), *spell sth out* (= explain clearly and in detail), *sum up* (= summarise), *take sth back* (= admit you were wrong to say sth), *talk down to* (= talk to sb as if they are stupid), *talk sb out of/into* (= persuade sb (not) to do sth), *touch on* (= briefly mention)

D More ways of rephrasing and summarising

We can use reporting verbs to summarise what somebody said.

allege, assert, challenge, confess, confirm, consider, deny, doubt, imply, maintain, proclaim, refute (= prove that a charge against you is false), *repudiate* (formal = say that something is not true), *state*

*James **refuted** the accusation that he broke the photocopier by proving that he wasn't at work that day.*
*The company **repudiated** the accusation of discrimination.*
These verbs can also be used impersonally.
*The company **is alleged** to be in serious financial trouble.*
*It **has been confirmed** that two hundred members of staff will be made redundant.*

Note
Noun forms can also be used.
***Allegations** concerning the CEO's integrity have been made.*

Language in use: general verb phrases; phrases with *come, go, make* and *take*; nouns from phrasal verbs (page 162)

A General verb phrases

Some verbs are part of fixed phrases that often include a noun or adjective and a prepositional phrase. Here are some examples that often appear in *CPE* exams. Add to the list any others that you find.

be at (sb's) disposal	*be of your own making*
be no comparison between	*be out of the question*
be no concern of (sb's)	*be short of*
be exempt from	*be taken aback by*
be no justification for	*put (sth) into practice*

B Phrases with *come, go, make* and *take*

1 *come*

come as a/no surprise	*come to a halt*
come in for criticism	*come to terms with*
come to a decision	*come to the conclusion (that)*

2 *go*

go from bad to worse	*go bankrupt*
go out of business	*go by the board*
go to great expense	*go without saying*

3 *make*

make do (with)	*make no difference to*
make a swift recovery	*make the best of*
make allowances for	*make it possible for (difficult/easy)*

4 *take*

take exception to	*take something on board*
take (no) notice of	*take something for granted*
take the opportunity to	*take something into account*

C Nouns from phrasal verbs

We can form nouns from phrasal verbs. The particle can be used as a prefix (e.g. *an **up**turn*) or a suffix (*a take**over***). Here are some examples. Add to the list any others that you find.

Phrasal verbs
break down   come in   draw back   feed back   go out   look out   put out   take in   take over   turn up
*The company didn't get the order because communications with the supplier **broke down**.*
*For a business to be successful, it must have more money **coming in** than **going out**.*
*The company is **looking out** for new opportunities and plans to **take over** one of its rivals.*

Nouns
breakdown   income   drawback   feedback   outgoings   lookout   output   intake   takeover   upturn
*The company asked for **feedback** on its advertising campaign.*
*In spite of some **drawbacks**, the company considers the **takeover** was a success.*

Note
The phrasal verbs and the nouns formed from them do not always have identical meanings.
*Financial considerations made the company **draw back** from its original plan. (= not continue with)*
*There was a **drawback** to the original plan. (= a disadvantage)*

Expert writing

Contents

Assessment

Acceptable performance at CPE is represented by Band 3. Candidates' writing answers are assessed in two ways: firstly by an overall impression and secondly, by the requirements of the particular task. The overall impression mark is based on the content of the piece of writing, the organisation and cohesion, the range of structures and vocabulary, the appropriateness of the register and format, and the effect on the target reader.
Candidates need to be aware of the following:

- All the content points in a question must be covered in the answer, otherwise candidates will be penalised.
- The length of the answer should ideally be within the word-length given. However, candidates will not be penalised for writing more than the upper limit stated.
- The accuracy of spelling and punctuation is taken into account in the overall impression mark.
- Handwriting needs to be legible! If communication is hampered by handwriting, this will be penalised.
- Candidates will be penalised for including content that is irrelevant to the exam question

Mark scheme

Band 5

For a Band 5 (outstanding realisation of the task) to be awarded, the candidate's writing should impress the reader and have a very positive effect. It should show a wide range of vocabulary and structures, including collocations and expressions that are completely relevant to the task. The register, format and style should be fully in line with the demands of the task. All aspects of the topic should be covered and the task should show coherence and excellent organisation. There should be very few errors.

Band 4

For a Band 4 (good realisation of the task) to be awarded, the candidate's writing should have a positive effect on the reader. It should show a good range of vocabulary and structures, including collocations and expressions that are relevant to the task. The register, format and style should be in line with the demands of the task. Most aspects of the topic should be covered and the task should show coherence and good organisation. There may be minor errors but these do not affect the overall impression given by the task.

Band 3

For a Band 3 (satisfactory realisation of the task) to be awarded, the candidate's writing should have the desired effect on the reader. It should show a reasonable range of vocabulary and structures. The register, format and style should be generally in line with the demands of the task. The topic should be adequately covered and the task should show coherence and clear organisation. Any errors will not impede communication.

Writing checklist

- Have you answered the question and included all the points? Read the exam rubric again to check.
- For Part 1 tasks, have you summarised and evaluated the writer's views? Have you used your own words?
- Have you organised your writing in accordance with the particular task? For example:
  Letter: have you used appropriate opening and closing phrases? Is the language you use appropriate to the task?
  Article: have you organised your article for maximum effect? Is it written in the correct register for the target reader or publication?
  Report: have you organised your report under the correct sub-headings? Have you covered all the points in the task?
  Review: have you used suitable descriptive and evaluative vocabulary? Have you included recommendations?
  Essay: have you used convincing arguments? Have you included the use of suitable discourse markers? Is your writing logically organised?
- Are you showing in your writing that you have a good knowledge of grammar and vocabulary, including collocations, phrasal verbs, prepositional and verb phrases?
- Are you using complex sentence structure, e.g. use of impersonal structures, conditional sentences, inversion?
- Have you used the appropriate register throughout the task or does it go from formal to informal?
- Have you written the correct number of words?
- Does your piece of writing show evidence of good organisation and paragraph use? Do you include an appropriate introduction and conclusion?
- Have you checked for any inaccuracies in your spelling or grammar that might prevent comprehension or lead to lack of clarity?

Part 1: Essay

Task

Read the two texts below.

Write an essay summarising and evaluating the key points from both texts. Use your own words throughout as far as possible, and include your own ideas in your answers.

Write your essay in **240–280** words.

1 Nature should be left alone

Nature, in its natural state, is a balanced system: larger animals prey on smaller animals, bigger fish eat up the smaller ones. Other animals feed on the vegetation which is allowed to grow thickly in the shade of the towering trees above. The laws of nature do not change but man's activities can very easily disturb that balance by destroying habitats and hunting wild animals for trade. It is fortunate that individuals, together with conservation organisations, campaign tirelessly on behalf of our natural surroundings and the creatures that live there. They have achieved great things but the struggle is ongoing. Nature needs our help and protection.

2 Nature as inspiration

Where would Art be without nature from which to draw inspiration? Throughout the centuries, so many artists, designers and architects have used scenes from nature in their works: the petals on a flower, the savage sea, the green knife-like shape of a blade of grass. And there's science too, drawing so much knowledge over the centuries from the study of plants and animals and how they function, proving how an understanding of this can deepen our understanding of humanity. Nature is our source of wisdom and it will only benefit all of us if we give it the due care and attention it deserves.

Model answer

> Identify the main point of each text, and explain them in your own words.

Both texts support the idea that it is important to protect the natural world but they give different reasons. The first mentions the necessity of campaigning to protect nature. The second text considers the benefits of nature.

> Summarise the key points of the first text in your own words.

The first text suggests avoiding any disruption to the balance of nature. It makes the point that the destruction of habitats can easily result from human activities. It warns against the depletion of natural resources, for example, by hunting wild animals. The second text suggests that we should protect nature because it inspires us. It outlines the importance of studying plants and animals and claims that the more we know about nature, the better we understand ourselves.

> Summarise the key points of the second text in your own words.

> Evaluate the key points of the first text, and add your own ideas.

In my opinion, the first text does not make a convincing argument. It makes particular mention of the balance of nature, and advocates leaving nature alone. However, it completely ignores the place of humanity. I agree that we should guard against the degradation of nature and try to avoid wiping out animals and plants. At the same time, we should recognise that we are part of nature and cannot leave it entirely alone. The second text makes a better case. It acknowledges that man interacts with nature and concludes that we can only learn from nature if we protect it.

> Evaluate the key points of the second text, and add your own ideas.

> Say how far you agree or disagree with the points made in the texts.

In conclusion, I think it's the benefit that we get from nature that is the stronger reason to minimise the impact we have on the natural world. The balance of nature is not a good thing merely because it exists. We should limit our consumption of the animals and plants that share our planet not only because they are natural, but also because we need them. [280 words]

Further practice

Read text 3 and text 1 in the task above. Write an essay summarising and evaluating the key points from both texts. Use your own words throughout as far as possible, and include your own ideas in your answers.

Write your essay in **240–280** words.

3 Nature is there to be exploited

There are many people in the world who believe that nature is there to be exploited fully so that businesses can flourish and people's desire for good living can be met. They see rare species as a source of highly expensive restaurant delicacies, the seas as a source of indiscriminate fishing so as to catch as much as possible, the forests as a source of wood for cheap furniture. In many areas of the world, people have no other option but to work in industries they may or may not like; they simply work in order to survive. The luxury of choice is fast disappearing.

Part 1: Essay

Task

Read the two texts below.

Write an essay summarising and evaluating the key points from both texts. Use your own words throughout as far as possible, and include your own ideas in your answers.

Write your essay in **240–280** words.

1 Making a case for computer games in the classroom

Playing computer games is second nature for today's children. Teachers can embrace this fact in the classroom in order to enhance their relationship with their students. By focusing on the positive aspects of games, teachers can use them as valuable educational tools. Games such as Restaurant Empire teach students problem-solving and business skills. Other games like Making History get them to role-play historical events, bringing history to life in a way that books cannot, and making it more attractive to less academic children. They face challenges that people of the past faced, and work together to find solutions. Thus, interaction in the classroom is maintained.

2 Should computer games be used in the classroom?

There is a danger that students who get used to learning via computer games will become intolerant of other learning tools such as books. Also, the predominance of computer terminals in the classroom may effectively destroy direct physical interaction between students. While children may create certain things on the computer, physical creativity such as handicrafts and play-acting may be lost. For many teachers, these are a fundamental part of classroom life. Virtual interaction via the internet detracts from real physical interaction, and could adversely affect children's ability to express themselves orally. We should not lose sight of the social role that the classroom plays in a child's development.

Model answer

> **Identify the main point of each text, and explain them in your own words.**

The texts consider the controversial issue of playing computer games in the classroom. The first text advocates bringing computer games into the classroom, and claims that they can be a valuable educational tool. The second text, on the other hand, says that one of the dangers of encouraging students to learn through computer games is that they may become unwilling to learn in other ways.

> **Summarise the key points of the first text in your own words.**

The first text outlines the benefits of using computer games in the classroom. It makes particular mention of an improvement in the relationship between teachers and students. It gives examples of computer games that it claims can develop learning skills and boost the educational experience. It points out that the collaboration required to solve problems and find solutions provides motivation for students to work together and interact with each other.

> **Summarise the key points of the second text in your own words.**

The second text argues that using computer games in class runs the risk of discouraging students from working together. It focuses on the different quality of interaction provided by computers and warns that physical activities, such as play-acting and crafts may be lost. It concludes that virtual interaction is not a substitute for talking to other students in the classroom.

> **Evaluate the key points of each text, and add your own ideas.**

In my opinion, there are weaknesses in both arguments. I think that teachers should take responsibility for making learning interesting without becoming dependent on computer games. As for rejecting computer games altogether, I think teachers would end up regretting such a decision. Allowing computers into the classroom does not make it compulsory to use them all the time. On the whole, therefore, I agree with the first text that it is wise to use all the educational tools that are available, including computer games. [279 words]

> **Say how far you agree or disagree with the points made in the texts.**

Further practice

Read text 3 and text 1 in the task above. Write an essay summarising and evaluating the key points from both texts. Use your own words throughout as far as possible, and include your own ideas in your answers.

Write your essay in **240–280** words..

3 The creativity of computer games in the classroom

At school, the challenge for children is to learn in order to progress to the next class. The current system demands they pass a series of tests in order to do this. Video games present children with challenging tasks which they must complete in order to progress to the next level. At the next level, they must employ skills learned in previous levels in order to continue playing. Thus, the need for testing is eliminated, because the process of learning is ongoing. Potentially, games designed to teach skills for specific subjects could revolutionise the way we teach children of the future, and enhance the performance of current low achievers.

Part 2 Essay (discursive)

Task

Your tutor has asked you to write an essay about the extent to which our lifestyle affects our health. You should focus on eating habits, work and leisure activities, and include examples to support your views.

Write your essay in **280-320** words.

Model answer

> Write an introductory paragraph, mentioning the points you intend to include.

This essay will examine the role played by diet, occupation and free-time activities in keeping fit and healthy. It will examine the positive influence of healthy eating and consider how different activities can promote fitness and a sense of well-being.

> Develop your first point, and give examples to support it.

The first part of a healthy lifestyle is a healthy diet. It's a good idea to eat organic food, because fruit and vegetables not grown organically retain large quantities of herbicides and pesticides. Organic meat doesn't contain antibiotics and growth hormones like normal meat. Reducing consumption of red meat is also a good idea. It's important to eat a variety of different foods. A healthy, balanced diet includes plenty of fresh fruit and vegetables, and food cooked from scratch.

> Relate your examples to the main point.

> Make your second point, and give examples to support it.

Exercise is another vital part of a healthy lifestyle. Studying doesn't provide many opportunities for physical activity, so it's important to find ways to get out of the house. Although joining a gym is a good way to get fit, it's expensive and if you don't keep at it, it can be money wasted. People who don't enjoy sports, won't manage to keep it up. An alternative is something like a dance class, which is great fun. Classes will not only help you to feel fitter, they also provide a chance to meet new people and make new friends. Members of the class socialise and let their hair down together. This creates a greater sense of community which is good for mental health as well.

> Relate your examples to the main point.

> Write your conclusion, referring back to the points you made in each paragraph.

To sum up, there are three aspects of a healthy lifestyle. The first one is diet, because without good food you can't be healthy. The second is exercise, which keeps you physically fit. The third and possibly the most important, is building relationships and developing community spirit, which keeps you happy. It's much easier to eat well and exercise properly if you have friends to help you maintain a sense of well-being. [318 words]

Further practice

Your tutor has asked you to write an essay outlining the value of including meeting places in public buildings and institutions, such as colleges, museums and libraries. You should focus on the social and economic effects such places have, and include examples to support your views.

Write your essay in **280–320** words.

Part 2: Essay (set text)

Task

Based on a book you have read recently, write an essay for your tutor comparing the main characters in the story and discussing your opinion of the way it ended.

Write your essay in **280–320** words.

Model answer

| Introduce your essay, saying which book you are writing about. | This essay will compare the main characters in *Persuasion* by Jane Austen. The heroine, Anne Elliot, is kind, dutiful and loyal, whereas her family are variously snobbish, vain, selfish and hypocritical. | Use adjectives to describe the characters. |

Say how the novel demonstrates the differences between the characters.

Aspects of each person's character are exemplified in different scenes. In Bath we see the vain and snobbish Sir Walter Elliot perplexed and angry that Anne prefers to visit a distressed friend rather than accompany him and Elizabeth to visit Lady Catherine de Burgh.

Elizabeth's extravagance is compared to Anne's sense of economy when Elizabeth offers the expensive luxury ice-cream in late summer, while Anne and Lady Russell are looking for ways for the family to economise.

Use the language of comparison and contrast.

Use different structures to introduce your points.

In all the encounters between Mary and Anne, we see Mary being selfish and petulant while Anne is kind and helpful. The contrast is most vivid when Mary's son has a fall just before a dinner party which they were both looking forward to and Mary readily accepts Anne's offer to stay with the boy.

Anne's qualities of constancy and loyalty are highlighted against Louisa's changeability. Louisa falls in love first with Captain Wentworth and then with Captain Benwick. Anne remains constant to Captain Wentworth, rejecting Mr Eliott even though he will inherit Sir Walter's land and wealth.

Keep the summary of the plot very brief. Your aim is evaluation.

The main plot of the story turns on Anne's initially thwarted love for Captain Wentworth. Her family persuaded her to reject him because they did not consider him worthy to be her suitor. When they meet again, and find that each has retained the same feelings for the other, they find the courage to defy her family.

State briefly how the story ends, and say how you feel about the ending.

The story ends happily, with the marriage of Anne and Captain Wentworth, but they have to overcome many obstacles on the way. Their love has overcome snobbery and hypocrisy. The ending is very satisfying because Anne and Captain Wentworth both show themselves to be loyal and courageous and they are rewarded. The Captain's friends and relatives are kind and pleasant so the reader is sure that Anne will be happier in the future. [314 words]

Further practice

Based on a book you have read recently, write an essay for your tutor discussing the use of descriptive language in the story and how the plot was developed.

Write your essay in **280–320** words.

Part 2: Article (formal)

Task

The History of Art department at the university in a city near you is carrying out some research into places of historical interest. They have asked for contributions which will describe places of historical interest in your area. You decide to write an article about these places, saying why you have chosen them and what visitors might learn from visiting them.

Write your article in **280–320** words.

Model answer

> Say what the area is, which places you have chosen and why they are interesting.

As a contribution to your research into places of historical interest, I would like to tell you about two very different places close to Blackfriars Bridge in London. On the south side, Shakespeare's Globe Theatre is a well-known landmark. On the north side, hidden from view, is Dr Johnson's house. Each place is associated with one of the most important figures of English literature.

> Describe the first place, saying what it looks like and what you can see there.

The Globe is actually a twentieth-century reconstruction, not a historical building. We don't know a great deal about Elizabethan theatres but the Globe is based on what information we do have, and building it contributed to the understanding of Elizabethan playhouses. The building is round, and partly open to the sky, 'a wooden O' as described in *Henry V*. The façade has black beams and white walls, and the roof is thatched. Watching a performance at the Globe takes theatregoers back over four centuries, and it's a very different experience from seeing a play in a modern theatre. As well as watching a play, visitors can take a tour of the theatre and see the backstage areas and the replicas of Elizabethan costumes.

> Say what visitors can learn by visiting it.

> Describe the second place.

Dr Johnson lived at 17, Gough Square, and this is where, in 1746, he began the work for which he is most famous, his *Dictionary of the English Language*. It's fascinating to climb the steep, narrow staircase to the long, light room at the top of the house and to imagine Dr Johnson and his assistants sitting around the long table, busy writing and copying. On the walls there are portraits of Dr Johnson and his friends, many of them women. One portrait of Johnson is by his friend Frances Reynolds, sister of Sir Joshua Reynolds, the first president of the Royal Academy. Visitors to the house can learn a great deal about eighteenth-century life in London and about Dr Johnson's life and work. [313 words]

> Give examples of what you can see there.

> Say what visitors can learn by visiting it.

Further practice

An educational journal has asked young people currently attending an educational institution to write an article for its quarterly publication. The article will be part of a series called *The educational system and the world of work*. It should describe your impressions of the educational system you have experienced and how well it has prepared you for a future career. The article should also mention other areas in which education is valuable.

Write your article in **280–320** words.

Part 2: Article (semi-formal)

Task

Your college magazine has asked readers to send in articles about social or sports clubs that they are involved in. You decide to write an article describing a club you belong to, what you like about it and evaluating its benefits for members.

Write your article in **280–320** words.

Model answer

Choose a snappy heading and a first paragraph that will capture the readers' attention.	**How the college sports and social club changed my life!**

How the college sports and social club changed my life!

Yesterday, I was unhealthy, unfit and painfully shy. I worked on my own in the library, bought ready-meals from the supermarket and ate alone in my room. When I had spare time, I watched TV or played computer games. I looked in the mirror and felt deeply ashamed. Today, I'm fit, healthy and perfectly confident in company. How did it happen? I joined a club, and I'm totally convinced that it changed my life.

Address the target audience, in this case fellow students at the college.

Choose the appropriate register (semi-formal) and style (in this case, anecdotal).

It didn't really happen overnight, of course, but I really have undergone a transformation. I saw the advert for the club on the college noticeboard, and I decided to join. The first time I went, I crept in, hoping nobody would notice me. Immediately, a friendly trainer came up and introduced himself. He worked out a training programme for me, and we got started. The first few sessions were an ordeal, and I became painfully aware of muscles I'd never thought about before. He encouraged me to keep trying and it gradually became easier. With his help, I kept at it. As soon as I overcame one challenge, he set me another, and then another. My trainer also recommended changes to my diet and I began eating more healthily. Remarkably, I kept going and eventually, my underdeveloped muscles responded and I got stronger. As I got fitter and felt healthier, my confidence improved. No longer do I feel totally inadequate in company. I started going to the social events organised by the club: my team scored well at the quiz night and I met a girl at the disco.

Use a wide range of interesting vocabulary, collocations, etc., plus evidence of an advanced level of grammatical knowledge.

Organise your content and sentence structure in a way which will make the greatest impression on the reader.

End with a recommendation, and refer back to the task.

Before I joined the club, I found social events unbearable. I found a reason to get out of every invitation. Now, I've overcome my shyness, and found a partner. So, take my advice – join the club! [305 words]

Further practice

A performing arts magazine has asked readers to send in articles about the use of special effects in the cinema and theatre, and whether they enhance the audience's enjoyment of the film or play, or not. You should give examples of films or plays you have seen recently to support your views.

Write your article in **280–320** words.

Part 2: Letter (personal experience)

Task

An English language magazine is doing a feature on travel, and has invited readers to send in letters describing personal holiday experiences where something unexpected happened. You have decided to send in a letter about a trip you went on, describing what happened that was unexpected and the effect it had on you.

Write your letter in **280–320** words.

Model answer

> Explain the reason for writing, referring to the magazine request.

Dear Sir/Madam,

I read the announcement in yesterday's magazine asking readers to send in descriptions of holiday experiences. Last summer I set out on an adventure. I didn't want to stay in a tourist trap and see the sights that everybody sees. I wanted to get off the beaten track, so I decided to go to the Outer Hebrides, off the west coast of Scotland. The Butt of Lewis is the most north-westerly point of Europe, so it's one of the far-flung corners of the Earth. Some of the islands are uninhabited, so they are a wild and pristine wilderness. This is one of the best places to go climbing, and some of the cliffs are only accessible by boat.

> Decide what type of letter to write, in this case a description of a holiday and a surprising event.

> Set the scene that led up to the surprising event.

The day we decided to go climbing was a beautiful, clear, sunny day. Four of us took a boat and set off early in the morning. We got to the foot of the cliff and looked up at the awesome, beautiful climb ahead. We couldn't wait to get started. After a long climb, we reached the summit and watched the birds swooping around the cliffs. It was wonderful. Then our problems began. The weather changed very suddenly. All at once, we lost sight of the beach below. We could hear the waves crashing on the rocks, but we couldn't see where we were going. What had been a challenging climb became a terrifying nightmare. We shouted for help but the wind was too strong and we knew that nobody could hear us. We didn't know what to do. It would be too dangerous to take the boat across to the next island in a storm. After what seemed like a lifetime waiting on the beach, we were finally rescued by helicopter. I think I got more than I bargained for. I've lost my taste for adventure. Next year, I'll take a nice, safe package tour to a familiar holiday resort.

> Describe the surprising event.

> Say what effect the event had on you.

Yours sincerely,

[321 words]

Further practice

An English language magazine has invited readers to send in letters sharing their experiences of trying something new. It may be a new sport or leisure activity, or the first day in a new school, college or job. You have decided to send in a letter describing a new experience, describing what happened, your feelings and the effect the experience had on you.

Write your letter in **280–320** words.

Part 2: Letter (factual information)

Task

A director of an international company is carrying out a survey to find the Entrepreneur of Modern Times. A local TV channel is organising the survey. Viewers are invited to nominate an individual for this title, explaining why they have chosen this person. The person should be well-known and should have had a significant impact on modern life in today's society.

Write your letter in **280–320** words.

Model answer

Annotation	Letter
Explain your reason for writing by referring directly to the TV channel's request.	Dear Sir/Madam,

I'm writing in response to your request to nominate an Entrepreneur of Modern Times. The person I would like to nominate is Mark Zuckerberg, the founder of Facebook. My reasons for nominating him are that Facebook has made a huge change to the way people communicate and keep in touch with each other all around the world.

Say who you have chosen and explain your reasons.

Choose the correct register, neither too formal nor informal.

Explain what the entrepreneur's business is.

Zuckerberg set up the business while he was still at university and it grew extremely quickly reaching 500 million users in just a few years. The success of Facebook was unforeseeable, and even Zuckerberg failed to predict its potential. His intention was only to allow college friends to contact each other easily and quickly using a computer programme. It became so popular among students at Harvard that he extended it to include other American universities. Zuckerberg and his co-founders decided not to sell out to big corporations, because they were more interested in the idea than in making money. The decision paid off because Zuckerberg became one of the world's youngest billionaires.

Explain the impact the business has had on modern life.

Facebook is a modern business: it isn't a product to buy, it's a tool to use. Communications is the fastest-growing and most important business of the 21st century. Facebook is innovative, it embraces technology and would be inconceivable without the internet. It is useful for personal life, helping people to stay in touch with friends, and it's useful for business. Any company that wants to build up its business has a Facebook account. Any prospective employee can get a lot of background information about the company they want to join by looking it up on Facebook. It gives companies a human face.

To sum up, Facebook has changed the way the world communicates in a very short time. It's undeniably the most successful business of the early 21st century. Facebook was created by Mark Zuckerberg, and therefore, I think you should choose Mark Zuckerberg as your Entrepreneur of Modern Times.

Close your letter using Yours sincerely, or Yours faithfully,.

Yours faithfully,

[320 words]

Further practice

Recently, a literary festival took place in your home town at which many major authors and other people associated with the literary world gave talks to the public over three days. Your college principal has asked members of the student body who attended the festival to write a letter describing the event, and giving their opinion as to the value of this type of festival for the general public.

Write your letter in **280–320** words.

Part 2: Report

Task

Following complaints from local residents about students' cars and bikes blocking the street, the principal of your English school has asked you to write a report on the means of transportation students use to reach their classes and the effects this has on traffic circulation outside the school. You should make recommendations for improving the situation.

Write your report in **280–320** words.

Model answer

> *Introduce your report. Say what it presents, what it examines and that it makes recommendations.*

This report presents the findings of research into the numbers of students who come to the school on foot, by bike, by bus and by car. It examines the impact of these different means of transportation on the circulation of traffic outside the college and the primary school next door. It makes three recommendations to improve the situation.

> *State the findings of the research.*

Generally speaking, there are two periods of time, morning and afternoon, when traffic is heavy outside the college. Traffic is heavy at these times because the time that students arrive for classes coincides with the time that children arrive at school and students leave college at the same time that workers leave their offices in the afternoon. This means that many people converge on the area at the same time in the mornings and evenings.

> *Say what the main areas of concern are.*

The main area for concern is the safety of schoolchildren. The amount of traffic in the area can lead to cars being parked on the pavement and immediately outside the school gates. This could result in accidents as children try to cross the road to enter the school grounds. Another problem is that residents complain that students' cars block the roads near to the college. It cannot be denied that too many students who live only a short distance away drive to college. Furthermore, many students who cycle to college leave their bikes locked to railings, in spite of the notices requesting them not to do this.

> *Give the recommendations.*

> *Organise your points.*

This report makes three recommendations. Firstly, that students living close to the college shouldn't come by car. Secondly, that the college extend and improve the facilities for cyclists, so that bikes can be safely left within the college grounds. Finally, it is proposed that the college approach the council to request that they improve the bus service between the residential area and the college.

> *Conclude with the benefits of implementing the recommendations.*

Implementing these recommendations would benefit local residents and schoolchildren as well as college students. [317 words]

Further practice

Your tutor has asked you to write a report on how students spend their leisure time. Your report should focus on entertainment, sport, hobbies and socialising, the time individuals spend on each and the benefits they receive from such activities.

Write your report in **280–320** words.

Part 2: Review

Task

A local magazine that gives information about what's on in your area has asked for a review of a local restaurant. The best review will win a meal for two at the restaurant of their choice. The review should be about a restaurant that has recently opened. Describe the location, the food, the service and the ambiance, and say whether you would recommend the restaurant, and why.

Write your review in **280–320** words.

Model answer

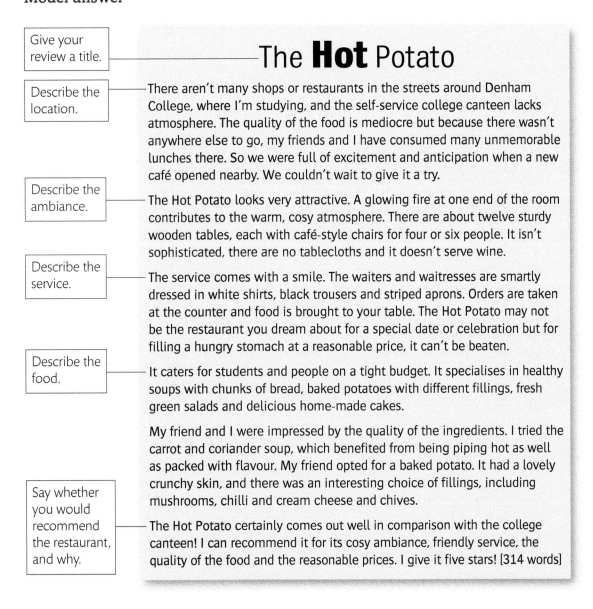

Give your review a title.

Describe the location.

Describe the ambiance.

Describe the service.

Describe the food.

Say whether you would recommend the restaurant, and why.

The **Hot** Potato

There aren't many shops or restaurants in the streets around Denham College, where I'm studying, and the self-service college canteen lacks atmosphere. The quality of the food is mediocre but because there wasn't anywhere else to go, my friends and I have consumed many unmemorable lunches there. So we were full of excitement and anticipation when a new café opened nearby. We couldn't wait to give it a try.

The Hot Potato looks very attractive. A glowing fire at one end of the room contributes to the warm, cosy atmosphere. There are about twelve sturdy wooden tables, each with café-style chairs for four or six people. It isn't sophisticated, there are no tablecloths and it doesn't serve wine.

The service comes with a smile. The waiters and waitresses are smartly dressed in white shirts, black trousers and striped aprons. Orders are taken at the counter and food is brought to your table. The Hot Potato may not be the restaurant you dream about for a special date or celebration but for filling a hungry stomach at a reasonable price, it can't be beaten.

It caters for students and people on a tight budget. It specialises in healthy soups with chunks of bread, baked potatoes with different fillings, fresh green salads and delicious home-made cakes.

My friend and I were impressed by the quality of the ingredients. I tried the carrot and coriander soup, which benefited from being piping hot as well as packed with flavour. My friend opted for a baked potato. It had a lovely crunchy skin, and there was an interesting choice of fillings, including mushrooms, chilli and cream cheese and chives.

The Hot Potato certainly comes out well in comparison with the college canteen! I can recommend it for its cosy ambiance, friendly service, the quality of the food and the reasonable prices. I give it five stars! [314 words]

Further practice

A radio programme is running a competition to find the best cultural night out. To win the prize, two tickets to the theatre, the ballet or a music concert, you must write a review of a cultural night out to celebrate a special occasion. Describe the type of place you went to, the standard of the performance and the overall value for money, and say whether you would recommend it, and why.

Write your review in **280–320** words.

Linking devices in writing

Part 1: essay

A Comparing two texts

Both texts present similar views ...
Both texts present similar views *with regard to the use of mobile phones in public places.*
The two texts illustrate different aspects ...
The two texts illustrate different aspects *of the issue.*
The two texts look at the subject from different perspectives: On the one hand, ... While text A suggests ...
While text A suggests *that computer games can be educational,* **text B advocates** *placing strict time limits on the amount of time children are allowed to spend on the computer.*
This point is juxtaposed with ...
Text A makes a case for social networking sites as a good means to make new friends. **This point is juxtaposed with** *the view presented in text B that teenagers generally spend so much time on online chat rooms that they find face-to-face interaction difficult.*
In contrast with this, text B places emphasis on ...
In contrast with this, text B *places emphasis on the value of training to improve your performing skills.*
Text B, on the other hand, argues for/against...
Text B, on the other hand, argues against *educating children at home.*
claims ...
supports the idea of ...
outlines the importance of ...
makes particular mention of/mentions/states ...
refers to/advocates/suggests ...
makes the point that ...
makes a case for ...
Text A **outlines the importance of** *play in helping children to learn social skills.*
Text B **makes the point that** *team games show children how to work together to produce a desired result.*

B Evaluating

Weighing up the points made in the two texts, ...
Weighing up the points made in the two texts, *it is clear that text A presents a more balanced view of the subject.*
Text 1 places emphasis on ... but ignores the fact that ...
Text 1 places emphasis on *the value of traditional education,* **but ignores the fact that** *it fails to cater for some children.*
Another point worth mentioning/considering ...
Another point worth considering *is the fact that not all children are academic.*
There is a correlation between/link between ...
There is a correlation between *ability in sport and a child's self-esteem.*
With respect to ...
With respect to *acting on the stage, text B makes a stronger case in favour of voice training.*
Similarly ...

Admittedly... but nevertheless ...
Admittedly, *young people can learn a lot from online courses,* **but nevertheless,** *the value of social interaction in education should not be underestimated.*
We cannot ignore the fact that ...
We cannot ignore the fact that *western societies produce vast amounts of waste.*
To my mind ...
There is no doubt in my mind that ...
There is no doubt in my mind that *the problem of waste needs to be addressed.*
While I agree with this point to a certain extent, there are other factors to consider ...
Undoubtedly, there is some truth in this view, but ...
In fact ...

C Using impersonal statements

It is often claimed/suggested ...
It is widely/generally understood/believed/accepted ...
Many/Certain people claim/assume ...
It has been pointed out that ...
It is common knowledge that ...
It seems as though ...

D Expressing grades of agreement

1 Agreement

Without a doubt, ...
Undoubtedly, ...
I'm (absolutely) convinced ...
I totally agree ...
I'm very much in favour of ...

2 Partial agreement

I tend to feel that ...
Most of the writer's arguments are plausible although ...
I'm fairly certain that ...
I'm inclined to agree with ...

3 Disagreement

I'm not (entirely) convinced that ...
It's doubtful that ...

4 Strong disagreement

I seriously doubt whether ...
It's highly unlikely that ...
I'm strongly against/opposed to ...

Parts 1 & 2

A Linking devices

1 Conjunctions

Addition: *and, as well as, not only … but also*
Not only *do people get fitter doing yoga,* ***but*** *they are* ***also*** *able to control their stress levels more effectively.*

Time: *before, after, as soon as, once, since, until, when, while, by the time*
The problem is that the current technology will have become outdated ***by the time*** *many teachers get used to it.*

Contrast: *although, despite, in spite of, but, even if, even though, while, whereas*
Mobile phones remain popular ***despite*** *efforts to warn people of the potential threat they pose to our health.*

Reason/Result: *as, because, so, since*
Many people prefer the cinema to the theatre ***as*** *they find action-packed movies more exciting.*

Purpose: *(in order) to, so that, so as to*
After climbing for three hours, we stopped at the shelter ***in order to*** *rest.*

2 Adverbials

Presentation: *at present, the current situation suggests, some experts/students/tutors believe, one view put forward is that, to begin/start with, firstly*
One view put forward is *that alternative therapies help you to take responsibility for your health.*
Some experts believe *that we should eat more raw food.*

Addition: *also, as well, besides, furthermore, in addition, moreover, too, what's more*
What's more, *it is thought that dogs benefit from eating raw meat rather than tinned dog food.*

Time: *afterwards, beforehand, eventually, finally, first, in the end, lastly, later, meanwhile, next, secondly*
Mum left for school rather hurriedly. ***Meanwhile***, *my brother and I began the preparations for her surprise party.*

Contrast/Change of direction: *even so, nevertheless, nonetheless, however, on the other hand, still, yet, in contrast, the problem with this, the question is, quite the opposite, contrary to*
Contrary to *criticisms that social networking sites are full of inane comments and useless information, they do in fact play an important role as advertising tools for both businesses and charity organisations.*

Example/Illustration: *for example/instance, for one thing, to begin/start with*
For example, *Greenpeace uses such sites to publish warnings against GM foods.*

Explanation/Clarification: *one reason for this could be, from this perspective, providing, as long as*
Looked at ***from this perspective***, *it can be seen that social networking sites are not all bad.*

Concession: *admittedly, few can deny that, it cannot be denied that, certainly, it may be true that, naturally, of course, that's not to say/suggest that*

Admittedly, *there are dangers that individuals may suffer harassment from unpleasant characters, but this can be avoided by not uploading too many personal or provocative photographs onto your page.*

Comment: *interestingly enough, surprisingly, thankfully, (un)fortunately, in my opinion/view*
Interestingly enough, *young people are generally becoming more cautious about how they use such sites.*

Reason/Result: *as a result, because of this, consequently, then, therefore, that's why*
Consequently, *reports of problems have decreased in recent months.*

Recommending: *In light of the current situation, it would be advisable to, the following measures could be taken to improve, it would be a good idea to … in this way*
It would be a good idea *for networking sites to offer advice on the sensible way to use their facilities. In this way, problems could be avoided more effectively.*

Conclusion: *generally speaking, all in all, whatever your views, I firmly believe, ultimately, to my mind, overall, to sum up, in view of this, in the light of this*
Whatever your views, *social networking sites are here to stay, so the best way to approach them is to show young people how to use them sensibly, by making them aware of potential dangers.*

Modifying/Hypothesis: *apparently, chiefly, evidently, in some respects, mainly, on the contrary, presumably, theoretically, to a certain extent, up to a point*

3 Discourse markers

Adding: *moreover, furthermore, in addition, as well as (that), what is more*

Clarifying: *I mean, that is to say, in other words*

Concession: *it may be true, certainly, granted, of course, if*

Concluding: *to sum up, in conclusion, briefly, in short, in a word*

Contrasting: *on the one hand … on the other hand, while, whereas, however, nevertheless, although, nonetheless, still, yet, in spite of/despite, even so, on the contrary, quite the opposite*

Generalising: *on the whole, it is commonly accepted, the general opinion is, broadly speaking, to a great extent, to some extent, apart from, except for*

Giving examples: *for instance, for example, in particular*

Giving your opinion: *in my view/opinion, as I see it*

Reference: *with reference to, talking about, regarding, with regard to, as far as … is concerned, as for, according to*

Result: *therefore, as a result, consequently, so*

Similarity: *similarly, in (much) the same way, just as*

Structuring: *to begin/start with, first of all, in the first place, then, lastly/finally*

Expert speaking

Contents

Assessment

Candidates are assessed individually on their performance in five main areas:

- **Grammatical resource**
  A wide range of grammatical structures should be used at *CPE* level and candidates should show their ability to use grammar correctly and effectively.

- **Lexical resource**
  Candidates should give evidence of a wide range of vocabulary and an ability to describe practical situations as well as abstract ideas. Opinions should be clearly expressed and candidates should not have to simplify their language, even when dealing with topics that they may not be familiar with.

- **Discourse management**
  Candidates should be able to maintain a monologue or dialogue in a logical and structured way, without too much hesitation. The length of their contributions should also be appropriate for the requirements of the task.

- **Pronunciation**
  Candidates should aim to produce spoken language that is easily intelligible, both from the point of view of the pronunciation of individual sounds and from the point of view of stress and intonation at sentence level.

- **Interactive communication**
  The candidates should show an ability to participate actively in a dialogue, initiating discussion where necessary or responding appropriately. Communication strategies should be used effectively in order to maintain the interaction. The assessor awards the above marks, and the interlocutor also awards an overall mark for global achievement, that is, how effective the candidate was in dealing generally with the three parts of the Speaking test.

Module 3B: Speaking, Exercise 8
Collaborative task

Module 4B: Speaking, Exercise 6

Individual long turn

Student A

Task card 1

How has technology affected the way people communicate?
• instant messaging
• video conferences
• cell phone applications

Question for Student B:
• Do you think such technological developments are ultimately beneficial or detrimental to our ability to communicate?

Student B

Task card 2

How has technology affected the way we travel?
• weather and traffic information
• booking and buying tickets
• convenience and safety

Question for Student A:
• Do you think people will travel more or less in the future?

Module 6B: Speaking, Exercise 3

Individual long turn

Student A

Task card 1

Which do you prefer, a package holiday or independent travel?
• convenience
• cost
• freedom of choice

Module 6B: Speaking, Exercise 5

Individual long turn

Student A

Task card 1

When choosing a holiday, which source of information is preferable?
• travel agency
• internet
• advice from friends

Student B

Task card 2

When deciding where to go on holiday, which criteria are the most important?
• price
• facilities
• respect for local community

Module 9B: Speaking, Exercise 5a

Individual long turn

Student A

Task card 1

What would you say are the main criteria for a healthy lifestyle?
• nutrition
• physical activity
• intellectual stimulation

Question for Student B:
• Would you say you have a reasonably balanced diet?

Follow-up question for Student A:
• How about you?

Student B

Task card 2

How far should we be concerned about where our food comes from?
• health reasons
• expense
• local producers

Question for Student A:
• What criteria do you use when choosing what to cook or eat?

Follow-up question for Student B:
• Do you agree?

Linking devices in speaking

A Agreeing and disagreeing

I can't disagree with that ...
I think we ought to take into consideration ...
That may be the case but ...
We can't rule out (the possibility that) ...
Have you considered ... ?
You've got a point but ...
I'd go along with that.
Absolutely!
Don't forget ...

B Structuring a long piece of speech

1 Starting off

Well, there are pros and cons to ...
I think I can safely say that ...
This is an important issue and one that is discussed a lot.
Well, this is an interesting question and it's not that simple to answer. Anyway, ...
To start off with, ...
Er, generally speaking, I think .../Er, let's see now ...

2 Linking

Another point we need to consider that should be taken into consideration is ...
Regarding/As regards/With reference to ...

3 Expressing personal opinion

Personally/Personally speaking, ...   *My opinion is that ...*
I (don't) tend to ...   *In my view, ...*

4 Giving counter-argument

I'm not sure to what extent this is true.   *Instead of ...*
Having said that, ...   *... whereas ...*

5 Summing up

So, in this sense ...   *To finish then, I feel that ...*
So, what I think is ...

C Sustaining a conversation

I think this is true.   *Anyhow, ...*
Absolutely.   *As a matter of fact, ...*
While I agree with you, of course ...   *Definitely.*
Not only that, ...   *Apart from that, ...*
Perhaps ...   *Actually, ...*
Mind you, ...   *This is the case.*

D Comparing and expressing opinion

The problem with ...   *I have to say ...*
Whereas ...   *I must admit ...*
With regard to ...   *I don't mean ...*
I'm not suggesting ...   *As for ...*
What does happen ...   *On the other hand, ...*

E Concluding and moving on

1 Concluding your turn

That's about it, I think.   *That's how I see things.*
That's my personal opinion.   *That's basically where I'm at on this.*

2 Moving on

How about you?   *How do you feel about that?*
What do you think?   *What's your opinion?*

F Adding points and expressing contrast

1 Adding

On top of that, ...   *And another thing is that ...*
What's more, ...   *Not only that, but ...*

2 Expressing contrast

But in fact/actually, ...   *X, on the other hand, ...*
In reality, ...   *X, meanwhile, ...*
The fact of the matter is ...   *When it comes to X, however, ...*

G Expressing opinions and responding

1 Expressing opinion

I think it's a matter of personal taste/choice whether you ...
Whichever type of holiday you prefer, the cost may affect ...
As far as freedom of choice is concerned, many people prefer ...
I feel that it is essential that young families be provided with ...
Personally, I'd sooner go ...
My own holiday decisions are always based on ...
Quite frankly, ...

2 Responding

Yes, I totally agree with you on that.   *You're absolutely right!*
Oh, I wouldn't say that!   *Yes, but isn't it better to ... ?*
But think of the benefits ...

H Communication strategies

... I mean   *sort of*   *well, when it comes to*
I suppose   *the thing is that*   *you know*
In that sense   *so to speak*   *you see*
not only that   *somehow*   *that's why*

I Discourse markers

after all   *in any case*   *on top of that*
at any rate   *in fact*   *to begin with*
at least   *in particular*   *well actually*
basically   *in the first place*
for one thing   *in the same way*

J Adverbs to describe how you do something

hurriedly   *painstakingly*   *pleasantly*   *thankfully*   *wearily*

K Sentence adverbials expressing surprise

Believe it or not, ...   *Incredible though ...*
To X's amazement, ...   *Difficult as it is to believe, ...*
Surprisingly enough, ...

Pearson Education Limited
Edinburgh Gate
Harlow
Essex CM20 2JE
England
and Associated Companies throughout the world.

www.pearsonelt.com

© Pearson Education Limited 2013

The rights of Megan Roderick, Carol Nuttall and Nick Kenny to be identified as authors of this Work has been asserted by him/her in accordance with the Copyright, Designs and Patents Act 1988.

First published 2013

Thirteenth impression 2021

ISBN: 978-1-4479-3759-3

Set in Amasis and Mundo Sans

Printed and bound by CPI Group (UK) Ltd, Croydon, CR0 4YY

Acknowledgements

The publishers and authors would like to thank the following people for their feedback and comments during the development of the material: Petra Pointer, Emily Bell, David Petrie, Mike Mills, Agnieszka Mlynarska, Jeannie Efstathiou and Rosalind Eden.

We are grateful to the following for permission to reproduce copyright material:
Cartoons
Cartoon Module2..2 from http://www.dailymail.co.uk/news/article-1254467/Battery-farm-cows-8-000-animals-housed-milk-factory.html, Daily Mail / Pugh, Daily Mail
Figures
Figure Module 4..1 from One photo from original article: www.guardian.co.uk/technology/2011/apr/24/jemima-kiss-twitter-facebook-emails?INTCMP=ILCNETTXT2387, Guardian News and Media Ltd; Figure Module 4..2 from http://thenextweb.com/shareables/2010/02/01/google-before-you-tweet-is-the-new-think-before-you-speak/, Design: Joe Newton Copy: Jon Parker Typeface: Olduvai, by Randy Jones; Figure Module 4..3 from http://www.facebook.com/www.thearomatherapycompany.co.uk?sk=wall&filter=1, The Aromatherapy Company
Text
Article Module 1. adapted from www.telegraph.co.uk/culture/theatre/dance/8554651/The-truth-about-life-as-a-background-dancer.html Will Storr /June 5, 2011, copyright (c) Telegraph Media Group Limited; Article Module 1. adapted from http://runninginheels.co.uk/articles/cinema-villains-classical-music/, Running in Heels / Ruth O'Reilly; Article Module 1. adapted from www.telegraph.co.uk/culture/music/classicalmusic/8585103/Queens-composer-calls-for-fines-on-artistic-terrrorists-who-allow-mobile-phones-to-ring-during-concerts.html Telegraph /Auslan Cramb June 19, 2011, copyright (c) Telegraph Media Group Limited; Article Module 1. adapted from www.independent.co.uk/student/magazines/performing-arts-no-business-like -show-business-427081.html Virginia Matthews, Independent Print Limited; Article Module 1. adapted from www.articlesbase.com/art-and-entertainment-articles/stage-acting-v-screen-acting-worlds-apart-1155932.html#axzz1RDFIw313, Brian Timoney; Article Module 1. adapted from www.american.com/archive/2008/march-april-magazine-contents/the-show-must-go-on// Jillian Cohan March/ April 2008, The American : The Journal of the American Enterprise Institute; Extract Module 2. adapted from http://en.wikipedia.org/wiki/Sustainable_development, Wikipedia:Text of Creative Commons Attribution-ShareAlike 3.0 Unported License, http://creativecommons.org/compatiblelicenses; Article Module 2. adapted from http://www.newscientist.com/article/dn20780-zoologger-the-most-athletic-ape-in-the-canopy.html, NewScientist Michael Marshall 10 August 2011, http://www.newscientist.com/article/dn20780-zoologger-the-most-athletic-ape-in-the-canopy.html; Extract Module 2. adapted from http://www.lionalert.org/pages/about.html http://www.lionalert.org/pages/why-act-now.html African Lion & Environmental Research Trust 2011, African Lion & Environmental Research Trust; Article Module 2. adapted from http://www.telegraph.co.uk/travel/safariandwildlifeholidays/8296668/Amboseli-Kenya-where-elephants-have-the-right-of-way.html, Daily Telegraph / Richard Madden / 1 Feb 2011, copyright (c) Telegraph Media Group Limited; Article Module 2. adapted from http://www.telegraph.co.uk/travel/safariandwildlifeholidays/8296668/Amboseli-Kenya-where-elephants-have-the-right-of-way.html, Daily Telegraph / Richard Madden /1 Feb 2011, copyright (c) Telegraph Media Group Limited; Extract Module 2. adapted from http://www.guardian.co.uk/theobserver/2010/mar/28/raising-chickens-eglu-alex-horne, The Observer / Alex Horne/ 28 March 2010, The Observer; Article Module 2. adapted from http://www.independent.co.uk/environment/green-living/they-tell-us-recycling-is-good-for-us-garbage-2297961.html, The Independent /John Walsh / 16 June 2011, Independent Print Limited; Article Module 2. adapted from http://www.guardian.co.uk/environment/2011/apr/03/last-stand-of-the-amazon, The Observer/ Edward Docx/ Sunday 3 April 2011, The Observer; Article Module2. from http://www.newscientist.com/article/dn9967-instant-expert-mysteries-of-the-deep-sea.html; Article Module3. adapted from When I Say No, I Feel Guilty, 1975 978-0553263909 Bantam USA (Smith, Manuel J 1975), From WHEN I SAY NO, I FEEL GUILTY by Manuel J. Smith, copyright 1975 by Manuel J.Smith. Used by permission of Doubleday, a division of Random House, Inc.; Article Module 3. adapted from Is Positive Psychology For Everyone? New Research Raises Doubts, Scott Lilienfeld / Jun 19, 2009, Scott O.Liienfeld Professor of Psychology; Article Module3. adapted from www.healthline.com/galecontent/dance-therapy-1, Gale Group, Inc. – Healthline.com / Barabara Boughton / 2002 p.1 - Origins, Material adapted from Cengage source.; Article Module3. adapted from www.life-coach-tips.co.uk/bookreviews1.html, David

Bonham-Carter, Life Coach David Bonham-Carter; Article Module3. adapted from www.guardian.co.uk/books/2011/jan/22/help-slightly-happier-oliver-burkeman-review?INTCMP=ILCNETTXT3487], Nicholas Lezard, The Guardian; Article Module3. adapted from www.accesstoexcellence.co.uk/html/feel_the_fear_and_do_it_anyway.html, Steve Unwin/ Feb 28, 2004, Feel The Fear And Do It Anyway: How To Turn Your Fear And Indecision Into Confidence And Action by Susan Jeffers; Article Module4. adapted from www.guardian.co.uk/technology/2011/apr/24/jemima-kiss-twitter-facebook-emails?INTCMP=ILCNETTXT2387 The Observer/ Jemima Kiss / April 24th, 2011, ©Will Whipple/The Observer; Article Module4.5 adapted from http://www.telegraph.co.uk/motoring/columnists/mike-rutherford/8632060/Mr-Money-driving-the-car-of-the-future.html, copyright (c) Telegraph Media Group Limited; Article Module5.. adapted from http://www.independent.co.uk/arts-entertainment/books/features/will-the-home-library survive-the-surge-of-the-ebook-2298751.html, The Independent / Alice Azania-Jarvis, Independent Print limited; Extract Module5.. adapted from http://www.bl.uk/learning/langlit/changlang/across/languagetimeline.html, British Library / David Crystal Geoffrey Hughes, (C) British Library Board ; Article Module6. adapted from www.guardian.co.uk/travel/2011/mar/05/technology-travel-jan-morris-iyer, Guardian / March 05 2011, The Guardian; Article Module 7. after www.noanoliveoil.com, www.noanoliveoul.com; Article Module8. adapted from http://www.telegraph.co.uk/property/interiorsandshopping/8789691/Shoestring-renovators-Interior-design-on-a-budget.html, copyright (c) Telegraph Media Group Limited; Article Module8. adapted from http://fashion.telegraph.co.uk/Article/TMG8677647/304/Fashions-most-influential-Petra-Nemcova.html, Daily Telegraph / Aurelia Donaldson /19 Oct 2011, copyright (c) Telegraph Media Group Limited; Article Module9.4 adapted from http://www.gq-magazine.co.uk/entertainment/articles/2011-06/03/gq-sport-wimbledon-nicolas-mahut-john-isner-tennis/wimbledon GQ.com, Edward Caesar; Article Module10. adapted from http://www.translatingtoday.com/index.php?option=com_content&view=article&id=50:translation-a-changing-profession&catid=36:feature-articles&Itemid=53, Translating Today magazine / Mary Carroll, Mary Carroll
The Financial Times
Article Module8. adapted from http://www.ft.com/intl/cms/s/2/22943b1c-d878-11e0-8f0a-00144feabdc0.html#axzz1ZPZaR9OB, Financial Times / Jonathan Foyle / Sept 19 2011

In some instances we have been unable to trace the owners of copyright material, and we would appreciate any information that would enable us to do so.